Wise Daughters from Foreign Lands

Wise Daughters from Foreign Lands
European Women Writers in China

Elisabeth Croll

PANDORA

London   Winchester   Sydney   Wellington

First published by **Pandora Press**, an imprint of the
Trade Division of Unwin Hyman, in 1989

© Elisabeth Croll 1989

PANDORA PRESS

Unwin Hyman Limited
15/17 Broadwick Street, London W1V 1FP

Unwin Hyman Inc
8 Winchester Place, Winchester, MA 01890

Allen & Unwin Australia Pty Ltd
P.O. Box 764, 8 Napier Street, North Sydney, NSW 2060

Allen & Unwin NZ (in association with the Port Nicholson Press)
Compusales Building, 75 Ghuznee Street, Wellington, New Zealand

---

British Library Cataloguing in Publication Data
Croll, Elizabeth, *1944 –*
Wise daughters from foreign lands : European women
writers in China.
1. English literature. Women writers. Special subjects. China
I. Title
820.9'3251

ISBN 0–04–440414–X

Typeset in 11/12.5 point Times
Printed by Billings & Sons, Worcester

Contents

To my mother, Joan, and my father, Bob, whose lives and ideals in a Presbyterian manse have aided me in the understanding and appreciation of the lives and works documented in this book

Now there are happily certain benevolent gentlemen and virtuous daughters of ability, wise daughters from foreign lands, *who have initiated a truly noble experience. They have addressed our women in animated exhortations. . .*

Kung Hui-cheng, lineal descendant of Confucius, 1895

Preface

I can remember the exact moment that this book was conceived. Lost in a fictional world of Beijing (Peking) at the turn of the century which had been unusually but faithfully depicted by an American woman writer, I reluctantly closed the last chapter late one Saturday night with the question: who was this woman that she could write like this? I decided to find out, and so was born a new hobby, discovering the persons and works of European women writers on China. The six women writers presented here were selected because of the inherent interest of their writings, their diverse but complementary experiences and their influence on contemporary and international images of China. Their biographies are based mainly on a study of their books, which are more non-fiction than fiction, their published articles, and for some their autobiographies. Their writings have revealed six vibrant and curious women who not only depicted many of the customs and practices affecting domestic and social life in Chinese society earlier this century, but also inadvertently left a record of their own attempt to pursue somewhat unconventional and independent lives in still-circumscribed times. Although there is a remarkable story behind each of these women, this book is more than a series of biographies of six women European authors who resided and travelled in China from the turn of the century. It is also about the China which they observed, their images, impressions and interpretations of Chinese domestic and social life and of the lifestyle of Europeans residing in China.

My acquaintance with the six European writers featured in this book began more than ten years ago when I was writing a history of the women's movement in China. During that study, it was frequently necessary to rely on the less formal of historical sources, and in particular to consult eye-witness accounts and interviews recorded in diaries, autobiographies, letters, magazine articles and books written by both Chinese and European women. Often they alone had documented the attitudes, responses and the experiences of the women who had either participated in or observed important movements, events and trends affecting the role and status of Chinese women in the twentieth century. Several of the books written by European women from the end of the nineteenth century to the mid-1930s proved to be especially interesting in that either they had better documented the domestic and social roles of Chinese women or because they had become best sellers in Europe and North America and were thus responsible for creating and nurturing many of the popular contemporary European images of Chinese society and Chinese women. As a result of my later training as an anthropologist, my initial interest in the books developed into a curiosity about the experience and perceptions of the European women writers and their own multiple roles in China as Europeans, as women and as writers akin to ethnographers.

British and American writers in China usually referred to themselves in their writings as Europeans, a practice to which this book adheres. Although European women in China as a social category might be made up of many different national-ities including American, they largely shared language, mean-ings, symbols, values and sacred and secular rituals. These reference points were important in providing them with a sense of common European identity in a strange and unfamiliar environment. Indeed it was the very novelty and strangeness of China which defined anew and strengthened their contrasting experience not only as Europeans but as Europeans with a definite interest in China. Following the conventions of their day they largely divided the world into the dual, separate but uneven halves of East and West (or sometimes Orient and Occident), a usage this book has followed. In writing of European women and allowing them to speak for and represent China and Chinese women, this study recognises that it is European rather than Chinese women who at this time had the greater capacity to write about Chinese culture for an international audience. It can only be said that the choice of writers, topics and incidents included here takes images and representations which reflect as accurately as is possible Chinese customs and practices as verified over long periods of anthropological study. The production of this book, a long-term hobby, has been accompanied alongside my publications of Chinese women's own stories and views of themselves and hopefully will be followed some time in the future by a companion volume which takes as its starting-point the autobiographies of six Chinese women writers.

Many people have helped me further my knowledge of these European women writers. I would particularly like to thank Mrs Wigan of Hallaton, Leicestershire, Lady Little and Mrs Little of Wheatley, Oxfordshire, for sharing their memories of their aunt, Mrs Archibald Little. Ms Linda Wrigglesworth generously allowed me to see the scrapbooks of Mrs Archibald Little which had passed into her possession. Mrs Mary Clarke, of the British Embassy in Beijing, and Vanessa and Ken Whinney provided helpful information on Sarah Pyke Conger, as did Carol Becker of the United States Department of State in Washington DC. Many libraries helped in procuring the works of each of the women writers and I would especially like to thank Frances Wood of the British Library and the staff of the School of Oriental and African Studies Library. Many friends have taken an interest in this project and passed on interesting and relevant materials. I would therefore like to take this opportunity to thank Helen Callaway, Peter Carey, Delia Davin, Ray Dawson, Felicity Edholm, Mark Elvin, Hilary Laurie and Maxine Molyneux. My thanks also to Philippa Brewster who as publisher and friend has given more than the usual encouragement to this long-term project, and to Marilyn Mastrandrea, Marcia Eedle, Anne Aggersburg, Gertrude Booty and Sharon Lewis, who have patiently deciphered and typed the various drafts of the manuscript.

In thinking about the ways and means by which these European women writers depicted Chinese society and its women and mediated their own and Chinese culture, I am particularly indebted to my colleague David Parkin for his timely suggestions, to Felicity Edholm for her comments on Chapter 1 and to Jane Hunter's very fine book *The Gospel of Gentility* which, taking European women missionaries in China as its focus, set an exacting precedent. As a long-time hobby the research and writings of this book have required more than the usual understanding and co-operation from Jim, Nicolas and Katherine Croll – for which I thank them. I would also like to mention my friend Jenny Mark who was tragically killed in the summer of 1988. With unfailing generosity, she always took a special interest in 'my ladies'.

In a very real sense these women writers are my own forebears in that I too have devoted the major part of my professional life to studying and writing on Chinese domestic and social life, albeit as a trained anthropologist. These women, their writings and persons, have contributed much to my own professional and personal interests over the past few years. I hope therefore that I have managed to convey some of this interest and most of all the pleasure and sometimes excitement that have accompanied the discovery of each of these women writers: be it the individual details surrounding the personal circumstances of their arrival and stay in China, their first impressions and longer-term depictions of Chinese domestic and social life, Chinese culture and European culture in China or their own and others' expectations of themselves as women and as writers.

Elisabeth Croll
London 1988

1

Depicting Domestic and Social Life in China: *Six European Women Writers*

It was not until the later decades of the nineteenth century that European women began to reside in large or significant numbers in China although the first treaty ports had been open to European residence since the 1840s. Indeed the early treaty port centres of commercial and consular activities could be likened to the trading posts and mining camps or transient stations of other continents which followed a predominantly masculine routine. Company days were punctuated by flurries of feverish activity attendant upon the arrivals and departures of mail, and vessels bearing consignments and diplomatic negotiations between Chinese and foreign representatives were interrupted by intermittent periods of sporting or shooting centred on the Club. Community life might make periodic allowance for the few European consular, company or mission wives, but outside of Shanghai their numbers were few until the foreign treaty port settlements themselves expanded as China's markets and China's millions became the object of European commercial hopes and missionary aspirations. As the number of concessions permitting the establishment of foreign settlements and foreign traders and missionaries to travel, trade and preach individually in the interior regions of China multiplied so did the numbers of European women resident in the country. Most commonly they came to China as wives accompanying their missionary, merchant and diplomatic husbands but they came also in smaller numbers as mission nurses, teachers or preachers and even as travellers in search of themselves and of adventure.

For each of the brides and wives newly resident in China there was usually an initial degree of culture shock during the period shortly after her arrival when she had to adjust the images and expectations which she had brought with her to China. Most had come with expectations shaped by romantic images of the exotic East. China was popularly thought to be a land of pagodas and pavilions, of fans and lanterns, of silks, satins and pigtails and other distinctive oriental material and cultural objects. Indeed their picture of a Chinese landscape was very much based on the blue and white willow-patterned plates with their delicately curved arch-bridges, streams and drooping willows – landscapes which in the traditional style of Chinese brush paintings dwarfed the tiny human figures as if the latter's presence was almost incidental. First time visitors then, as today, admired the curve of the roof, the grace of the pagoda and the artistry of the gardens, but they had been also less prepared for the endless brown of mud, waters and earth, the equally common dust, dirt and disease and the swiftness of a typhoid or cholera death. They were frequently unprepared for the endlessly crowded village and city streets where, as members of a small intrusive and privileged European minority, 'superior' in their Christian beings and secure in their European heritage, they were not always welcome. They were frequently unprepared for the violence of a divided nation that was also the China they inhabited. Indeed the century of European settlements in China was marked by periodic outbursts or bouts of violent xenophobia and there were few resident European women who did not at some time experience fear. During their stay many were forced to flee their homes for the very safety of their lives. It was these factors as much as the strange, romantic and aesthetic which shaped the lives of European women in China in the first decades of the century.

Most European women in China had to come to terms not only with a strange culture, with unfamiliar languages, gestures and meanings, but they usually had to come to terms also with leaving the comfortable homes and life patterns for which their socialisation had invariably prepared them and with the absence of familiar and significant others. Mothers, sisters, friends and very often their own school-age children were absent in far North America and Europe, so that they were several months away from even the fastest return letter or packet. For some, their newly-married lives of loneliness and isolation in a different and strange land, away from all things familiar, initially – or even permanently – assumed a quality of 'exile' and sent them rushing to recreate familiar domestic rituals in a foreign environment. For so many resi-dent women, homemaking and the arrangements of familiar objects within a company, legation or mission house assumed greater proportions than they might have done 'back home'. Gardens too came in for an inordinate amount of loving care and attention partly to fill new-found leisured hours and partly as a reminder of 'home'. The retreat into the domestic refuge by most European women in China was not only a practical gesture embracing or clinging to the familiar, but also a symbolic gesture consciously or unconsciously signalling their retreat into an inviolate private domain protected from things Chinese. The same defensive attitude towards the strange, the unfamiliar and the alien might be displayed by the small foreign communities established in the city treaty ports from the turn of the century.

Many European women, faced with the strange, appro-priated anew their own culture and sought the company of others with like backgrounds within the small foreign communities. These foreign enclaves were usually located in small land concessions set aside for the purpose of European settlement alongside ocean or river anchorages with a bund and promenade for evening walks, a church, a club and a race course. Set among these might be several houses of assorted but recognisable national architectural styles, and indeed it is still a fascinating exercise today to identify the boundaries of the concessions and the nationalities of their inhabitants by their distinctive styles of architecture – at least of those that have survived the planning rigours of the last thirty-five years. Within a treaty port, much of the social life of the community centred around a strenuous regime of male sports such as rowing, rackets, fives, cricket, bowling, riding and pheasant shooting, but women were permitted to join in the tennis and the bridge and they were delegated to organise the numerous social occasions celebrating the various national festivals of the calendar year. They had their own entertainments with elaborate rules detailing the rituals of 'calling cards', receiving 'at home' and entertaining. Despite the tensions inherent within them, these taut foreign communities were nevertheless close-knit enclaves whose members tended to seek reassurance in their cultural heritage and 'superiority' during times of peace and mutual protection when under threat from Chinese anti-foreign outbursts.

Although several of the women writers featured in this book were also conspicuous for their loving recreation of a succession of European homes and a European environment, they looked beyond the boundaries of home and treaty port communities and took a novel interest in Chinese culture and Sino-European relations. Indeed what distinguishes the women writers featured in this book is their relative detachment from their own domestic and foreign community affairs especially when compared to other European women of their acquaintance. It is true that the six women writers were frequently physically located in scattered homes or in towns without foreign concessions, but when they resided within and did participate in the affairs of treaty port communities, they did not allow themselves to be fully encompassed by the smallness of enclave affairs, preferring instead to observe them with a slightly humorous air. A constant theme in many of their novels and books was the fatigue and spiritual ennui of European women who, longing for the familiar in home and children and custom and entirely encompassed by the affairs of their heart, home and foreign community, neglected almost entirely the world of Chinese culture and society of which they were also part.

What equally distinguished the women writers presented here was their curiosity about Chinese domestic and social customs and especially the life patterns of Chinese women. It is in their depiction of these that they have left valuable ethnographic records of their time in China. It was and is still fashionable for foreign travellers and residents in China to write of their travels and experiences in that country, however brief, and a number of European women have left records of their stay in China. Out of these I have selected six women and whether their writings took the form of fiction, personal narrative or letters, they frequently wrote in comprehensive detail of both Chinese and Sino-European domestic and social life. Once published, many of them contributed to the accumulating public knowledge of China and the more popular images of the China of their times. Although all of the six women writers in this book played a full and wide-ranging role in mediating, observing and depicting Chinese culture in Europe and North America, each of the six women's experience in China and of Chinese culture was also different and in some cases unique.

The British Mrs Archibald Little, who lived for several years in a Chinese town in the far western interior province of Szechwan (Sichuan), is best known for her founding of one of the first anti-footbinding societies in China and for her record of the campaign to 'stand the women of China on their feet'. Sara Pike Conger, wife of the American minister in Peking at the turn of the century, befriended the Empress Dowager and a number of noble ladies of the court. As one of the first and frequent visitors to their homes, she made the most of every opportunity to record their customs. Grace Seton Thompson, traveller and journalist, has left a unique written and photographic record of her interviews with the first generation of Chinese women to acquire new public roles in the professions, commerce and industry. Chicago-born Alice Tisdale Hobart first wrote of her travels and homesteading experiences as a young company wife in China and then a number of novels which thoughtfully explained the experience of young European traders, missionaries and company men and women in China throughout the turbulent twentieth century. Young Nora Waln, an American student of Chinese in Philadelphia, had the good fortune to be invited to live as an 'adopted daughter' within a large and extended gentry household. *The House of Exile* which closely documents the daily and domestic arrangements and practices of the household has long since informed and given enjoyment to students of Chinese domestic and social life. Finally Pearl Buck, the daughter of missionary parents in China, wrote the best-selling novel *The Good Earth* about peasant life in China. She also wrote numerous other novels, her own autobiography, the biographies of her missionary mother and father in China and several works of non-fiction and translations so that for a generation of Europeans it was she who almost single-handedly depicted Chinese domestic and social life. In a recent study of American attitudes towards China, it was her writings which were designated one of the most important sources of American images and expectations of China in the twentieth century.

Although each woman writer's experience of China was very different, they had a common curiosity which caused them to take advantage of every opportunity to travel in China. Their books reveal a fund of experiences and adventures from the relatively advantageous position, if not always the comfort, of the sledge, mule cart, litter or sedan chair in environments ranging from far-flung Tibet or the northeastern frozen waste to a Chinese coal mine. Mrs Archibald Little, smothered in a large fur coat to look like any Mandarin, ventured as the first European woman to travel in far-western China and in unknown parts of Tibet. Alice Tisdale Hobart set off on sledge trips in the frozen north of China for weeks on end in so many layers of clothes that she could barely move. Others were less ambitious, but all contrasted the day-time sights and the gentle swaying of the sedan chair with the nightly indignities of the dirt-ridden, bedbugged Chinese inns when fearful of being objects of curiosity or sometimes hostility they could not undress to reveal their foreign identity let alone their sex. Away from the crowds and inns, however, they explored the mountain tracks and farmed parts of the Chinese countryside, observing a China quite unlike that of the treaty ports and cities and towns. They saw the coolie woman bearing heavy baskets hung from her shoulders; they stopped to stare at the neatly dressed mothers sitting on their low stools in the narrow alleyways patching clothes, fondling their children or preparing foodstuffs; and they saw and heard the boatwomen as they wove their sanpans in and out of the crowded canal and river traffic. In China at this time though, even the most imaginative travellers were constrained. However much the travellers might glimpse and observe, to foreign eyes in the early decades of the twentieth century, the lives of Chinese peasant and gentry women still lay hidden from all but the most privileged, curious and determined. There were few opportunities for foreigners to observe informally the daily life of gentry and village women for their activities largely took place within enclosed family compounds behind high solid brick, adobe or stone walls. Consequently, there were few occasions for informal contact between European women, largely confined to public spaces, and Chinese women, largely confined to their domestic affairs.

Perhaps the most striking feature of Chinese social life generally was the segregation of the sexes and the domestic seclusion of women. From earliest times all women had been taught that they should not concern themselves with public affairs: 'A wife's words should not travel beyond her apartments' and 'a woman does not discuss affairs outside the home'. Women were denied any formal participation in any of the government or local community institutions and all the significant Confucian ceremonial roles in society could only be fulfilled by men. Even within family and kinship units all the leadership and ceremonial roles had been reserved for men. Only they could perform the ancestral rites of such importance in the clan or lineage. The absence of women in public spaces and their confinement to the domestic sphere was further reinforced by the concern for and almost obsession with the preservation of their virtue and honour. The practice of binding feet, which could devastatingly restrict mobility, the cult of feminine chastity and ideal of segregation had led to the virtual isolation of women within their own households. Indeed the very word for *woman* was *neiren* which literally meant 'inside person'. Within the confines of the women's apartments in richer and gentry households women were occupied with their toilet, embroidery, the management of household affairs and parlour amusements. In peasant households, which afforded women less seclusion, working women frequently laboured on their doorways on the village or city street, gathered water from the well and shopped and marketed, but even so the movements of most village women were restricted. It was frequently observed that women had rarely travelled except on their marriage day and they were known to have referred to themselves as 'frogs in a well'. The common saying, 'A man travels everywhere while a woman is confined to the kitchen' and 'an incompetent man can get around nine counties but a competent woman can only get around her cooking stove', arose because appearances of women outside their household yards were rare. One working woman recalled that the greatest compliment a woman could receive from her neighbours was that they 'had never seen her'. The denial of a public self was even reflected in the domestic domain where the customary answer in northern peasant households to the question: 'Is anybody at home?' was 'No, there's nobody in', given by the housewife herself!

Not only did Chinese women inhabit few public spaces; few European women themselves ventured on to the city or village streets to shop and gossip at the markets or wash and collect water from the communal wells. Should they have done so, they would still have had the problem of communication for most European women made little attempt to learn the Chinese language. In an attempt to breach the communications gap several of these curious woman writers attempted to speak Chinese and their success in grappling with the difficult language ranged from the case of Mrs Little who managed to speak a little to Pearl Buck who as a child could shock Chinese strangers with her command of and fluency in the Chinese idiom and written word. Even for those who persevered, the problem of local dialect remained. Within her 'adopted' family, even Norah Waln, a student of Chinese, was initially banned from the presence of the senior lady of the household until she had sufficiently mastered the intricacies of the local language to be understood by her. In addition to the language, however, foreign wives found it even more difficult to breach the physical and cultural barriers when it came to observing domestic and social life away from the streets and public places.

Such were the divisions and separate spheres of Chinese and Europeans that for all the women writers, with the exception of the privileged Norah Waln and the child Pearl Buck, any form of interaction had a long gestation. To glimpse behind the walls of a family compound required a formal invitation, and in the ordinary course of events it was not customary for the heads of Chinese families to receive visitors who were neither kin related nor of long-standing friendship into their own homes. As is still the custom today, foreigners were more usually treated to receptions or meals in restaurants or tea houses by their Chinese hosts, acquaintances or friends. For many months, Sarah Pike Conger, who attended many an official reception, despaired of ever penetrating behind the walls of Peking's family compounds. For her the walls visibly symbolised the invisible cultural barriers separating and blocking more intimate interaction between herself and Chinese women. Apart from the racial segregation that was such a deeply entrenched factor in treaty port traditions and which made it very difficult to have a foot in both worlds, differentials in status and power between the 'privileged' European and 'colonised' Chinese were such that they affected almost every facet of interpersonal or intergroup communication and relations. Although most of the women writers would have agreed with Sarah Pike Conger that these invisible barriers were every bit as formidable as the walls of bricks and mortar, after some time most of them did receive the longed-for invitations.

Given the very formal rituals which surrounded visits to Chinese homes, however, it was often quite difficult for the European women, at least in the first instance, to engage in more than the politest niceties of enquiry and reply. They also found themselves to be the novel objects of curiosity and attention so that they could nearly all recall an occasion when their female attire right down to their chemises was very much the object of enquiry and touch! Even when it looked as if some rapport might have been established, there were instances of culturally-derived misunderstandings which could beguile the unsuspecting foreigner. For example European wives often thought quite incorrectly that they had been privileged to meet the wives of their husbands' business or official acquaintances even though it was not usual for the women to accompany them to tea-house or restaurant meetings. Alice Tisdale Hobart thought she was meeting the wife of one of her husband's business acquaintances only to find afterwards that a flower girl had been hired especially for the occasion. Moreover by taking his own wife with him, Earl Hobart was advertising to the assembled company how little he respected her. Sarah Pike Conger thought she had established a privileged rapport with the Empress and ladies of the Imperial Palace, but it was later revealed that the Empress disliked their undue prying to the extent that she frequently had her rooms redecorated or her personal effects rearranged so as to maintain the Chinese conventions of domestic privacy. When Mrs Little thought she was to be granted an unusual opportunity to live alongside a Chinese farm household, relations between them so badly deteriorated after a robbery of their rooms that they were glad to return to the city.

It was perhaps the initial difficulties of gaining access to the domestic and social life of other households that commonly turned the attention of the women writers to the one group who could be closely observed and befriended within their own home – the servants. Indeed it was within their homes that most European women first came into direct contact with Chinese customs. No European household in China was without a goodly number of servants to take charge of the cooking, cleaning, clothes, garments and other needs of the European employers. Below stairs there was a well-developed and highly stratified and rationalised mode of interaction defining relations both among the servants and with their European employers. Within the house, the allocation of the space for the European and Chinese inhabitants was very well defined as were the rules and regulations governing the responsibilities of each. Any attempt by the European mistress of the household to modify or adjust these regulations and relations usually failed and any differences of opinion were almost always resolved in favour of the servants. Nevertheless relations between the European mistress of the household and her servants were frequently very warm and cordial with a degree of loyalty on both sides that could be sorely tested during anti-foreign outbreaks. As books, diaries and novels reveal, the daily and life-cycle activities of servants offered a wonderfully direct opportunity for observation and learning if the European mistress had a mind.

Outside of their own homes, intimate and longer-term opportunities to observe Chinese domestic and social life were thus often hard won and having won them, the very novelty of their experiences and the knowledge that they had stepped beyond the formalised and polite conventions normally governing such interactions encouraged each of these six women to write of her experiences. Until the twentieth century there had been few European books about China that had either described the lives of Chinese women or attempted to document and relate women's experience. Previous writers on China, mostly male scholars and travellers, focused on the Chinese language, politics and places with much emphasis given to the flora and fauna. Most alluded briefly to practices such as bound feet, female infanticide and prostitution but ignored women's experience of these and the details of domestic and social life. Around 1920 when one European male author was questioned as to why there was so little writing on the subject of women in China, he had stopped, looked puzzled for a moment and then replied, 'I believe no one ever thinks of them except perhaps that they are mothers of Chinese men!' This study of the works of women writers reveals how different were the observations and emphasis of female and male writers of the same times and situations.

In one respect however women writers had an advantage over their male counterparts in that once admitted to Chinese households they had exclusive access to the domestic spaces, inner courtyards and female domains. Their very sex, so often a disadvantage in other respects, had in this case created a privileged space for female ethnographers. In all cases each of the six women defined her purpose in writing on China quite differently from those of her male contemporaries. They alluded frequently to their new and unusual knowledge of the 'hidden' or 'inner' spaces, the 'dark' or 'secluded' corners of China – interestingly all adjectives used to describe the cosmological private, dark, hidden female 'yin' as opposed to the light, public open male 'yang' domain. Mrs Little called her first book on China *Intimate China* precisely because she felt that she had seen families in the *intimacy* of their homes and could therefore record the unusual and the private for her British readers. Sarah Pike Conger thought that she had been placed in the unique role of being able to relay 'intimacies' or 'heart stories' in which she was able to illustrate the 'real' character of her Chinese informants. Grace Seton Thompson exhorted her readers to listen to the 'talking of hearts' and in her book entitled *Chinese Lanterns* she thought of herself as lighting for her readers the dark corners of home, street, town and village. Several years later and from their vantage point within Chinese households, both Norah Waln and Pearl Buck felt that they could draw uniquely for their readers the intimate and domestic details they had personally observed and experienced. In describing and reporting on the hidden domestic and social life of Chinese households, these women writers have much in common with modern ethnographers.

Although personal narrative plays a much larger part in their writings than is usual in ethnographies today, their observations are based on informal conversations and on formal interviews and acquired on the basis of their own direct first-hand experiences over a long-term period of personal involvement with their informants and respondents. To learn, they placed themselves frequently in the 'polite' role of pupil or student, and while many of their writings were more descriptive than analytical, the description was often unusually latticed and the underlying meaning solicited. Many a modern ethnographer would sympathise with Sarah Pike Conger who, aiming to render intelligible to her reader the social behaviour she observed and participated in, felt initially overwhelmed in that all she could see was 'confusion, lack of method and lack of meaning'. Only as she struggled to make sense of the puzzles around her did she begin to realise that the customs and rituals were made up of a rich symbolism of such continuity and depth of meaning that she developed not only a greater curiosity but also a greater respect for the customs and rituals themselves. It is in the books of these women writers that European readers were first able to learn in detail of the daily or annual bathing rituals, dress and attire, the seasonal cycles of food production, preparation and consumption, the recording of time, the household accounts or genealogy and the arrangement and distribution of domestic labour including the nurturing and socialisation of the younger generation. Here too the European reader can learn of the practical and ceremonial preparation for conception and birth, the rituals of betrothal and marriage and the anticipation and preparation for, or even rehearsal of, death and the subsequent promotion to ancestor.

What had always attracted the attention of the European writers on China were the various means by which Chinese women were kept in their subordinate position. Already the technicalities of the bound foot had been much described and frequently criticised. Indeed in Europe and North America the bound foot had become symbol of all that was deemed to be culturally backward about China. Victorian readers, despite the oppressions in their own countries, read with shaking heads of the crippling of Chinese women, the horrors of female infanticide and the plight of young girls sold into slavery, prostitution and as child daughters-in-law. The six women writers depicted these practices too, but they were also more concerned to reflect the experience of women by relaying the tears and pain of their first footbinding, the crippling of physical mobility and the resultant ill-health. In contrast too, their writings provided fragments of women's rich and various relationships in secluded and domestic domains. They provided insights into the interpersonal relations between women of the same generation and across the generations, they revealed the intimate messages that were transmitted from mothers to daughters, and they revealed the strategies by which women survived or acquired a degree of personal influence and power. Young Chinese maidens might have their own means of subverting an arranged marriage, a woman of the older generation might simultaneously cite and instil the old adages of obedience, virtue and submission and exercise a degree of personal control and authority within the household which would be the envy of many a patriarch.

As the twentieth century progressed, the writings of European women increasingly vividly portrayed the changes in the emerging public lives of younger and older women. After the turn of the century, a generation of young women grew up at a time when traditional and modern, Chinese and western influences jostled for supremacy in the minds of the literate and urban-educated young. They lived through a period of cultural renaissance during which there was some fundamental questioning of traditional Chinese philosophies and customs and a powerful first acquaintance with new political and literary influences from abroad. Within gentry households it was a time when the ideal of romantic love was set against arranged marriage, agility and mobility against footbinding and seclusion, and new forms of female education and occupation against domestic service and dependence in marriage. How to reconcile the individual quest for personal freedom and fulfilment with the old Confucian obligations on daughters and wives rooted in the traditional patriarchal family system was a central dilemma for modern young women. It was this generation of young women who were the focus of Grace Seton Thompson's attention in 1920 although she also interviewed peasant and working women. Although each of the six women writers had established a rapport with the Chinese women of their acquaintance very much on the basis of their common interest in the domestic and felt that they therefore had a special responsibility to write of China's women, it would be mistaken to assume that they were not also interested or indeed very concerned with more general Sino-European relations.

Any European women or men in China who were of receptive and reflective disposition could not help but find themselves confronted by a smouldering political and cultural revolution as late-nineteenth and twentieth-century China struggled to come to terms with its changing self and its semi-colonial encounter with European and North American nations. Europeans arriving and residing in China from the turn of the century regularly found themselves part of an uncertain and turbulent sequence of events affecting not only China but also Sino-European relations. The few decades before and after the turn of the century had been marked by the questioning of and challenges to the old and traditional ways and a search for new and modern social and political institutions. Much of the source of inspiration for the attempted imperial reforms of 1898, the toppling of the Dynasty and founding of the Republic in 1911 and the subsequent new thought and cultural renaissance known as the May 4th movement of 1919 were all in their various ways attempts to redefine social and political institutions in China after examples derived from the western nations. During this Chinese crisis of confidence, it was the western powers of North America and Europe which seemed to hold the secret of wealth, power and stability. These decades thus saw the height of western influence in China and a preoccupation with emulating European social, political and economic thought, institutions and practices.

At the same time, however, this age of foreign privilege, penetration, aggression and violence was depicted by the *Punch* cartoons in which China was frequently shown as the enticing cake, melon or other treat available and ready for portioning between the foreign powers at the party table. The increasingly apparent incapacity of China's governments of the day to respond to this challenge fed the reform republic and anti-foreign patriotic movements of the first two decades. A second semi-colonial phase opened in the 1920s and was marked by the further penetration of foreign presence and capital and a steady decline of the power of the central government in the face of competition and fragmentation from a number of regional warlords. Banditry, the extreme vagaries of China's

climate and the flood of machine-made goods contributed to
the decline of the rural economy while the growth of new
industries and commerce based on cheap labour in the larger
cities created a new class entirely dependent on either casual
or below-subsistence wages. In response to deteriorating conditions and the disaggregation and colonial status of the once
proud Middle Kingdom, there emerged a single new nationalist
movement combining a number of political groups and parties
under the leadership of first Sun Yat-sen and later Chiang
kai-shek. Its immediate goal was the defeat of the regional
warlords and the establishment of a new strong and central
government to defend China's national interests. It was the
wave of nationalism and anti-foreignism which accompanied
this movement that threatened non-Chinese residing in China
including both Alice Tisdale Hobart and Pearl Buck.

The attitude of most Europeans travelling and residing in
China towards the reforming patriotic and anti-foreign movements of this period was dictated by their own enormous
confidence in European civilisation reinforced by the visible
decline and convulsions of the once great Chinese civilisation.
Such a juxtaposition lent credibility to the European cause in
China be it to save souls or expand commercial and trading
interests. With such an inherent culturally derived confidence,
a lamentably large number of Europeans thought of China as
little more than an ancient nation irretrievably sunk in an
outworn culture, the political and economic spoils of which
were up for auction. Out of this enormous confidence in
their own culture and cause, there developed a general air
of superiority among Europeans which came to characterise
inter-personal relations between individuals of the two races.

Colonial attitudes can certainly be detected in the writings
of the six women authors and although not one of them was
immune from the prevailing attitudes of confidence in and
superiority of their own culture, they seemed to have been
unusually sensitive to the hierarchical nature of the power relations between China and Europe and to China's own response
to and point of view about this uneven power relationship.
They did achieve a certain degree of detachment in the face

of cultural chauvinism and blindness commonly displayed by Europeans in China and which they depicted and denounced in their books. At one extreme they portrayed the Sinicised individual who, having appropriated the attire of a Chinese Mandarin, lived in a Chinese house with a Chinese wife and children in an explicit rejection of his European heritage. At the other extreme most of their books feature the culturally blind, the European residents who never set foot out of the foreign concession or were 'twenty-years-in-China-and-not-know-a-word-of-the-language' people. Some of the very amusing incidents related in their writings centre around the exaggerated cultural chauvinism within the all-encompassing inherently taut and isolated foreign concession even when it involved no more than deciding the common Christmas menu which could quite suddenly exaggerate ever-present gossip, rumour and tensions along nationalist lines.

Interestingly only two of these authors, Nora Waln and Pearl Buck, had any children. They each had a daughter but Nora Waln left China soon after her birth and Pearl Buck for very special reasons did not bring up her own retarded daughter in China. Although they therefore did not suffer the ambiguities of European motherhood in China, they all sympathetically depicted the plight of mothers who acted in the interest of preserving their children's own European cultural identity. Mothers, wholly responsible for the socialisation of their children in China, not only created European-centred homes, but they also took up an increasingly defensive position to protect their children against the vicissitudes of a Chinese environment with all its physical dangers and cultural encroachments. Having raised them to be as aware as possible of their own European cultural heritage, they sent them home to be educated; the loss entailed in the pain of separation frequently deeply affected their own attitude to and experience of China. The significance attached to letters, photographs and tea-time hours long after their children's departure prompted bouts of depression and ambivalence and created barriers in the hearts of even the busiest foreign mothers, even for those who had come to China of their own free will.

Spared such agonies, and with a degree of good sense, these women writers all attempted to explain for Europeans the Chinese response to the European presence with its explicit threats to Chinese cultural traditions and to its sovereignty. Mrs Archibald Little frequently wrote to the British papers putting the Chinese point of view and explaining and legitimising the Chinese government's response to some action of the foreign powers. Sarah Pike Conger often observed that it was not so very surprising that China should react against the foreigners who had not only come to China unbidden but had also forced their presence, their customs, their habits and their guns on the Chinese. She forecast that China and the European nations were on a collision course or a war of ideas with the Chinese striving to sustain their own cultural identity. In the early 1900s Sarah Pike Conger was uncertain what the outcome of this conflict would be. Not so Alice Tisdale Hobart whose pessimistic conclusions twenty years later suggested the impossibility of an equitable reconciliation and resolution of the cultural differences. As Pearl Buck finally departed from her girlhood China she was both relieved to be escaping the accumulated guilt which her European heritage had laid upon her and pessimistic that any form of equitable Sino-European relations could be worked out in the near future.

Despite this note of pessimism, each of the women writers would have disagreed vehemently with the sentiments of the eminent Mr Rudyard Kipling. Although they recognised differences and that 'East is east and West is west', they would have gone on to argue not that 'the twain shall never meet' but that the two should and must meet. In their books they did not minimise the differences between the two cultures or even necessarily repudiate the superiority of their own culture, but they did argue that it was important, indeed imperative, to develop a peaceful working relationship based on mutual understanding and respect. This they thought could only be based on an increasing knowledge and new appreciation of Chinese culture and in this regard they each quite consciously adopted the role of cultural mediator. In their day and even still today in some quarters, China was very much reported as a puzzle and an inscrutable one at that, dominated by images that were alien in some exotic or oriental and mysterious manner unique to the East. In making the hidden visible and the strange familiar and comprehensible, they sought to explain meanings behind customs and practices and to interpret apparently exotic concepts and beliefs within their social context.

In common, these women writers did not always avoid the many difficulties in representing other cultures for their readers. When they sought to render the strange or the foreign familiar they sometimes succumbed to the temptation to reduce the differences and in subscribing to common or universal motivations they tended to deny cultural differences. In drawing attention to these differences they likewise either asserted or exaggerated the foreign or the strange in depicting the 'other'. Most of the women writers were at some time or other accused by critics of following one trend or another. In describing the peasant world of China in her famous book *The Good Earth* Pearl Buck was frequently accused of attributing familiar American attitudes, motivations and responses to her Chinese peasants. Alice Tisdale Hobart found it difficult to get her first book published because she had not depicted the sufficiently novel or unique oriental world of American fantasy. They refused to subscribe to the distillations of essential ideas or stereotypes about China or to edit out what might offend European sensibilities of the time. Despite such problems, however, some of which modern ethnographers still find very difficult to overcome, their books were greatly welcomed by the reviewers and the public precisely because in very readable non-fiction and fiction forms, they commonly presented a 'different' China in that they humanised the experience of and created sympathy for individuals of another culture.

It is interesting to conjecture that it might have been their own experience as women in a peculiarly male colonial or semi-colonial world which contributed to their cultural and political sensitivity towards China. They frequently referred to the constraints and circumscriptions surrounding their female persons, likening themselves to 'islands' in the 'seas' or 'rivers' of men's affairs or as the 'oil' confined in flow and expression within 'the lamps of China'. In common with the Chinese they perceived themselves to be different, inferior and muted in a framework constructed on the basis of their biological differences by the European male. In challenging their own position as women within this framework, they also challenged colonial conventions and gave voice and ascribed value and status to the culture and persons of China.

Finally, and in addition to creating knowledge, interpreting custom and fostering widespread popular images, they wrote for themselves and in their texts their selves are mostly to be found. It is now widely acknowledged that any description or interpretation of another culture is very much a personal creation as much dependent on the culture, personality, values and choices of the observer or writer-ethnographer as on those whom in the society they happen to observe and question. There is now rightly much greater significance attached to the relations between observer and observed, interviewer and informant, and writer and text in studies of the process by which knowledge in the form of the written text is constructed. In attempting to discover the identities of these women writers, it has been fortunate that their books incorporate, as was fashionable at the time, a narrative that is personal so that much of these women is written into their books. In a certain sense their writings tell us as much about the authors and their culture as they do about Chinese women and China itself. They tell us something about the expectations of European girl and womanhood which each brought with them to China in one form or another. In their books we learn much of their prior expectations, their personal hopes, apprehensions and ambitions in China, and also of the frustrations and rewards attendant upon their taking up a writing career.

Although they each had begun to write of China because they felt they had something unusual to say, in nearly every case they took up writing also as a means of preserving their very selves in the face of exile or adverse and tragic circumstance. With servants and without children, some found themselves with a new or greater leisure than hitherto. Alice

Tisdale Hobart for example took up writing to counteract the effects of a very painful spinal condition and to escape from the oldest of 'eternal triangles' in which she found herself in competition with her mother-in-law for the attentions of her husband. Pearl Buck took up her pen to ease the absence of the much beloved retarded toddler daughter and the pain of an increasingly disappointing marriage. As for any woman author in Europe, the space to pursue their writings was frequently hard won. As symbolic in a European household in China as elsewhere was the ability of the woman of the house to take charge of and occupy a room of her own. In her house in Nanjing, Norah Waln made elaborate plans for the transformation of an attic room into her own room for writing. Despite her determined efforts, the Chinese servants of the house refused to carry out her plans for redecoration and furnishing until her husband returned home and as master of the house gave his permission. Pearl Buck only escaped to her own room and to the secret life of her books once her house of many rooms was organised for the day. If for some, the space to write was hard won, for others the struggle for independence came later when the hurried scribbling in the attic became a profession with its own discipline and demands.

If subsequently fame also followed professionalism then personal and family relationships often had to be redefined to take account of this success. Frequently the isolation and loneliness of out-port and even treaty port life had bound husband and wife into a closer relationship than might have been developed back home, and certainly the majority of the women writers enjoyed their husbands' company and determined on working at maintaining a valued relationship. However most of their husbands had also married in the expectation that their wives would conform to the norms of the times and that they would receive from their wives both help and support in pursuing their own careers or hobbies. Each therefore had to make adjustments of one kind or another once their wives became writers of some renown. Alice Tisdale Hobart's very supportive husband refused to see the film of her bestseller *Oil for the Lamps of China* in case his wife should be spoiled by too much attention. Both Pearl Buck's husbands made all-consuming demands on her very considerable personal talents and on her material resources to the detriment of her own writing career.

What these women writers wanted to do was to evolve a way of living which combined both personal and professional interests and a certain degree of independence within a sharing relationship. On the basis of their common interest in the domestic and the social, they each succeeded in establishing an intimate rapport with women of another culture, which was often followed by respect and recognition in other domains including Sino-European political and cultural relations. In pursuit of these personal and political goals, each of the six European women writers featured in the ensuing chapters constantly defined and redefined their own lives. They found themselves expressing very decided views, challenging the narrow conventions and expectations surrounding European womanhood. The women writers presented here are perhaps only representative of the unusual women of their times who disregarded or overcame the constraints of their Victorian girlhoods and of Edwardian women be it at home or in foreign lands. In so doing, they left behind them writings which were widely read in their time and their texts are still unique records of traditional and twentieth-century domestic and social life in China; thus the historical importance of the authors as cultural mediators is assured, not so much of European culture in China as of Chinese culture in Europe.

2

An Intimate View of Chinese Women: 'The Chinese Goddess of Mercy' and against Foot-binding, Mrs Archibald Little

'You are just like the *kwanyin pusa* (the Chinese Goddess of Mercy). Hitherto we Chinese have had but one *kwanyin*. But now we have two. You are the second.' The European woman who was given this honorary title by a senior Chinese official was the British Mrs Archibald Little who, determined to set the women of China on their feet, founded one of the first anti-footbinding societies there in 1895. She was its first president and organising secretary and for ten years until her departure from China in 1906 she worked energetically for its cause. Within China she played a more public active role than any of her European contemporaries, and outside of China she was probably one of the best known authors writing on China around the turn of the century. In 1887 at the mature age of forty-one years, the novelist Alicia Bewicke had arrived in China as the bride of Mr Archibald Little, a merchant of some twenty-five years standing in China who had been on leave in England for a few months. For several years she lived in a Chinese town in the far western interior province of Sichuan where, isolated from the amenities of any treaty port, or significant foreign settlement, she continued to write fiction and non-fiction in which she documented both the domestic and social life of Chinese families and of European families in China.

Alicia Bewicke had been born in Madeira in 1845 where

her parents had migrated to the warmer climate after her
father, Calverley Bewicke of Hallaton Hall, Leicestershire,
had sustained an injury while stroking for the Oxford Eight.
She was the second of six children, the first three of whom
were daughters. Their arrival had so shamed the parents that
they had given each of their subsequent sons names which
variously meant 'gift of God'. Daughter Alicia grew up and
was educated in Madeira where family photographs show large
smiling gatherings given to festive celebrations and sporting
recreation. Her books suggest that she had been educated in
the classics and was well-read in the literature of a number
of European countries. She travelled widely and probably
sometime in her early twenties she returned to England to
be entered into the debutante social circuit appropriate to
acquiring a suitable husband. Photographs of the time show
a very poised young lady of the season but with fewer of the
conventional attributes. Her hair was rather severely pulled
back in a large chignon to highlight a strong profile, definite
features and a determined gaze. Perhaps she was a woman
with too much spirit to be confined to the social round for
it does seem that she was soon bored by the customary entertainments and preoccupations of the social season and instead
took to writing down her sharp observations and astute perceptions of its limitations and foibles.

At twenty-three years of age she published her first novel,
called rather provocatively *Flirts and Flirts or A Season in
Ryde*. In it, the new young author, with an eye for nuance
and detail, is gently scathing but pointedly critical of the season
in Ryde which, concentrated on its pier, was characterised by
the manoeuvrings and manipulations of mothers and daughters
in viewing the turn of the ankle, the size of the bonnet and
the length of the dress, or the dash, the cut and the fortune
of young men as the chief prerequisites to a good marriage.
Her main ambition in this and her subsequent novels was to
lay bare the collusion of Victorian mothers in the socialisation
of their daughters for the sole purpose of delivering them into
the hands of men about whom they knew very little beyond
the size of their fortune, their good looks and the art of

their conversation. In her books she is highly critical of the circumscription placed by the demands of the season on young women's lives and talents, and their subsequent confinement to husband, health and home.

In *Miss Standish*, which is probably the most autobiographical of her novels, the author apparently speaks from the heart when she writes of what it feels like for a woman to step outside the narrow domestic role prescribed for her and come to terms with 'the real world'. Emelia Standish, a poetess of some note, is interested in the political and social questions of the day, from women's franchise to the fate of pauper children, and in pursuit of this interest often attends the Ladies' Gallery to listen to the parliamentary debates. She refuses to think only of marriage or to relate to men of her acquaintance merely as potential marriage partners. She is chastised by all and sundry about being interested in subjects 'not fit for women'. One of these subjects which Alicia Bewicke thought should be of particular interest to women was made into a little shilling book of pamphlet size written in support of the Married Women's Property Act. The story, entitled *Mother Darling*, may have been inspired by the fate of her own older sister Caroline who like Lady Caroline Norton was said to have married the best dressed man in town to whom she later lost her children and her property and fortune following the breakdown of her marriage. Alicia's aim in writing this story of a young mother who finds to her absolute horror that her wayward husband is entirely within his rights not only to take away the children but also deprive her of all access or even knowledge of their whereabouts was to shake women out of their state of ignorance and lack of concern with the social and political issues of the day. She thought that women would continue to be left without adequate protection so long as they avoided knowledge of and about such issues. This is the last of the fiction written by Alicia Bewicke, for like all her heroines Alicia herself eventually married although for her it came much later than was customary for the times.

In November 1886 at St George's, Hanover Square, she married the son of a London surgeon, Archibald Little, who

had first gone to China in 1859 where he had established
a trading company in a far western province of Szechwan
(Sichuan). Although he was a merchant by accident of career,
he was however a scholar and traveller by bent of character and
preference. He had indeed written several books all of which
reflected his keen interest in China and his observations on
its language and its people. He had travelled widely, collected
many materials and his fluency in the language had given him
a store of information, anecdotes and reflections which had
contributed many interesting touches to his writings, the best
known of which was a book on the Yangtze river gorges.
As his wife of twenty-two years was to write on his death,
he was something of 'an innocent dreamer', full of weird
and interesting ideas and schemes; some, such as taking
the first steamships up the Yangtze River worked; others
never matured in practice. Shortly after her marriage, Alicia
Bewicke began a new life in China as Mrs Archibald Little
and it is interesting that she embraced that life so completely
that in her later writings and press interviews on return trips
to England her English novels were never again referred to.
Only the research for this book has uncovered her previous life
as the novelist Alicia Bewicke. As for Mrs Archibald Little,
she became very well known as a writer on China and for her
reforming zeal in unbinding the feet of Chinese women.

Mrs Little's first glimpse of China in May 1887 was of
European Shanghai with its fine European houses fronting
the river, the well-known public gardens and the wide streets
with their electric lights, carriages and great European stores
'in which everything that could possibly be wanted could be
bought and only very little dearer than in London'. Indeed Mrs
Little thought that but for the density of the crowds of Chinese
inhabitants jostling with Europeans in the thoroughfares of the
European concession and the proximity of nearby Chinese
towns she might have imagined herself still in Europe. Even
today vestiges of the European remain more in evidence in
Shanghai than in any other city. Mrs Little's first years in China
were however largely spent away from European treaty port
settlements in the relative isolation of Chungking city located

in distant Szechwan (Sichuan) province, about as far west from Shanghai as it was possible to travel while staying within China. As Mrs Little rather wryly wrote, the sense of isolation in Chungking was very much heightened by the thought that it took longer to get a letter the 1500 miles from Shanghai to Chungking than it did to get a letter the 13,000 miles from England to Shanghai! In an ordinary run and with good luck, an answer might be received from a letter to England within four months.

The city of Chungking boasted no settlement for the exclusive use of the few Europeans who resided there, few European houses and no European shops. In terms of layout the city reminded Mrs Little of Edinburgh or Quebec in that it lay at the junction of two rivers and in terms of size she thought of French Lyon. The city was walled and built upon a rock which as the summer progressed warmed up until the heat was very great indeed. Very crowded and closed in by walls, the airless, steep and stepped streets were mostly covered over, both as a protection against the fierce summer and the frequent rains. If outdoors were hot and stifling, the temperature was no different indoors so that sometimes whole days had to be spent in the cellar in order to gain relief from the incessant heat. As much as Mrs Little found the lofty-roofed and pillared houses to be picturesque – with their black rafters and white plaster, their highly decorated exteriors with little black and white paintings under the eaves, and richly carved and heavily gilded beams – she soon realised that Europeans could not hope for health in them because of the draughts and damp in the winter and the heat and damp in the summer. Given the shrinking partitions, doors, windows and floorboards which let in the draughtss on rainy wintry days, she understood why their Chinese friends wore heavily padded and fur-lined clothes the very bulk of which not only made it impossible for them to take exercise but gave the day-long impression 'of lolling about' much as if in bed! For European women in their flimsier clothes, the relentless heat of the summers and wet, cold winters caused nearly every one to be ill at some time and sometimes very seriously so.

From the time of her arrival in China, she had made it clear
that she intended to lead no ordinary life and certainly not
one typical of European women in China. Indeed, if anything,
in the spirit of the heroines of her novels, she was rather
impatient with their leisured preoccupation with fashion, the
shortcomings of their servants and the distractions, deferences
and niceties of treaty port life. She was even more scornful of
their lack of interest in street life, the 'native' city and Chinese
affairs. She thought it to be symbolic that most European
women, serviced and sedan-chaired, did not even set foot on
Chinese soil! She had no time for those who because of the dirt,
the 'horrible sights' and 'still more horrible smells' felt unable
to leave the comforts of the foreign settlements. She fancied
that those that talked this way could know very little of the East
End of London and nothing of the towns of the south of France
and Italy. However although Mrs Little might wish to avoid the
insularity of a regular treaty port life, at home in Chungking
she could not entirely escape the poor health, the tedium, the
triviality and the depression that were the European women's
lot during the long hot summer and even longer wintry days. As
she wrote rather wryly: 'Chungking is not a place for a woman
without occupation.' Fortunately she found plenty to occupy
her. When not exploring her surroundings or travelling afar
with her husband, she tackled the Chinese language, taught
English, continued to write novels and published several travel
books which were and are still noted for their adventurous
spirit, colourful and astute observations and the quality of the
many photographs, most of which she took herself.

In her immediate environs she thought that to miss out on
street life was to miss out on a most important experience of
Chinese social life. To this end she disregarded all the dire
warnings and determined on finding the ways and means to
walk, observe and even photograph as anonymously as possible. In one of her books she describes the street life immediately outside of her own Chungking house-wall and gate:

> The streets although wide for a Chinese city, are very
> narrow in comparison with English streets, being only

eight feet at the widest and extraordinarily crowded. Passing through them is a continual pushing through a crowd of footpassengers; its sedan chairs, carried by coolies, with sometimes one or two men running before to clear the way, and if it be necessary, beat back the crowd; of mules, donkeys or ponies with loads; and of numbers of carrying coolies, a bamboo across their shoulders and from either end a basket hanging by strings. Everything that can be done in the streets is done in them: pedlars go by with great quantities of goods for sale; men are mending broken china with little rivets after a fashion in which the Chinese are great experts; here is a barber shaving a man's head, there one or two women menders, on little stools very neatly dressed, pursuing their vocations; here is a man working at an embroidery frame, there a cobbler mending shoes; here some pigs, there some children; here a baby in a hen coop, there a pussycat tied to a shop counter; and in the evenings street preachers, in the afternoons vast crowds passing out from the theatres. At night in going out to dinner we used always to pass at least three street preachers. . .there is always a little crowd listening, though often a small one. In the better streets every attention is paid to decency! In the lesser streets none is apparent. At the street corners there are often large tanks full of water, as a precaution against fire. These are invariably grown over with weed. A vast army of coolies is everyday going down the steep flight of steps to the river to bring water, which drips from the buckets as it is carried along. Another army is carrying out the sewerage of the city to be used as manure. A very soft coal is used for fuel: and baskets of coal are constantly being carried in, two dangling from a pole across the coolies' shoulders.

On her arrival in Chungking she had been advised that because of the crowds, coal, dust, smoke and dripping water, not to mention the manure, it would be 'absolutely impossible' for an

English woman to walk the streets. With typical determination she set about to accustom the crowds of Chungking to her presence. After showing herself as much as she could in a sedan chair with the curtains up in order that all those in the streets would have done with their stares and curiosity, she then took to walking in the streets. Despite the fact that she had her sedan chair follow her to show that she had some claim to respectability, she still had to be rescued from the crowds several times before the Chungking residents became used to the sight of her and she was able to walk unattended. If familiarity provided her with some acceptability in the streets of 'her city', elsewhere she had to accept the constraints of her race and sex. The excitement of her first night in a Chinese city was heightened by the secrecy of her presence and the enforced anonymity of her person. As she later recalled:

> One of the most exciting moments of all my life in China when I first found myself shut up within the walls and barred gates of Wuchang, the provincial capital of Hupeh, one of the rowdiest provinces of China. . . I remember still the thrill with which, when I went to bed that night, I stood at the window and listened to the strange, unfamiliar sounds from the street beyond the compound or garden. There was the night-watchman crying the hours, and clacking his pieces of bamboo together to warn evil-doers to keep off. But he did it in a way I had not yet heard. Then there were the curious long drawn-out street cries, all unknown, and sounds of people calling to one another, and the buzz of a great city. And I suddenly realised with a choking sense of emotion, that the gates were shut, and I was within there with a whole city full of Chinese so hostile to foreigners, and especially to foreign women, that it had not been thought safe to let me walk through them to the missionary's house. Even the curtain of my sedan-chair had been drawn down, so that I might not be seen by anyone.

The anonymity of her first night in a Chinese city set a familiar pattern for future travels in which Alicia Little had to get used to denying her female presence. Certainly she came to feel that men had great advantages in travelling. Not only could they show themselves openly during their travels, but curiosity in their persons was less and facilities more common even in well-travelled parts of the Yangtze valley. On one of these mountain trips there had been a great wondering as to what she was, and she had often heard the country people beseeching the coolies to tell them. When she sat in her chair in her long fur coat, and her husband rode the pony, alongside, bystanders had no doubt at all that she was a man, and a mandarin or official at that, and he her outrider. In the accustomed manner they stood with bated breath while 'he' was carried by. But with the heat and discarding of her fur coat, which is generally only worn by mandarins, her dignity departed and then on foot or on horse-back, she was altogether an anomaly. 'The hair seemed to be the hair of a woman; but, then, the feet were surely the feet of a man.' Old-fashioned Chinese inns with no women's quarters frequently refused to have her overnight and only the servants' categorical pretence and denial that she was a woman found them all beds for the night. As her servant advised:

> No man must see you. And you no must say anything. My have say all a mistakey, you no belong woman, you are man. . . The last inn say no got any room, because no will have one woman. So my go on very fast, and say you are man.

Given the public nature of Chinese inns such pretences made it very difficult for her to undertake her toilette, undress and go to bed let alone talk and be with her fellow-travellers. How she envied her husband his freedom of person and talk on these occasions. It also must be said, however, that both husband and wife never really knew what reception to expect on their travels. They might be pelted and hit with earth as part of local anti-foreign sentiment or they might be welcomed by the curious and invited into peasant homes. Like many ethnographers past and present they hit upon a device which enhanced communication. Having no babies or young children, they took along with them a succession of small dogs as travelling companions. Their presence aroused everywhere an enthusiastic response; of one such dog she says:

> Mothers brought out their babies who cooed in delight; boys danced backwards down the street before him, clapping their hands and even the pallid faces of the most hardened opium smokers relaxed into a smile. Everywhere we marvel to a chorus of 'him-dog, lion-dog!' and general happy smiles.

In fact they had many offers to buy him for why else would a dog be travelling with them if he were not being taken to market for sale? Mrs Little could also recall several occasions on her travels when onlookers thought that at least foreign animals were good-looking and well kept even if their owners were not!

Although Mrs Little had many adventures and travels including journeys in the first steam-ships up the Yangtze gorges, in the far western provinces and in Chinese Tibet where she was one of the first European women to travel, what made her books different and caused them to be greeted in England with special interest were her observations on Chinese families', and especially women's, domestic and social life as she had personally experienced it. In her books she aimed explicitly to use anecdote and description rather than the facts and figures of a reference book to encourage her readers to feel the sights, sounds and smells and become acquainted with the people whom she had had the good fortune to observe intimately in their homes and at their dinner parties. In this, her most important aim in writing her books, she succeeded. As one reviewer said of her first non-fiction book on China, entitled *Intimate China*, 'it enabled people to become acquainted with a thousand and one little peculiarities of dress, of speech and customs that other books leave out'. In writing of such details and to allow the readers to feel themselves part of the scenes and sights, she combined various techniques or styles, sometimes giving them the very words in which she dashed off her instant impressions, 'all palpitating with the strangeness and incongruity of Chinese life' while at others giving them the results of subsequent serious reflections.

In presenting China to her readers, Alicia Little was well aware of how difficult it was to observe and write of another culture, country and society 'with quite unprejudiced eyes'. She thought that while persons of each nation got accustomed to their own problems and shortcomings they still had wide-open eyes for their neighbours' deficiencies. Deficiencies of which she herself was most conscious and fought hard to overcome included her first and greatest disappointment on arriving in China and seeing so much brown mud and dirt and dust. She was not sure that she really had expected it to be the blue and white of the willow plate, but she was greatly disappointed to find it all so brown and muddy. Like many visitors today, she retreated into the aesthetically landscaped gardens with their exquisitely planned pavilions, lakes, walls and trees to find the romantic East of which she had dreamed. Elsewhere she found it very hard to ignore the dirt and to rise above this to appreciate the physical landscape around her. To this end she constantly reminded the reader of the problems of the urban fog and other similar shortcomings in European cities. On the whole she was rather brusque and matter-of-fact in expressing her own attitudes and views. She did not wince at describing the dirt, cruelty and strange customs in China which were not to her own taste; at the same time however she drew attention to the hard-working, good-humoured, kindly, thrifty and astonishingly conscientious cultural attributes. She also found that she had to overcome her own ethnocentric-bound definitions of valued physical and personality attributes. At first she did not find the Chinese women of her acquaintance either attractive or charming in their presentation of themselves. Indeed she went as far as to say that there was no single facial feature that Europeans would call 'pretty' and their feet and legs were like two sticks. Moreover, because in accordance with Chinese etiquette the face is entirely devoid of expression, she found among the well-bred a want of manners and charm.

She was also honest enough to remind the reader that she like other Europeans with her larger facial features and large feet was similarly found wanting by her Chinese friends and acquaintances. If in her works of fiction she mainly portrayed the European in China, in her works of non-fiction she turned her ethnographic eye toward Chinese domestic and social life.

In China she continued to write a number of novels which were set within both the large and small foreign communities. Their plots and stories tended towards the fanciful or melodramatic and were characterised by sets of circumstances and coincidences which seemed quite improbable. They are more notable for the sharp, detailed and humorous observations and sketches of European settlement life in both the larger bustling treaty ports and the lonely isolated out-ports or out-posts. In her novels, Alicia Little (like many of the other women writers in this book) conveyed the sense of isolation and insulation which she thought caused European residents to become unduly impressed with their own affairs. She was intrigued by their separation from and yet encapsulation by the Chinese town and city and the uncertain influence of the Chinese on those who from choice or necessity had made their homes in China. Each of the novels has a large cast of supporting characters representing the 'various types' of treaty port residents – the missionaries, the consuls and commissioners of customs, the merchants and their wives. She had open sympathy for the missionaries who, hopeful and idealistic, came to China with a yearning to do something to better the lives of the Chinese. Yet so often they ended up frail and ill and depressed in the face of the continual isolation, hostility and the small returns. Alicia Little thought that the Chinese had much more influence on the missionaries than vice versa, and that although as a group the latter were much maligned, as individuals they were each impressive in their own way. She concluded that the wreckage of missionary lives and hopes might be one of the greatest tragedies of Europeans in China. Apart from the missionaries there were also the kindly and slightly odd consuls who laboured over their reports for the government back home and the merchants, in China to make their fortunes, who accused their Chinese counterparts of being interested only in money! Both of these groups boasted frequently never to have set foot in Chinatown nor to speak a word of the language and yet they had the nerve to pontificate in great detail on everything Chinese. Mrs Little dubs these the 'twenty-years-in-China-and-not-know-a-word-of-the-language-men'; so sure are they that nobody can grapple with the Chinese language and remain balanced that they take the precaution of not ever opening a single Chinese book!

As befits her previous writing career as Alicia Bewicke, Mrs Archibald Little's novels set in China reveal her interest in the lives of European women and their lot in that country. Within a very short time of her arrival in China, she was struck by the weary and worn looks of the European women in Shanghai, contrasting these with the ruddy good health of the men who commonly had a fitter and more sporting life at their clubs in China than back at home. Not only were the clubs rarely open to women but in their tight-fitting clothes and their shoes designed for an English climate rather than the hothouse air surcharged with moisture, these women were excessively at risk from temperature changes. Moreover they took little exercise, preferring to be carried in their sedan chairs. No wonder, she thought, given the climate and their poor health that they had such pale cheeks. She was struck by these sad expressions conveying their sometimes overwhelming sense of isolation and separation from their families, their loved ones and especially their children. One of the themes of her novels is the difficulty with which young brides and women learned how to use and enjoy the greater leisure and an accompanying absence of constraint that were quite unknown in England. She thought that their lack of intellectual interests and occupations meant that the long hours their husbands were at work were unduly given over to reflections on the merits of servants, characteristics of husbands and habits of small communities. She writes rather wryly that more husbands would be in favour of intellectual pursuits and occupations if they realised how few of their own characters and habits could stand up to such microscopic inspection! To remain occupied and interested she herself continued to write. Her novels, popular and well-received at the time, are rarely read today. However, her non-fiction books in which she determined to pass on to a wider audience her observations, experiences and impressions of China – the country, its people and particularly its women – were more popular and well-reviewed at the time and are still today consulted by students of Chinese society.

Alicia Little was particularly fascinated by the Chinese family and its role in Chinese society as a 'co-operative, working and living unit'. She was intrigued by the large Chinese household, perhaps composed of scores of family members spanning several generations resident in houses arranged around picturesque inter-connecting courtyards. If economic conditions permitted, if there were sufficient land or other forms of income-generating activities to employ family members and produce a ready income, then married sons, their wives and children were indeed likely to remain under a common roof or within the family compound, with joint management of property, income and expenditure. However, the large household of foreign literary image and stereotype, requiring as it did wealth and property, was common only among the large landowners and well-to-do merchants; the average household of the majority of the population, the peasants, urban artisans and petty traders, numbered between four and six persons. The smaller nuclear or two to three generational family of grandparents, parents and children was much more common in the small houses of one to two rooms built of dried mud packed hard, fired brick or stone, with tiles or thatched roofs, that clustered in rural villages or lined city streets. What Alicia Little found interesting about each household, small and large, rural and urban, was the plurality or wide range of its activities and the complex division of labour it generated. She noted how each household aimed to be as economically self-sufficient a unit as possible by cultivating its own rice, beans, Indian corn and pork, producing its own silk and cotton, and weaving and sewing its own clothes. It not only raised but also educated its own sons and sometimes daughters by either engaging tutors or establishing small schools for family and kin members.

What impressed Alicia Little most was the practice of co-operation which she observed between members of small and large family units which not only generated income for their members but also provided for their permanent welfare and support. She thought it difficult fully to understand Chinese society unless the dependence of the individual and her or his encapsulation by the family were recognised. Such were the family links of mutual claims, responsibilities and guarantees that no one who had family stood alone in Chinese society. Significantly, the very name for an individual without any family links meant 'a bare stick'. Alicia Little thought that the very solidity of the family unit possessed many advantages for its members including its elderly, its needy and its women. She observed the benefits for aged parents and grandparents who, as honoured, respected family members, were carefully tended to and nurtured at home. Needy relatives were usually taken in and assisted in times of hardship. She was especially intrigued to note the position of concubines and prostitutes. It was surprising to a Victorian woman long versed in the ambivalent, hidden and muted position of the European mistress to learn of the contrasting position of her Chinese counterpart. Once selected by a man of the household a concubine, although never fully admitted to the rank of wife, was taken permanently into her lover's household where she and her children were as much a charge to him for the rest of their days as were his first wife and her children. With such family responsibilities there was no notion that he might be permitted to enjoy her fleeting years of youth and beauty before setting her adrift with a small sum of money for services rendered. Alicia Little was interested to note the shocked overtones in a conversation between two Chinese women of her acquaintance who were discussing the fate of a concubine who had been forced by the reduced circumstances of 'her family' to move out of the household. In a similar manner, she more than once pointed out that many of the numerous prostitutes of Shanghai were girls abandoned or sold by their families who had not enough income to support them or rice to feed them. A secure and stable economic base was not available to all households, and outside the family unit there were few resources available to support daughters, wives or mothers.

Much as she admired the solidity and interdependence of the Chinese family, she was fully aware that these admirable characteristics could be offset by the exaggerated authority claimed by the head of the household be it the senior male or after his death his eldest son. All members of the household were subject to his authority; hence there never came a time when the voice of youth could make itself heard. Was it the same with the household's women? Many foreign observers from Alicia Little to myself have been intrigued by the discrepancy between the rules of the patriarchal Chinese household and the personal confidence and authority of Chinese women outside the home.

In classical Chinese literature, most of the women whose behaviour was celebrated and who were held up for emulation were those who were ideal daughters, wives and mothers resolved on denying themselves in favour of either male or older family members. As examples of such paragons of virtue, Alicia Little selected two women recommended by the Board of Rites for commemorative honours whose stories were reported in the old and reputable *Peking Gazette* in 1891. One was of an old lady of eighty-two who, described as 'of singular purity and simplicity', had seen seven generations of her family, including six sons, forty grandsons, one hundred and twenty-one great-grandsons and two great-great grandsons. The second was of a daughter renowned for her docile disposition and filial piety who tenderly nursed her ailing mother, going to the lengths of cutting off a piece of her flesh to make soup for the invalid and taking her own life after her mother's death to serve upon her mother in the 'shades'. These two cases were chosen to represent the domestic virtues honoured by Chinese tradition.

Yet like most other foreigners of the time Alicia Little found it difficult to reconcile such ideal female roles with the behaviour which she observed around her. While it was not in accordance with the rules of etiquette that women should talk to any men not their own kin, she was struck by the fact that whenever men had been in the company of Chinese women they displayed an ease of manner and quiet dignity that was a pleasure to observe. While it was true that Chinese women were rather given to rising to address a man, as if he were a superior being, they in no other respect conveyed the impression that they were accustomed to consider themselves either in the service of or for the pleasure of men. She found the relationship between husband and wife difficult to fathom given that their marriage had been arranged and that they were rarely seen together and certainly did not travel together. Yet she was frequently touched by the soft and caressing references of one for the other and the excessive efforts men went to to celebrate the warmth and fondness of their relationships especially after the untimely death of a wife.

Mrs Little thought that the domestic position of the married woman was hard to describe in any society and that in China it was especially difficult because of the unusual nature of marriage in which the groom does not see his bride until she is his wife. As a new wife, or more importantly daughter-in-law, she then tended to become more of a household servant of her mother-in-law, wore poor clothing in comparison to the daughters of the household and waited upon her mother-in-law. Often and often had Alicia Little wished it was not so, and that in going to a house she could talk directly with the wistful young daughters-in-law who glanced at her from under their eyelids and yet looked as though they would be receptive to new ideas, spirited or even quite ready for revolt of some sort. In contrast the honoured older lady of the household who regulated its affairs and entertained the guests seemed conservative and even docile, for who was 'more set in her ideas than a grandmother of many children?' Mrs Little's views on the position of the daughter-in-law were prophetic, for forty years later in the villages of China it was the young daughter-in-law who in their bid for independence became the most vociferous of village supporters of the Red Army. Least likely to support their independence were the grandmothers and women of the older generation who had risen to a position of relative eminence and authority whether in the peasant or gentry household.

Although Chinese men were the acknowledged source of authority, on closer observation Alicia Little came to appreciate that informally Chinese women had 'some influence over their husbands and their business affairs'. She had first become aware of this influence when her husband, in transacting some intricate business with a merchant, would frequently and suddenly find that the ending of the negotiation would be postponed until he had gone home and consulted with his wife. Contrary to foreign expectations moreover, it was also the custom of an official or merchant absent on business to hand over his official seal or his keys and account books to his wife. In these circumstances Chinese women did not seem to avoid direct negotiations with their husbands especially when they deemed it to be in their own or their husbands' and sons' interests. On one such occasion Mrs Little noted: 'I must add that for all her being a lady, she went on her knees to my husband on arrival, and tried to do so again on going. But in conversation with him she was anything but on her knees.' Soon after her arrival in Chungking Mrs Little herself was importuned by the wife of a formerly wealthy merchant who hoped that some place might be found in Mr Little's business for her now impoverished husband. As Mrs Little proceeded to ascertain the details and found her knowledge of Chinese to be less than sufficient, she called on her cook who had spent a lifetime in service of foreigners to interpret for her. To her amusement she heard him intone conclusively: 'I don't know why you trouble my mistress about all this. Foreign ladies are not like our ladies; they don't understand anything about business, and take no part in their husband's affairs.'

Alicia Little contrasted the leisure, fatigue and ennui of the women of the gentry and merchant classes with the incessant and hard demands on peasant and working women. In far Sichuan, Mrs Little was struck by the lack of learning and serious occupation of women of the richer households in contrast to cities like Peking and Shanghai where gentry daughters often shared their brothers' tutors and acquired literary skills. In Chungking around the turn of the century she met one young woman who quite unusually could both read and write, and she was much talked about and admired. All the other leisured women of her acquaintance looked after their children, played cards, gossiped, went to dinner parties and looked forward to going on pilgrimages to distant shrines. To be sure of this pleasure it was sometimes stipulated before marriage that a wife was to be permitted to go on so many pilgrimages each year, during which the nuns of the shrines invited them to visit and enjoy themselves drinking wine, smoking and playing cards; not uncommonly, because of the poppy fields of the west of China, smoking included opium-smoking. Frequently on social occasions Mrs Little herself was asked by the women of the household to share an opium couch with all its elegant accessories. In their homes women who were regular opium-smokers told Alicia Little that they had usually taken to the habit to counter the effects of poor health. Most sat up late through the night and often did not get up till five or six in the evening, and at ladies' dinners Mrs Little observed that the opium-smokers tended to return from the couch with their eyes very bright, their cheeks very red and talking a great deal of nonsense very excitedly. Within a short time however they looked yellow, sunken cheeked and most unhealthy, but she also thought that they seemed no more ashamed of their habit than ladies were of taking wine in England.

Mrs Little had a unique opportunity to observe at first hand over some months farm family life. To escape the oppressive heat one summer she and her husband rented a house on a Chinese farm across the Yangtze River from Chungking in an area where they eventually hoped to build a house. During the very hot days when she was confined to her farmhouse sitting room, Mrs Little kept a diary in which she noted down interesting details of family life that went on around her on the farm. There was plenty to observe and participate in for the two houses both opened onto a common concrete threshing floor which, shaded by a fine walnut tree, was variously covered by yarn stretched on long frames for spinning and weaving, peas, the blazing-coloured Indian corn still unhusked, crimson peppers drying in the sun or the freshly threshed tall millet. In the hot season, the threshing floor became common living ground. It was here that the wife washed the clothes in a large wooden tray which was brought out for the occasion and stood on a frame. At meal times the farm family ate their food sitting on low benches around a little low table with the children all busy with their bowls sitting on the high threshold. Certainly the farm seemed to produce everything its members consumed and this was largely the result of the labours of the mother of the household for the farmer was away for much of the time engaged in carrying coal from a large nearby mine and retailing it in Chungking. In his absence his energetic wife managed the farm and the children. She was regularly up at 4 am to begin the day and still chatting and chopping up the leaves of the grass cloth plant for the pigs at 10 pm. This did not make for much of a peaceful night for the hot and tired foreigners who had taken refuge outside on the coolness of the threshing floor!

In no less of an energetic and noisy manner the busy peasant woman managed the younger children, one of which was sure to be chased and beaten with a decent-sized stick at least once each day. The older married daughters returned from Chungking to help their mother with shoemaking and weaving of grass cloth. One frequently arrived bearing the same sad tale of unhappiness and beatings at the hand of her husband. One one occasion she returned beaten and in an emotional state because she had ordered new clothes from a tailor without insisting that the material should come from her own husband's shop. When the bill had come, her husband had refused to pay and beat her instead. This daughter, who was well known for her fine embroidery skills, developed very bad eyesight which put an end to the deployment of this her sole skill. The farmer's wife acted as a go-between for Mrs Little's cook who was persuaded to overcome his reluctance to purchase a Szechwanese wife. He knew that she might be cheaper, but he had no way of having her parentage and ancestors checked or of knowing whether she smoked tobacco or opium as he would a woman from his native province of Hupeh. And how could he know beforehand and not waste his money if he did not check her out himself prior to marriage! The intimate knowledge of and interaction with this farm family next door extended to include village neighbours. Some little distance from the farm, there was a richer peasant family in which the chief item of display and interest was a large coffin which had been prepared for the great-grandmother of seventy-seven years of age although it was not yet clear when she would need it. It excited much admiration, but not from Mrs Little. She noted in her diary that although it was etiquette in China and her husband also exhorted her to tell the old lady that she had seen it and compliment her upon it, she really could not bring herself to touch upon such an indelicate subject.

In her writings on Chinese society, Alicia Little many times reminded her readers not to make snap judgements based on fragments of information or necessarily to subscribe to the stereotypes which abounded in the existing literature on China. There were numerous customs and rituals which each culture practised differently and she alluded constantly to both the differences and the similarities between China and Europe and the need for mutual recognition and respect between the peoples of different cultures. In her writings she challenged European ethnocentric attitudes which commonly condemned 'the Chinese' for their 'bad qualities' and yet simultaneously identified individuals of that race to whom they would trust all in sickness or in danger. If individuals could be regarded as 'the embodiment of all virtues' then how could they collectively be written off as a decadent race? As to Chinese morals, which the European missionaries found so suspect, Mrs Little thought it was well to be reminded that the Chinese sense of decency was so often stricter than the European. European ladies who went up country frequently had to alter their dress if they wished to make the acquaintance of Chinese women and in support of her views she quoted the story of the wife of a French consul who was obliged to take down the painting of an old master, such an outrage was it considered to be to the Chinese sense of decency. There was one custom however which Mrs Little could neither understand, explain, tolerate nor accept and that was the practice of footbinding.

In the first days after her arrival in Shanghai it was the contrast between the health, mobility and laughter of young boys and the pallor, immobility and tears of the girls of the same age which first drew her attention to the harms of footbinding. Later she was to hold it responsible for much of the helplessness, ill health and ennui of women of all classes including the footbound beggars on the roadside, the servant girls who could not sweep a floor or stand up properly to do their mistresses' hair without leaning against something to prevent themselves falling, the peasant women in the far northern fields labouring on their knees and the reclining small-footed gentry women who could not even take a walk in their courtyarded gardens. The practice of footbinding was believed to have dated from the fashion of small bowed feet current among the court dancing girls of the tenth century. Much admired by the Emperor and men of the court, the practice was first taken up by the gentry and extended to include other social classes as small feet increasingly became associated with wealth and status. Indeed they became a prerequisite to an advantageous marriage and any form of social mobility. Matchmakers were asked, not 'Is she beautiful?' but 'How small are her feet?' Many an aspiring mother thus subjected her daughter to this painful process and girls of all but the poorest families and some specific non-Han ethnic groups lost their freedom and agility to a greater or lesser degree.

The age at which footbinding began and the methods utilised to achieve the desired foot size varied from region to region throughout China, but for all bound-footed girls the process had certain characteristics in common. As Mrs Little described it for her readers:

> The cloth is drawn as tightly as the child can bear, leaving the great toe free, but binding all the other toes under the sole of the foot, so as to reduce the width as much as possible, and eventually to make the toes of the left foot peep out at the right side and the toes of the right foot at the left side of the foot, in both cases coming from underneath the sole. Each succeeding day the bandage is

tightened both morning and night; and if the bones are re-
fractory, and spring back into their places on the removal
of the bandage, sometimes a blow is given with the heavy
mallet used in beating clothes; and possibly it is, on the
whole, kinder, thus to hasten operations. Directly after
binding, the little girl is made to walk up and down on
her poor aching feet, for fear mortification should at once
set in. But all this is only during the first year. It is the
next two years that are the terrible time for the little girls
of China; for then the foot is no longer being narrowed,
but shortened; by so winding the bandages as to draw the
fleshy part of the foot and the heel close together, till it
is possible to hide a half-crown piece between them. It is
indeed not till this can be done that a foot is considered
bound.

Most feet were bound within the secluded women's quarters,
hence few outsiders witnessed the pain and suffering and the
intimate effects of footbinding on the health of young girls
and women. Mrs Little, as an unusual visitor to the women's
courtyards and quarters, observed that the girlhood of China
presented 'a most melancholy spectacle' during the three years
in which the bandages were progressively tightened to narrow
and shorten the feet.

Instead of a hop, skip and a jump, with rosy cheeks like
the little girls of England, the poor little things are leaning
heavily on a stick somewhat taller than themselves, or
carried on a man's back, or sitting sadly crying. They have
great black lines under their eyes, and a special curious
paleness that I have never seen except in connection with
footbinding. Their mothers mostly slept with a big stick
by the bedside, with which to get up and beat the little
girl should she disturb the household by her wails; but not
uncommonly she is put to sleep in an outhouse. The only
relief she gets is either from opium, or from hanging her
feet over the edge of her wooden bedstead, so as to stop
the circulation.

The more she travelled and observed, the more Mrs Little was able to confirm the popular saying that for every pair of bound feet, there was indeed a bucket of tears. The more she questioned European missionary doctors, the more she learned of the mutilations wrought by footbinding and the devastating effect it could have on the health of women.

It was the medical and women missionaries who were the first Europeans to have intimate acquaintance with both the intricacies of the bandaging process and its effects on women's health. During the nineteenth century the missionaries had been somewhat divided in their attitudes towards footbinding. Some like the Roman Catholics and the American Episcopalian Church had at first thought it wiser to accept and conform with Chinese customs including footbinding. Thus in some of the mission schools, the missionaries had continued to tighten the bandages of pupils rather than have parents withdraw their daughters from the schools. In some schools however the process was too painful for outsiders to supervise. One Italian Mother Superior at a Hankow School for girls told Mrs Little that not only had the girls to be exempted from class on bandaging day, but the Italian Sister who had to be present suffered so much from witnessing the little girls' suffering that she had to be continually changed for no Italian woman was able to endure the pain of observation week after week.

The missionaries were not only in a position to witness and publicise the suffering, but those with some medical training repeatedly observed and reported the effects of footbinding on the health of girls and women. Many were called on to treat cases of infection, ulceration and mortification which resulted in the loss of a foot or feet, and they concluded that, unless the process were very carefully and hygienically supervised, the bound foot was itself directly liable to disease or through the consequent imbalance in body movement, was indirectly responsible for a number of internal maladies and problems in childbirth. It was the missionaries who first drew attention to the health problems associated with binding, and it was they who estimated that the death rate due to binding was around one in ten. It is evident from her own writings that Mrs Little not only questioned missionaries closely on the physiological processes and common ailments linked to binding but that she also strongly supported missionary attempts to end the custom.

Although there had been a number of unsuccessful attempts in the seventeenth and eighteenth centuries to end the practice by the Ching dynasty government who as Manchus had never subscribed to the custom, in the latter half of the nineteenth century it was the turn of the Europeans and particularly Protestant and women missionaries to become increasingly active in the anti-footbinding cause. Many began to make admission to their Christian schools and churches dependent on ending the custom. Girls were only recruited into mission schools if parents consented to natural feet, and to reduce parental and girlish fears that they would not be able to marry, many missionaries found themselves taking the role of matchmaker – locating spouses for their natural-footed pupils and providing dowries to make them more acceptable as brides. The activities of one, the enterprising Reverend McGowan who with his wife founded a society for natural feet in Amoy, particularly impressed Mrs Little. He had first approached the local gentry and officials to become members of the society and to pledge themselves to marry or have their sons marry natural-footed girls. The society, which also produced a very neat shoe to show the natural foot to advantage, was in existence for some twenty years, and Mrs Little was later to acknowledge her debt to the example of the Reverend McGowan and his Natural Feet Society in Amoy. After travelling about and listening to missionary accounts of the horrors of footbinding and applauding their first steps in ending the custom, Mrs Little decided it was time for European women resident in China to add their efforts to those of the missionaries and endeavour to expand the anti-footbinding movement beyond the small Christian Chinese communities.

In April 1895 at the behest of Mrs Little, ten European women of different nationalities including the wives of the various consuls and merchants founded the Natural Foot Society in Shanghai. Mrs Little was elected to the most important post of president and organising secretary. She expressed the

hope that the Society would 'offer a splendid opportunity
for genuinely benevolent work to European ladies in China
who not infrequently must have felt the need of something
to usefully occupy them beyond domestic chores'. She had
been very gratified to find that the first ten women she had
approached were apparently 'willing and eager' to serve on the
committee, although it also had to be said that in general the
establishment of the new society was greeted with some scep-
ticism and ridicule. Its very founding prompted some debate
as to whether Chinese customs were proper objects of foreign
reform and intervention, while others thought that even if they
were, it was doubtful whether the goal was attainable given the
Herculean task of demolishing such an age-old custom. Many
were the jokes likening the self-imposed task of the Society to
'an egg beating against a rock'.

In founding the Society, Mrs Little had several aims in mind.
She hoped to establish an international, non-denominational
and umbrella organisation to co-ordinate all the efforts to end
footbinding in order that the issue would not become aligned
with any one mission or indeed with the missionary movement
at all. She made every effort to ensure that mission property
was not used for the meetings of the Society. According to
Mrs Little's second annual report to the Society there were
two reasons for the separation of Christian missions from the
anti-footbinding cause. The first was that if mission influence
was prominent, natural-footed women might subsequently
become the focus of anti-foreign and anti-Christian violence
which was becoming increasingly common towards the turn
of the century. Second, the missions were mainly associated
with the poor and the humble, while the new society aimed
to influence a quite different category of persons, namely high
government officials and women and men of wealth and status.
This bias towards these latter groups was a direct consequence
of Mrs Little's belief that the practice of footbinding did not so
much derive from a religion, faith or ideology, but was simply
a matter of custom and fashion. Hence its abolition, a mere
matter of inducing a change in fashion, was something best
undertaken by those with wealth and status.

Interestingly, although the bound foot could be said to symbolise *par excellence* the subjection and immobility of women, there was little attempt to link anti-footbinding explicitly to any campaign for the general emancipation of women. Rather there was much talk about the practical improvements in women's health which would ensue if the custom were abolished. Finally, although Mrs Little and her ladies' committee were certainly aware that their very mention of the word 'foot' raised a delicate subject, they thought that in this instance European women could best act as spokeswomen for the women of China, given that only they could speak of it without endangering their reputations. To fulfil all these goals, the anti-footbinding society prepared publicity and educational materials for distribution, aiming at both soliciting women's support for the unbinding of their own and their daughters' feet and men's support for boycotting brides with bound feet.

In Mrs Little's own words, the Society began its work 'very timidly' with the distribution of two poems written by Chinese women which had been passed on to them by missionaries, and the publication of a tract written by a mission pastor which had to be translated into Chinese. Mrs Little relates that this was no simple matter but raised complex questions of language and priorities:

> It is difficult for English people to understand what anguish of mind had been suffered by all the ladies on the committee, before we could decide into what sort of Chinese we would have our tract translated. There were so many alternatives before us. Should it be into the Shanghai dialect? and then, should there be other translations into the dialects of the other parts? The women would then understand it, but, then, the women could not read. And were we appealing to the men or the women? And would not our tract be thought to be very low and vulgar in such common language? Should it be translated into ordinary mandarin? But would not the learned even then despise it? We knew of course – we all sat sadly weighted by the thought – that feet are

the most 'risque' subject of conversation in China, and no subject more improper can be found there. And some of us felt as if we should blush before those impassive, long-tailed boys, who stood behind our chairs and minister to our wants at tiffin and at dinner, when the latter knew that we – we, their mistresses – were responsible for a book upon footbinding, a book that any common man off the streets could read. In the end we took refuge in the dignified Wenli of the Chinese classics, confident that thus anti-footbinding would be brought with as great decorum as possible before the Chinese public, and that at least the literati (learned gentry) must marvel at the beautiful style and learning of the foreign ladies, who, alas! could not read one character of the little booklet, whose type and red label we all examined so wistfully. We circulated our books as well as we could; we encouraged each other not to mind the burst of ridicule with which we were greeted by the twenty-years-in-China-and-not-know-a-word-of-the-language-men. Our one French member was most comforting. . . But, to use the Chinese phrase, our hearts were very small indeed; for we knew the custom was so old, and the country so big. And what were we to fight against centuries and millions?

What raised the spirits of the ladies and took the Society beyond its timid beginnings were the positive response and support of a number of Chinese officials who themselves wrote placards and tracts which could be displayed and publicised by the Society. The first to lend his support in such a way was an official examiner from Peking who, on his way home to fulfil mourning obligations on the death of a family member, had come by one of their tracts. He thought he could write something much better on the subject, and after having done so arranged for several of his friends to sign and add their seals in support of anti-footbinding. He then had what is commonly referred to as the 'Suifu Appeal' written on placards and put up in his city where the thousands of students sitting examinations for entrance to the government bureaucracy could read it. Shortly afterwards one of the lineal descendants of Confucius applied to the Society for copies of all their educational materials so that he might compile a book out of the best ones and circulate it. A number of Viceroys including the famed Chang Chih-tung and Li Hung-chang were also persuaded, some more willingly than others, publicly to acknowledge the cause and express their written support for the anti-footbinding society.

Mrs Little recounts with some humour her interview with the high and great official Li Hung-chang in which she attempted to gain his support for her cause. She reported how Li Hung-chang first tried to avoid any talk of footbinding much preferring to talk about her husband's pioneering trips on the Yangtze River. This busy eminent official was reluctant to commit himself in any practical way in support of unbinding, but on the spur of the moment Mrs Little had the bright idea of asking him to write a few words on her fan which acknowledged the importance of the anti-footbinding movement. He did so, although on her leave-taking he rather grumblingly forecast that the end of footbinding was likely to make the women and men so strong that they would end up overturning the dynasty. The fan, without his accompanying prediction, was shown at every public meeting subsequently attended by Mrs Little. As a foreigner, she had an advantage in that it is doubtful whether the old and venerable Li Hung-chang would have consented to receive Chinese women at such an audience or whether they could have solicited official support on such a personal basis.

Most of the publications of the anti-footbinding society consisted of tracts written by both Chinese scholars and some women which were re-published and distributed as evidence of support for the cause by both women and in high places. The second annual report of the Society held in Shanghai in 1897 listed the poems and leaflets which had been published and circulated in the city the year before. These included upwards of 8,000 copies, and what is particularly interesting about the list is the number of poems written by Chinese women. These poems alike express the pain, confinement and lack of mobility associated with the custom which reduced women's enjoyment of nature and out-of-doors activities and in times of violence caused them to become blameless victims unable to escape an untimely fate. The more scholarly appeals written by Chinese officials expressed their opposition to the practice in terms often reminiscent of those used by some of the earlier Ming and Qing dynasty critics who variously represented binding as a barbarous punishment inflicted on innocent persons or as a physical handicap responsible for the weakness and ill-health of the mother and the reproduction of weak sons. A new element in the critiques at the end of the nineteenth century was the contrast between the bound-footed Chinese woman and her counterpart in countries beyond the seas in England, France, Germany and America who, free from pain, was strong and daring and able to defend herself in times of trouble.

If the Society under Alicia Little's leadership had some success in soliciting support from a number of Chinese officials in high places, it was less successful in seeking the support of the Empress Dowager and Emperor who as members of the Manchu race did not subscribe to the custom and might therefore be expected to take the lead in abolishing the practice as their forebears had several times attempted previously. The Society petitioned the throne according to procedures of the time. It sent a memorial to the Emperor written in characters of gold on white satin which was signed by its President on behalf of nearly every lady residing in the East and enclosed in a silver casket. Despite the diplomatic efforts of the American Minister in Peking on their behalf, it seems as if the foreign ministry did not dare to present the memorial to the Empress, much preferring to keep its existence from her to collect dust on their shelves! The Society was discouraged by this as it had rather hoped for an Imperial Edict in support of unbinding. Instead it had to be content with circulating copies of the memorial sent to Peking and showing it at its many meetings.

Anti-footbinding meetings were held in the main cities in preparation for the establishment of networks of local anti-footbinding societies in villages, towns and cities. Mrs Little played an important role in setting up and speaking at such meetings, first in the large cities like Shanghai and

Chungking and later on tours of the southern provinces. At the turn of the century she set off on a tour which took her from the Yangtze Valley to the southern provinces and to the cities of Hankow, Canton, Hong Kong, Swatow, Amoy and Foochow and later to Hangchow and Soochow in the east. Armed with a free pass from the steamship companies and a number of introductions to leading Chinese officials in all the cities, she embarked on her speaking tour rather nervously and not without some trepidation. As she wrote at the time:

> Those who remember their sensations as children, when first taken to plunge into the cold sea, can realise a little of the feeling, with which I contemplated starting off on a tour south of China among complete strangers to oppose footbinding, one of China's oldest, most deep-rooted, domestic customs.

She took with her a number of visual aids: the fan on which Li Hung-chang had personally inscribed his support for the cause, samples of normal-sized embroidered satin shoes which illustrated that larger feet also could look dainty and attractive and the usual numbers of leaflets and pledges for distribution. The reception she received and the response of the audience varied from outright rejection to warm hospitality and seemed to be very much dependent on the degree to which footbinding was locally practised and whether or not there had been any earlier attempts there or meetings to end the custom. She attended and spoke at meetings both for men and for women.

Some of these occasions were awe-inspiring events for this sole European women speaker addressing large numbers of Chinese officials. At one meeting in Hankow held to attract the support of local officials, Mrs Little described how official after official entered the audience: some with retinues, some without and 'some also with that tremendous swagger, that makes one feel as if the man who thus walked would think no subject in heaven or earth worthy of his interest'. At this meeting:

> The Consul introduced me in brief words, and then I had to stand up and front them, realising to the fullest

extent how strange, how unheard-of, these Chinese officials must consider a woman addressing them at all, and
especially on that, to them, exceptionally indelicate
subject – women's feet.

She did not wonder that her Chinese interpreter's courage gave
way and that he became to all intents and purposes voiceless for
'to him those officials were far more awe-inspiring personages
than even to me'. Fortunately on this occasion a well-known
missionary 'with a fine knowledge of colloquial Chinese and
a powerful voice' came to her rescue and eventually over
2000 leaflets and tracts against footbinding were carried off
from the meeting. Audiences were also asked to pay a small
subscription in support of the anti-footbinding society, and
if they were men to pledge their support for the unbinding
of the feet of the women in their household and to avoid
bound-footed women in their marriage negotiations. It was
acknowledged that if this move, tantamount to a masculine
boycott, became widespread it would directly hit at the basic
social tenet that bound feet were a necessary prerequisite to
a good marriage. A few years later the *North China Herald*
paid tribute to the influence of natural-footed societies when
it concluded that the custom first received its deathblow when
a growing number of Chinese men joined the societies and
took the oath that neither they nor their sons would marry
a small-footed woman. In the meantime and until this stage
was reached, the society arranged for a portion of its received
subscriptions to be used to provide dowries for natural-footed
brides to encourage men to marry them.

There were special meetings for women to encourage them
to unbind their own feet and not to bind their daughters' feet.
A meeting for women alone was in itself a novel occasion for
women accustomed to seclusion seldom met outside of the
family courtyards for any other purpose than to celebrate the
rituals associated with life passages. The formalities of these
meetings with speeches, chairpersons and even pledges thus
struck many of them as very unusual and strange and they
were unsure how to respond. This was evidently the case at

a meeting attended by Mrs Little in Chungking which she described as a 'most brilliant affair':

> The wealth of embroideries on the occasion was a thing to remember. . . All the Chinese ladies laughed so gaily, and were so brilliant in their attire, that the few missionary ladies among them looked like sober moths caught in a flight of broidered butterflies. Every one came, and many brought friends; and all brought children, in their best clothes too, like the most beautiful dolls. At first, in the middle of the cakes and tea, the speeches seemed to bewilder the guests who could not make out what they were meant to do. . .

Once the speaker went on to discuss regional variations in the practice, the ladies present from different provinces were eager to tell of their acquaintance with groups or areas where ladies did not bind their feet. They also very much appreciated a talk on the effects on health of footbinding when a missionary lady explained in fluent Chinese the circulation of the blood and with an indiarubber pipe showed the effect of binding some part of it. There were no interruptions then. This seemed to the Chinese ladies very practical and useful information and it was quite striking to see how attentively they listened. This speech was afterwards a great deal commented on and at the end of the meeting several Chinese women admitted that though they could all agree that footbinding was 'of no use', perhaps the practice itself could only be given up by degrees. On the other hand the little girls present avidly listened and to Mrs Little 'seemed almost eager in their attentiveness'. As for the husbands, one was afterwards heard to comment rather crossly that of course the women liked the meetings as 'they didn't want to bind their feet!'. A response which in itself seemed to Mrs Little to contain something of an admission!

The gathering and meeting together of women at the behest of the anti-footbinding societies seemed to have played an important role in the mutual support necessary to the encouragement of individual women to unbind. Even the wives of officials who had surreptitiously made ready socks and shoes were reported to put off unbinding until they could find other women to join them. It was not only the case that some feared discrimination in that 'no man would want to marry a girl with big feet', but that the actual process of unbinding, especially after a few years of narrowing and shortening, necessitated much physical discomfort and courage.

When Mrs Little visited England in 1898 and 1899, she was interviewed in the British newspapers and periodicals and gave many speeches about her work on behalf of the Natural Foot Society. She also took the opportunity to collect funds to further its work. Newspaper reports of the time reveal that there was a concert in aid of the anti-footbinding society in Manchester and still today one of her nieces can remember hurrying through the streets of the East End of London carrying the lantern slides showing the effects of binding on the bones of the feet to illustrate her aunt's speech. For her niece, the East End itself was like a foreign territory. It was the first time she had entered cafés where the knives and forks were tied to the tables, and the dirt was quite something. To her aunt, long used to China, the dirt was nothing out of the usual. The public opinion which she and others roused outside of China had some effect for it meant that footbinding came to be increasingly viewed by Chinese officials, students and diplomats travelling abroad as an outmoded vestige of the past which made China appear 'barbaric' or 'half-civilised' thus causing some loss of international face. Many prominent official Chinese reformers took up the issue of footbinding as part of their bid to strengthen and modernise China. In the last decade of the nineteenth century the leader of the reform movement, Kang Yu-wei, noted that in the eyes of foreigners nothing so much as footbinding made China appear so currently backward:

> There is nothing which makes us objects of ridicule so much as footbinding. . . With prosperity so weakened, how can we engage in battle? I look at the Europeans and Americans, so strong and vigorous because their

mothers do not bind their feet and therefore have
strong offspring. Now that we must compete with other
nations, to transmit weak offspring is perilous.

It was perhaps fortunate that the efforts of the foreign-inspired
Society coincided with a crisis of confidence in many of the
traditional social customs and a period of reform when the
desire to discover the success of European strength and power
was paramount. If nationalist sentiment had urged that China
differentiate itself from other cultures and retain its own distinctive customs, then the result might have been somewhat
different. Unexpectedly the movement in favour of unbinding
received Imperial support in 1902 when the Empress Dowager,
trying to appease officials and foreigners alike following her
humiliating escape from Peking at the time of the Boxer Rebellion, issued a decree exhorting 'gentry and notables of Chinese
descent to influence families to abstain from footbinding and
by this means abolish the custom forever'. Although it was to
take some time for the custom to be eroded, particularly in
rural areas and in conservative families, the cause had become
official, respectable and winnable. This was due in no small
part to the activities of Mrs Little and the Natural Foot Society.

It is difficult to identify and assess the separate contribution
of the activities of Mrs Little and the Natural Foot Society in
ending the custom for they became part of the much larger
Chinese sponsored anti-footbinding movement. Mrs Little and
the European Society's activities certainly contributed towards
the creation of favourable public opinion and provided some
kind of precedent in terms of organisation which other Chinese societies later followed. Mrs Little herself was a good
organiser and speaker in support of the cause. In newspaper
and magazine interviews, reporters comment constantly on her
exceptional vitality, vivacity and wit, good sense and power of
expression. In composing her anti-footbinding speeches she
believed in making as many comic points as she could on
the assumption that 'it was far easier to make people reform
when already moved to laughter'. Interviews and reports to
the annual general meetings of the Society suggest that she

was a good speaker and her materials and presentations well organised and accompanied by illustrations and humorous anecdotes. Today one of her nieces can remember how as a Surrey school girl at the turn of the century, she waited with some trepidation for the end-of-year speech that year to be given by her rather eccentric great aunt. She felt nervous and sensitive about the response of her peers. In the event she need not have worried, for so much enjoyed and appreciated was Mrs Little's speech that she afterwards quite reflected in her glory and was for a time the most popular girl in the school!

Much of the efficiency of the anti-footbinding society was due to the personal talents of Mrs Little as its president and organising secretary. The records suggest that few other members played such a prominent and active part although they did donate funds and attend its annual and special meetings called in Shanghai. Without doubt it took a particular kind of courage, determination and commitment to set off for distant and unknown inland parts to proselytise, but personal courage and commitment or determination were only two of Mrs Little's attributes. The cause was dear to her, and years after starting the campaign she still could not bear to see the suffering and hopeless agony of the small girls. She often said that if she was tempted to abandon the course or flag in her efforts, the memory of one small girl in particular would 'alone spur me on to redoubled efforts to do away with a custom, that had been more than so many children can endure, and that must have saturated so many childish souls with bitterness'. Mrs Little surmised correctly, for one of the interesting observations recorded alike by Chinese and foreign researchers on footbinding has been the minute detail with which women of any age could remember the day and the hour when the process of binding began, its tortuous progress, the depths of the pain and their hostile feelings towards those who inflicted that pain – normally their mothers. Indeed, Mrs Little herself went as far as to believe that perhaps God had deprived her of the joys of personal motherhood in order that 'all possible tenderness for childhood may be expended on the tortured children of China without the diminution from it of one iota, reserved for some sheltered, guarded child by my own fireside.'

Certainly in China her name became well-known not so much in association with her books as with the identity and activities of the Natural Foot Society and many were the appreciations of her activities expressed by both her European and Chinese supporters alike. Mrs Little herself left a careful record of her attitudes to and activities on behalf of the anti-footbinding cause. But as she herself once pointed out, it was the habit of foreign residents to attribute much more importance to their own actions than Chinese observers and foreign analysts would necessarily allow. In her own case however there are also on record a number of European and Chinese official reports and posters acknowledging and appreciating Mrs Little's work. A descendant of Confucius wrote to Mrs Little that although he could not have ventured so publicly to express his unquiet thoughts about footbinding, he supported the efforts of 'the wise daughters from foreign lands who had initiated a truly noble enterprise in addressing Chinese women in animated exhortations' by founding a society for the prohibition of footbinding. It was in Foochow that Mrs Little was likened by a senior official to the 'Chinese Goddess of Mercy' which she thought was probably 'the grandest compliment she would ever hope to receive'. In the annual general meetings of the anti-footbinding society continuing support for Mrs Little was repeatedly and generously expressed and endorsed. At one meeting she was likened to Moses by a Chinese pastor. He described how he had been in American when he had first heard of the foundation of the Natural Foot Society and the efforts of Mrs Little. He at once had felt that China was going to have a Moses to deliver her girls from bondage. The pastor went on to appeal for more and further support from his countrymen for Mrs Little and the Society she represented and he ended by saying how much he hoped that she would not leave the country until she saw her work accomplished.

By the time Mrs Little did leave China in 1907 she thought that the work of her own and other anti-footbinding societies had already set the women of China on their feet:

The women of China give me the idea, that, if once set upon their feet again, they will become a great power in the land – not wrenching men's hearts away, but guiding them in childhood in the way in which they should go, and in after years proved eminently calculated to be companions, counsellors and friends.

It was consistent with her writings as a young woman that Mrs Little thought that the terms companion, counsellor and friend should ideally define the relations between women and men friends be they friends, husbands and wives. Her own twenty-two years of married life with her 'Archipuss' came to an end in 1908 when after several years of failing health he died within a year or so of returning to England. In a Falmouth cemetery in Cornwall she had a small rough-hewn rock erected as a memorial which simply stated: 'Archibald Little, Pioneer of the Yangtze'. In her introductions to a volume of his essays which she collected and edited after his death, Alicia Little described her husband as a man of marked individuality and force of character who was the 'best of companions'. She thought that he was a writer of repute although in business he was often beset by troubles and anxieties, so guileless and unsuspecting was he. He was the first person to put steamers on the upper Yangtze, he did obtain a concession for and worked the 'best coal mine in the world after Cardiff' and he would never carry on business in any but the most honest activity. She honoured his support of her in all her endeavours and particularly in her activities on behalf of anti-footbinding:

The general anti-footbinding movement owed much of its inception to him. He had grieved over the agonies of footbinding, years before I ever saw China. He inspired and supported all my hesitating efforts; he first suggested my interviewing Chinese viceroys on the subject, then facilitated the interviews and always readily spared me for any work the movement entailed. Indeed from the moment I became his wife, he always insisted that I must fear nothing, neither danger nor fatigue while by his side, never finding fault with but always applauding every humblest effort – Can any of us do more for one another?

She was right to acknowledge the importance of his support for it is doubtful, given the expectations of men and the norms of the time, whether she could otherwise have continued as a married woman to write and campaign so much. Certainly her own nieces both remember the marriage as being somewhat unusual for its 'fond independent relationship'. But then they thought that their aunt was a very unusual woman and the phrase 'ahead of her times' was used by them frequently to describe her. As children they remembered with fondness a rather eccentric elderly aunt who was largely vegetarian and who took no interest in her clothes, often combining tennis shoes and green stockings! After she was widowed she lived in Campden Hill, London, and remained keenly interested in international affairs. She entered into all kinds of activities, becoming a member of both the Oriental and International Women's Clubs. She would write frequent letters to the newspapers on topics both to do with China and of general political import. She travelled, especially to Eastern Europe where her sister, a Sister of Mercy of St Vincent and St Paul, had lived and worked for most of her life. She was often short of money and borrowed from her husband's trust much to the later chagrin of his nieces and nephews. They do however remember with fondness and respect their spirited and 'never dull' Aunt Alicia who could nevertheless embarrass them with her free and frank opinions and directness of manner whether it be in conversation with the local policemen, a stranger on a bus or with themselves.

As she neared her death in 1926, aged eighty-one, she used to tell members of her family how she had lived a very satisfactory life with her many efforts rewarded. On her return from China she had protested alongside Mrs Pankhurst in favour of votes for women which they had later won. She had campaigned for and seen the women retain their rights to their own wealth and property after marriage. These were the two causes about which she had felt keenly in her youth and in her later years in England. She remembered with satisfaction that she had been part of a crusade against footbinding in China which as she had forecast in her writings would prove to be the beginning of a new era for Chinese women. At the turn of the century no other European woman or organisation had played such a public role in Chinese affairs or was to intervene so fundamentally in the domestic and social lives of Chinese women. Today however she is equally known among European students of China for her written records of the domestic and social lives of persons among whom, she said, 'I have lived on somewhat intimate terms for eleven years'.

3

At Home in the American Legation: *Diplomatic Wife and 'Friend of the Empress Dowager', Sarah Pike Conger*

S arah Pike Conger, self-styled friend of the Empress Dowager, arrived in China in 1898 as the wife of the new American Minister. She resided with her husband Edward Conger in the United States Legation in Peking for seven eventful years. Along with six other diplomatic wives, Sarah Pike Conger was a member of the first group of foreign women ever to enter the Imperial Palace and be granted an audience with the venerable and all-powerful Empress Dowager of China, Tzu Hsi. Her stay in Peking was made even more eventful in that she was caught up in one of the most violent and widespread anti-foreign movements of the century. In 1900 the xenophobic Boxers stormed Peking and she has left a record of the famous fifty-five day siege of the Legations in Peking. Afterwards and amid some controversy, Sarah Pike Conger still felt enough sympathy for China's dilemma and plight at the hands of the foreign powers to befriend and become a firm favourite of the Empress Dowager, visiting her 'at home' in the Imperial Palace many times. With the encouragement of the Empress, Sarah Pike Conger extended her circle of friends and acquaintances to include the imperial princesses of the Palace and the women of many of Peking's noble households. Perhaps more serious and earnest in her attempt to understand Chinese customs and meaning than most, it was a dream come true that she might enter Chinese households to learn of the domestic and social rituals of Chinese women's lives. During her seven-year stay, she also watched China open her doors to foreign contact and ideas; close them drastically after the attempted reform movement of 1898; attempt to eradicate all foreign influence and foreigners; and, finally humiliated and defeated, open them once more. As Sarah Pike Conger said, her story proved to be both unique and of extremes and it was her personal experience in and observations of these pivotal events around the turn of the century that caused her to collect together and publish her letters written to her daughter, nieces, sisters and many friends.

American Sarah Pike Conger was no stranger to foreign lands. She had arrived in Peking direct from the Brazilian Legation where she had delighted in the rich luxurious foliage and vivid colours of the trees, vines, orchids and ferns and feasted her senses in the tropical flowers and fruits of the then capital Petrópolis. Most importantly though, she felt that there she had learned a lesson in ex-patriate living which was to be of great value to her in learning to appreciate China – the place, its people and its culture. When she first went to Brazil in 1890 she had begun by always comparing and contrasting that country and her people with her own which were found to be 'always superior'. When returning home on leave a year or so later, she had had time on a long journey to review and reflect on her experiences, observations and thoughts on Brazil. To her surprise she had accumulated few and when she came to account for this lack, she thought that it was probably he own attitudes of superiority which had made it impossible for her to appreciate her opportunities for learning about Brazil. When she returned from home leave she descended from her 'imaginary height with the determination to seek with open eyes and a willing heart'. As she wrote in her first letter from Peking this experience had taught her the importance of shedding superiority and prejudice so that:

> now in 1898, I have come to this far-off land and am
> somewhat prepared to seek, to detect, to learn, and to

bring into my life perhaps a little of the knowledge of
the customs and home life of China and her people.

However, although she was more prepared and more aware
of the importance of symbolism and meaning to custom than
most, she assumed from her first impressions that she would
be indeed fortunate if she was to realise her dream.

On Sarah Pike Conger's arrival in China she had been
unprepared for the contrast between the 'open nature' of
Brazil and China where initially she felt that everything seemed
'beyond the reach of foreigners'; she felt very shut out and
excluded by the walls which seemed to surround all things
Chinese and separate them from the inquisitive and curious
eyes of the outsider. Indeed she wrote in her very first letter
from the American Legation dated 23 July 1898 that China was
a 'country of walls'. Just as the Great Wall was to protect her
vast empire from outsiders so city and village walls bounded
local residents and palace, compound cemetery and temple
walls alike protected families in their homes, in death and in
worship. It seemed to her that Peking could be described as a
'city of men'. It is the same long, low, grey anonymous walls,
still today the most obvious feature of old Peking's streets,
which symbolised for Sarah Pike Conger circumscription and
seclusion of Chinese women and foreign exclusion from the
social and domestic life of China's families. She felt pessimistic
about her chances of observing family life:

> How I long to go behind these high walls and see some-
> thing of the Chinese home life! Can it be that good fortune
> will ever open these locked gates and invite me to enter?
> I dare not cherish one hope in this direction; the recorded
> history of more than thirty centuries tells me 'No'.

Little did Sarah Pike Conger realise that she was soon to
be singularly privileged in her bid to penetrate the walls of
Peking, including those of the Imperial Palace itself, and
enter the domestic domains of royal and gentry women. In
the meantime, and behind her own walls in the Legation

Compound, she set about establishing the Legation home and her own patterns of domestic and social life as befitted the wife of the American Minister in Peking.

Sarah Pike Conger's own letters record the domestic and social details of diplomatic life in China at the turn of the century. She describes her home and the patterns of daily life, the festive cycles of the year and the unique combination of national and domestic rituals which characterised the life of American Ministers abroad. The American Legation, where her husband Edwin H. Conger was envoy extraordinary and Minister Plenipotentiary, consisted of a walled enclosure divided into courtyards in which resided all the Legation staff and servants. It was not unlike a large courtyarded Chinese compound made up of many gentry families and their servants although it had originally been an old temple compound; composed of many courtyards and buildings it was very much to her liking. The Minister and his wife had four courts for their personal use. In one of these which opened off from their drawing, dining rooms and kitchens, a set of chairs and sofas were placed in groups to receive day and after dinner guests. Photographs in her book show this temple court to have been both gracious and aesthetic at the centre of which stood an immense bronze incense burner and a temple bell surrounded by trees and groups of handpainted pots with large flowering and foliage plants. In the evenings these were all lit by fifty to a hundred small and large differently coloured lanterns hanging high and low and by globed candles upon the tables. One visitor to the American Legation at this time described how she found the combination of Chinese style and American comfort irresistible:

> While distinctly American as to its artistic comfort and furniture, the interior construction and decoration of the drawing room were purely Chinese, which gave a brush of oriental 'couleur locale' to this pleasant haven of hospitality where Mr and Mrs Conger dispensed their hospitality.

Early in their stay, Sarah Conger and her husband established a daily routine which began before breakfast with coffee and an early two to three hour pony ride in both summer and winter. On these rides they followed well-worn routes either on the narrow city byways past the camel caravans making their way from Mongolia in winter or through the parks and woods in the summer. The ponies were as much a part of the Legation as their owners, and a staff of both 'boys' and 'coolies' was always in the outer court ready to help the Minister and his wife dismount and pet and reward their ponies with cubes of sugar and vegetables. The rest of the day was passed in domestic or social activities, the range of which much depended on the season and the demands of protocol. As Mrs Conger described, social duty in the diplomatic service required its own book-keeping which had to be as accurately performed and balanced as that of a cash book in the bank. Thursdays were her 'days at home' when she found her rooms well-filled with a medley of foreigners who sipped tea, partook of simple refreshments and exchanged news and gossip. She delighted in the individuals and personalities representing the different nations resident in Peking who, though frequently involved in the same round of tiffin and dinner parties, were refurbished constantly by a stream of visitors to the capital from elsewhere in China and from abroad. During the social season the Congers customarily gave two official dinners each week in addition to the number of less formal dinners at which they received relatives, friends and fellow Americans. Visitors staying for rather longer periods provided the Congers with an excuse for local sight-seeing trips in Peking and its environs and expeditions to farther sights.

Mr and Mrs Conger themselves ordinarily took a keen interest in the Peking landmarks noted for their historic significance and/or scenic beauty. One of Sarah Conger's favourite haunts was the Peking Observatory with its 300-year-old astronomical instruments, nicely posed on axes or pivots with mountings in the shape of dragons, which were wonderful in design, execution and material. Even their large gold complicated mathematical dial plates were perfectly preserved and still today they can be admired by travellers along Peking's main thoroughfare. A second favourite local sight was the examination halls where many thousands of young men of learning assembled every two to three years to have their textual knowledge of the ancient Confucian and other classics tested. These examinations were the main means by which the higher officials of the Chinese civil service were recruited and gentry families all aimed to have at least one of their sons pass the degrees. To illustrate something of the examinee's ordeal, Mrs Conger described the examination halls in one of her letters. They were long, shed-like buildings about six-foot wide and 200 to 300 feet long, all facing the south. The open-fronted halls, which had a passageway of four foot between them and a roof which extended so far as to keep out the intense heat of the sun, were divided into compartments about three and one half feet square and furnished with a broad seat and a bench in front of the occupant upon which to write. Scholars were confined to these compartments for three days at a time and all necessities were brought to them. It was a popular visiting place for China's foreign residents and many must have pondered the system of examinations as a route to office. Many British visitors could have been surprised to learn that their own examination system for the recruitment of civil servants introduced in the mid-nineteenth century had been modelled on this Chinese example.

The number of nearby temples on the outskirts of Peking also provided an excuse for a sight-seeing party. On one typical occasion described by Sarah Conger a party of twelve set out from the American Legation on their ponies and in sedan chairs for the Yellow Temple and the Bell Temple some six miles distant. The object of great interest at the Yellow Temple was a large marble tower built in memory of Buddha which was adorned with carvings and bas reliefs depicting his life both on this earth and hereafter. The attraction of the Bell Temple was, as its name suggests, a great bell cast five centuries before which weighed just more than fifty-three tonnes. It was reputed to be the largest hanging bell in existence. It was completely covered inside and out with Chinese characters, extracts from the Buddhist Canon, and its melodies and resounding chords quite entranced Mrs

Conger and her visitors. Some idea of the elaborate planning and nature of these periodic sight-seeing expeditions can be gained from Sarah Conger's descriptions of the preparations for picnic tiffin. First the accompanying *mafoos* (stable boys), one for each horse, walked their charges and watered, stabled and fed them. Then the chair coolies dropped down in the shade for a time before they washed and ate their tiffin. Finally, the guests who had been preceded by their servants were escorted into the temple proper where their own washing bowls, pitchers and towels brought from home awaited them as did a table of twelve plates and real home-hot tiffin with its customary number of courses. Everything upon the table from the pickles, sweets and flowers to the ice and distilled water had been transported by the coolies for the comfort of the travellers.

During the long, hot and dusty Peking summers, most of the members of the diplomatic community removed their households to the temples of the Western Hills some fifteen miles from the capital city where each foreign Legation had been allocated a temple. In turn, members of staff were allocated one of the numerous courts and one-storey buildings located within the walled enclosure of each temple. Many of these temples can be visited today and are still favourite Sunday picnic places for the diplomatic community in Peking. The priests of the temples continued to worship their gods and monastic life co-existed alongside the daily life of its foreign guests for whom every furnishing and personal item had to be brought from their Peking household. Foreign families enjoyed the temple homes which were cool, quiet and peaceful, surrounded as they were by open fields dotted with stone walls and cemetery groves. A distant view of the city could also be viewed from their high broad verandas. The Congers, like other diplomatic and missionary members of the foreign community, daily partook in long strolls and donkey rides. A more ambitious and favourite expedition from their Western Hills homes was a visit to the famous and historic Great Wall and the Ming tombs. Then it was a four-day round trip instead of the few hours of today.

When Mr and Mrs Conger and their daughter and niece set off on such a journey their procession included four donkeys for themselves, one donkey for pack and four donkey men; two carts, two men and eight mules each pair of which carried a large chair on their backs. In addition they took three ponies, a stableman, head boy, second boy, first cook and a coolie. After passing by the small farms producing corn, beans, millet and buckwheat and which seemed like mere gardens and so different in scale from their native Iowa, they tiffined each day with the same foods, table linen, dishes and flowers as at home. Each evening they put up at a Chinese inn which was quite unlike anything they had ever seen. The inn was a compound combining many courts and one-storey buildings, each room furnished with a *kang* or Chinese platform-bed across one of its sides or ends. It was from five to seven feet wide, about two feet high and walled and covered with brick. The *kang* was covered with reed matting and under it a fire was lit in the winter to heat the travellers. Aside from the local furnishings of a table, two chairs and two stools within the bare brick floored room with paper windows and doors, all other needs had to be catered for by the travellers themselves. They found that their nights were hardly peaceful with the crowing of cocks, the braying of the many donkeys, the bleating of the sheep and the constant ringing of the bells worn by the moving laden camels in the endless caravans.

On the road to the Great Wall the travellers met hundreds of fine camels travelling the direct road to Mongolia and the West which rested during the day and travelled with their packs at night; at least five flocks of sheep; and hundreds of mules laden with wool, hides, tea, fruits, grain, fodder, cotton and other commodities. As they met pack-cattle from Mongolia, numbers of mule litters, carts and many men riding donkeys all bent on business, they were forcibly impressed and reminded that only the foreigners and not the Chinese sought their pleasure in travel! Like visitors to China today they were much awed by the dimensions, the labour and the timelessness of the Great Wall, and the strangely imposing avenue of twenty-four large yet exquisitely carved priests, warriors and animals leading to the walled tombs of the Ming Emperors.

Once the summers in the Western Hills had given way to autumn and the return to Peking the domestic and social rituals of the Legation were punctuated by annual festivals frequently celebrated with more aplomb and ceremony by foreign residents abroad than at home. On that peculiarly American festival day, Thanksgiving, the American Legation was bedecked with flags and opened its doors to all the American residents in Peking so that as many as seventy persons might join in the hymns of praise and listen to a patriotic sermon before sitting down to a turkey dinner. Another uniquely American celebration was Independence Day, a day on which the stripes and stars were much in evidence, which Sarah Conger thought did much to remind small groups of Americans residing in a foreign land under the protection of the American flag of the timeless thrill of being American. Celebrated throughout the foreign community in the middle of winter were Christmas and new year. Christmas Day was marked by the exchange of presents between the families of the foreign community and between foreign families and their Chinese servants. As the Congers opened their front door one Christmas morning, they saw on either side of the steps a small evergreen tree planted in a painted porcelain pot and decorated with many styles of the most intricately cut paper people, animals, birds, bats and flowers in colours, and clay birds beautifully enhanced with feathers. On New Year's Day there was any amount of formal visiting and salutations between the Chinese officials of the capital and the Legation staff. On their first New Year's Day, three companies of ten to twelve officials, men of wealth and high standing, came to pay their respects to Mr Conger each in his own sedan chair lined with fur and carried by four chair-backed coolies in uniform. They were not due to meet the women of the Legation, but the women in the Legation made sure that they saw them! Mrs Conger described the rich and colourful procession with each official dressed in the finest long noble garments of rich heavy silk satin, and velvet, fur boots and sable hats with official buttons and peacock feathers.

Each also wore a long string of valuable beads rich with jade and costly jewels.

All the time that Sarah Pike Conger enjoyed the novelty of her own domestic and social life in China, she also wanted, and more and more, to learn of Chinese domestic and social life. At first it had seemed to her that there was no method 'in their ways of doing', but gradually she became aware that there was indeed a 'great method' and that it was all-pervasive if at times apparently incoherent and contradictory. Like most foreign women, Sarah Conger's first contacts with the 'way of doing things' in China was with the servants within her own Legation walls. Mrs Conger's interest in the lives of her servants is revealed in her letters where she writes in great detail about their domestic and family affairs. It was from them that she first learned of the importance of sons in caring for the elderly in life and the departed souls after death. Her own *amah* or maid, who had no children of her own, purchased a boy child so that she might have sons and grandsons to care for her in her old age, visit her grave and tend the ancestral shrines. The adopted infant was not brought up by the *amah* herself within the Legation but was sent to the *amah*'s sister who had a son of the same age. On another occasion, her head servant appeared at the table with a white cord braided into his queue. He had just learned by letter that his wife back home had died. After a mere two to three weeks Mrs Conger was very surprised to be introduced to his new second wife who had been chosen for him by his mother and brought to him by his grown-up son. When it emerged that the new wife was but a singsong girl who though she had little feet had cost her new husband a great deal of money, the head servant had sent her back to his mother.

Although Sarah Conger appreciated the interest of the talk and gossip and the wonderfully quiet and gentle willingness of her servant to please, she was conscious of the power relations between foreigners and their Chinese servants, though like other first-time foreign women in China it took her a little while to learn the true nature of these. From the outset she was aware that while she was studying her servants, they were also studying her but with a perception that was keener and quicker.

> Their most unerring memory, their quick discernment, and their ready adoption of 'this' and of 'that' is a power to them. And all this is but another expression of their marvellous economy. This economy extends even to their thought processes; nothing is lost; anything is used to advantage. They read your varied expressions of face and tones of voice, and when it is well to understand you they are wise; when it is better to be ignorant they are blank.

The most likely source of contention between back and front rooms was the size of 'the squeeze', or the system of bonus payments by which each servant was entitled to a percentage of household expenses. In the Legation household, the servants were numerous and each had her or his exclusively defined tasks and did no other. On the basis of this division of labour the servants had their own elaborate hierarchies and methods of organisation so that all the houseboys and coolies were supervised by either the first cook in the kitchen, the first washman in the laundry, the first stableman or the first gardener. Each department under the overall supervision of the head boy or servant managed its own tasks and its own daily accounts which were each day checked by the mistress of the household. Although a small amount of squeeze or commission on every object which passed into the Legation household was deemed to be acceptable by all parties, it tended intermittently to get out of hand at which time the mistress of the house intervened, unable to tolerate any longer the rising amounts. In one letter Sarah Conger recounts how when she first came into contact with the system of the squeeze, she thought it wise to make some changes. In the interests of economy and efficiency, she arranged to have the coal required by the Legation delivered in bulk rather than for each department to order its own small supplies as had been the custom. Apparently there was no objection. It was not long however before there were complaints. The cook found he could not cook well; the washman could not wash and iron well; grates could not warm the house well. On enquiring into the cause of all the problems, Sarah Conger found that each must have his own coal. 'Don't like this coal.' She understood. The coal squeeze had been cut off from these departments and once it was reinstated to them, all proceeded as before and harmony was restored. Like foreign mistresses before her, Sarah Conger soon learned that it was a rare foreigner who could purchase daily necessities from the market as cheaply as could the servants despite their commission and usually an acceptable compromise was found. Rarely was it the sole basis for tension and the cause of dismissal. It was unusual for a foreign mistress to dismiss a servant, for they usually did not allow relations to deteriorate to such a degree without themselves first resigning. Sarah Conger soon realised it was best if servants came to her and said their father, mother, grandparent or anyone else was sick and it was best if they went, just to let them go. She noticed many times that it was less the problems between foreigner and servant than trouble among the servants themselves which forced some to depart. She learned after her first few months when she was inclined to interfere and attempt to introduce innovations and direct her household actively according to her own prescriptions and methods, that it was best if she left well alone and merely gave directions to her head boy. She was rarely disappointed and usually delighted with the results.

For some months, the domestic and familial affairs of the servants were the only form of sustained contact which Sarah Conger had with the Chinese way of doing things although she continued to wish otherwise. She had few opportunities to observe China's domestic and social life let alone street life, for the Congers, like other foreign residents in Peking, tended to take a frequent stroll along the city walls of which only fragments survive today. Unlike Mrs Little in far Chungking, Sarah Conger enjoyed few strolls in the street for it was not thought to be safe for foreign women to go out alone not least because of the numerous beggars. Although Alicia Little on one of her visits to Peking was horrified by the constraints on walking and somewhat scornful of the attractions of the rather overgrown and narrow city wall, Peking foreign residents thought that this wall, set aside for the exclusive use of foreigners, was a quiet and chosen vantage point from which to enjoy the sights and sounds of the crowded streets below and the panoramic views of the four walled cities that made up the city of Peking. The native and the Tartar cities were graced with many gates and temples, while in the Imperial and Forbidden cities the unusual and uniquely yellow-tiled and carved roofs tantalisingly glinted in the sun. Today in Peking visitors can stand within the Imperial Palace or walled Forbidden City and admire at close quarters the wonderfully memorable carvings, colours and curves of these roofs, but at the turn of the century the far view of these imperial gateways and roofs was all the foreign community knew of the Imperial Palace. Few foreigners had ever been admitted to the Imperial Palace although there was much interest in and talk among the foreign residents of the happenings and intrigues in the Imperial household headed by the Empress Dowager Tzu Hsi and a succession of young Emperors. Quite unexpectedly and quite dramatically within a few months of her arrival in Peking however, Sarah Conger was to achieve the pinnacle of her ambitions had she dared to so wish. She was granted the unique opportunity of joining the first small group of foreign women to pass through the Imperial gates and have an audience with the Empress Dowager herself.

The visit by a small number of women of the diplomatic corps was suggested by Lady Macdonald, the wife of the British Minister, shortly after a similar visit had been arranged for the Ministers, and quite why the Empress Dowager decided to receive the wives of the foreign Ministers in Peking was the subject of much debate. According to an account of the visit written by the Empress Dowager's lady-in-waiting it was probably due to curiosity as much as anything else. The Empress Dowager had apparently never seen a foreign lady before that time. The ladies of the diplomatic corps were to be invited to pay their compliments to the Empress Dowager on the occasion of her sixty-fourth birthday. For this most exciting and nerve-racking of occasions each of the seven women dressed in their finest attire and on assembling they were carried through the Peking streets in procession, each in a sedan chair with five chair bearers and two mounted riders. At the first gates of the Imperial Palace they were transferred to red upholstered court chairs with six eunuch chair bearers plus many escorts. To their great surprise they were thus transported to a railway coach, a gift made some time before by France to China, which had been installed within the palace gates. After a little rest and tea-sipping, they were received within the room where they stood according to rank decided by length of residence in Peking, they bowed and they were then each in turn presented to the Emperor and the Empress Dowager.

During the visit the Empress Dowager clasped the hands of each lady several times and presented her with many presents. They feasted with the princesses, all gowned in rich, finely embroidered bright-coloured satins, watched a Chinese theatre and had several opportunities to gather closely around the Empress Dowager and talk cordially with her. Sarah Conger was surprised to find her bright, happily communicative and glowing with goodwill with not an observable trace of the cruelty for which she was reputed. Indeed she several times welcomed the foreign women to the palace as 'fellow members of one family'. All in all the foreigners were well pleased with the visit and on their return to the British Legation they had their photographs taken and reflected on 'the happenings of this most momentous of days', the historic importance of which was not lost on Mrs Conger. She wrote in a letter to her niece:

After this wonderful dream day, so very unreal to us all we reached home, intoxicated with novelty and beauty. Everything had been done for us! Only think! China, after centuries and centuries of locked doors, has now set them ajar! No foreign lady ever laid eyes on the Rulers of China before, and no Chinese ruler ever before saw a foreign lady. We returned to the British Legation and in happy mood grouped ourselves for a

picture that would fix in thought a most unusual day
– a day, in fact of historic import. December the 13th
1898 is a great day for China and for the world.

Mrs Conger could not know that within six months she
would be participating in events in China of far greater
import in the eyes of the world and that her impression
of the goodwill of the Empress Dowager was to be sorely
tested.

The pattern of daily life at the American and other foreign
Legations in Peking was broken dramatically by the Boxer
Rebellion of 1900, the climax of which was the fifty-five
day siege of the British Legation within which much of the
diplomatic and foreign community in Peking were confined.
Prior to the siege, Mrs Conger increasingly mentioned reports
of very serious and tragic anti-mission and anti-foreign incidents at the hands of organised anti-foreign bands called the
Boxers who roved the countryside and the provinces for some
months before they eventually reached Peking. Although there
was some general uneasiness among the foreigners in Peking
including members of the Conger household, Mr Conger as the
American Minister was later criticised for his lack of foresight
in thinking that there had been no immediate danger to foreign
residents even up to a few days of the siege taking place. Only
as it became apparent that the Boxers might enjoy the support
of the Empress Dowager and Imperial Court and as the foreign
community became more and more isolated and cut off from
the outside world did Sarah Conger prepare for anti-foreign
violence within the city itself. She, like many others, began to
set in stores of flour, corn meal, beans, rice, sugar, chickens
and other supplies in case of an emergency which seemed
increasingly likely by the middle months of 1900. On 11 June
Mrs Conger wrote that it seemed that day by day they were
being forced into narrower and closer quarters. Little by little
all connections with the world beyond Peking were severed as
telegraph lines were cut and the railroad stopped. As they grew
increasingly isolated, she likened the position of foreigners to
one where they were 'on board ship in unknown seas and

battling with a terrific storm'. The subsequent flight of foreigners, missionaries and foreign-influenced Chinese converts
to the three-quarter square mile Legation quarter in Peking
in order to escape the rough and fury of the Boxers brought
the crisis directly into the Legations themselves. By the middle
of June the Legations were making elaborate defence plans
centred on the British Legation, the largest and most securely
fortified of the eleven, and it was there that the foreigners
finally gathered and set up their defences which unknown to
them would have to withstand the Boxers' siege for fifty-five
days.

The siege officially began on 19 June, the day on which the
Chinese government notified the diplomatic community that
it could no longer guarantee its protection from the Boxers.
At that time there were close on 900 persons barricaded in
the British Legation which amounting to seven acres housed
the entire foreign community in Peking, at that time made up
of diplomats, customs officials, servants, missionaries, troops,
women and children and the odd individual who happened by
chance to be visiting Peking. The British Legation, presided
over by Sir Claude and Lady Macdonald, normally provided
residence for only sixty persons in a small number of houses
which were now redistributed among the members of the foreign Legations, each ministerial family usually being allocated
one room for eating, sleeping and living and the common use
of a kitchen. Others were crowded into smaller houses or in
open pavilions. Alongside, Chinese converts were crowded
into an adjoining much smaller property which became even
more crowded and claustrophobic as the siege progressed.

A carefully planned division of labour was organised by the
Ministers who took responsibility for the overall management
of the siege and its negotiations with Chinese government
officials. The few troops augmented by male Legation staff and
customs officials fought off the Boxers at the barricades with
little respite or relief. They took time away only to sleep and
eat. The missionaries undertook a variety of tasks depending
on their skills, but they knew the Chinese language well and
hence it was they who took charge of the Chinese converts in

building barricades and fortifications, digging trenches, filling and carrying sandbags, and looking after sanitary conditions both by day and at night. The Chinese converts did much of the manual labour and many a time Sarah Conger expressed satisfaction at the mutual interdependence of Chinese and foreigner: foreigners saving the lives of the converts by giving them protection, the converts now in turn contributing much to the saving of foreign lives.

There were 300 foreign women and children in the British Legation and Mrs Conger recorded how many of the former were kept extremely busy overseeing food and medical supplies. The hospital too had to be supplied with linen, pyjamas and dressings. In Mrs Conger's own room the sewing machines whirred all day providing such items, for keeping the hospital supplied with linen was a constant source of worry. Fortunately Mrs Conger had just returned from America with bolts of new cotton, creton, sheeting, pillowcasing, new table cloths, napkins and towels which she turned over to the common store. For the barricades the women also made thousands and thousands of sandbags which were variously fashioned out of the monogrammed brocade dressing gowns of the Ministers, Liberty prints from England and bolts of silk and brocade abandoned in nearby Chinese houses. The fastest lady was said to complete and stuff one sandbag every four minutes or so. According to one eye-witness 'the butterfly colours and textiles of the brocades were quite memorable' and relieved the greyness of the atmosphere. The women were kept fully occupied by these activities together with nursing the wounded, caring for the sick and for children. Dysentery was rife and mosquitoes abundant given the seeping dampness and intense heat which measured 110 degrees in the shade. Most were too busy to give in to the constant fear that the barricades might not hold for another day although, according to several different reports written after the siege by the survivors, a few women did succumb and withdrew behind closed doors only emerging during each new attack to indulge in a fresh bout of hysterics.

As the siege continued without an end in sight, there was a constant problem of providing sufficient food and arranging for its distribution to maintain the health of so many for a seemingly indefinite period. Initially the staple diet was rice, beans and flour with some pony and mule meat, supplies of which had either been accumulated before the siege began or lifted from shops within the Legation quarters during the first days of the siege. As a last resort, the ponies and mules belonging to the foreigners met their fate one by one as the weeks passed. By chance there was no shortage of champagne which seemed to provide a nightly accompaniment to the evening meal – perhaps to celebrate the survival of yet another day. By the last few days of the siege, all food supplies had dwindled, and rations were short for all and shorter for some. By 9 August the Chinese converts were recorded as eating dog meat and cauldrons of broth made up of slippery elm leaves, grain and a little meat. On the one occasion the Empress Dowager had flour, watermelons, vegetables and ice sent to the foreigners they did not dare to eat the flour fearing that it might be poisoned. Certainly they did not want to admit to any shortages or request food for fear that it might reveal a weakness to be exploited by their enemies.

On the whole, Mrs Conger and other women who wrote their own accounts of the siege did not dwell on the dangers and privations to which they had been subject day in and day out although they were under constant firing from the Chinese guns. As the offensive-platform structures of the Boxers grew higher and higher so the foreign barricades had to increase in height to prevent the Chinese enemy from looking down and shooting to advantage. Fortunately much of the shooting was at too high a level and the bullets very much tended to whizz overhead – that is, until one of the foreigners, showing signs of insanity, escaped to the Chinese side and suggested that they fire their bullets a good deal lower! It was more the constant fires, the whizzing sound of the bullets and the incessant noise and shouts of 'Kill the foreigner' and 'Eradicate all things foreign!', the growing shortage of ammunition once the temple bells, vases, bronzes and all things that could be melted down were exhausted, and the depressing deaths among the small bands of men who stood between them and the invaders

– all these affected morale and after some weeks tested everybody's limits of endurance. Mrs Conger herself was not one to indulge in weakness or submission, and throughout the siege she kept very busy and was known for her words of cheer and encouragement. She had offered her services as a nurse, but that task was thought to be better performed by the wife of the Russian Minister who earned high praise for her devoted care of the wounded. Instead Mrs Conger turned her attention to managing hospital supplies including the provision of fresh linen and filtered and boiled water.

In her own account of the siege, Sarah Conger attributed much of her own courage to her religion, which gave her great consolation. Its importance in her life is revealed in her own diary letters about the siege in which she notes how she found great comfort in choosing biblical passages appropriate for the situation in which she found herself. At one point she acknowledged that 'she loved her religion as she never before knew how to in that it was surely a refuge and strength in times of need!' Her own religion, although this does not explicitly emerge from her diaries and her letters, was Christian Scientist and Mrs Eddy Baker, its founder, was at once both a friend and confidante of Sarah Conger. Many times during the siege Mrs Conger attempted to comfort her daughter and others by encouraging them to think of other things although some of the stories of her cheer suggest that her determination to put her own faith to the test and to find evidence of the constant goodness of God led her sometimes to strange fancies. On one occasion she apparently ascribed to God what should have been attributed to the Boxers! When, according to one contemporary account, a room full of women and children was surprised and shocked to find a bullet whizzing in its midst and narrowly missing a baby in its cradle, they flew to the other side of the room with the exception of Mrs Conger who

> conspicuous for her concise manner and Christian Science faith earnestly assured us that it was ourselves and not the times which were troublesome and out of tune and insisted that while there was an

appearance of warlike hostility, it was really in our own brains. Going further, she assured us that there was no bullet entering the room; it was again but our receptive minds which falsely led us to believe such to be the case. With these calming admonitions she retired and I can honestly say that we were more surprised by her extraordinary statement than we were by the material bullet which had driven us from the room.

Her refusal to give in to idleness and fear and her readiness to meet all contingencies were also illustrated during one fiendish attack near the end of the siege which had gone on long enough for everyone to get up and get dressed. Mrs Conger found one woman still lying in bed and not attempting to get dressed for what most of the women present believed to be the 'beginning of the final fight'. Mrs Conger couldn't resist asking her if she minded being found in such a state of undress when the end came. It floated through this woman's mind that it really did not matter if she was massacred in her pink silk dressing gown or grey skirt and shirtwaist. This argument however failed to make any impression on the American Minister's wife. On the whole however the siege conditions were such that the individual foibles of the women and the many tensions which the isolation and claustrophobia of the siege must have generated were kept in check by the hopes that the relief forces were on their way to aid them and end the siege.

Daily were the rumours that the relief troops were on their way and perhaps it was just as well that those in Peking who lived by this hope did not know that the departure of the troops had been frequently delayed. It was not until fifty-five days had passed that the besieged eventually heard the sounds of the relief forces they had been so eagerly awaiting. Most of them were so exhausted that although they were relieved and happy, most contemporary accounts of the relief suggest that it was the rescuers rather than the rescued who felt the emotions of the moment. Many had not survived; in addition to the numbers of Chinese who died, sixty-six foreigners had been killed, two women and six babies had died and over one hundred and fifty persons had been wounded. The feelings of the survivors that they were indeed among the fortunate were strengthened when they saw the devastations elsewhere in Peking and heard of the terrible end that had befallen countless others including the seventy children who had in vain sought a safe refuge in the Peking cathedral.

In the aftermath of the siege Mrs Conger could only think of 'going home' to the American Legation and the wonderful uplifting sound that those words now had. The Congers were fortunate in that they were one of the few who had a home intact to return to, although it took several days to clean up the now dilapidated Legation. The Legation also became 'home' to the American troops of the relief forces much to the enjoyment of Mrs Conger's daughter and niece who each married an officer. The daily round of social and diplomatic life was resumed much as before despite the fact that it remained very difficult to procure food, fuel and other daily necessities. As a result of the devastation wrought by the Boxers, the flight of the Imperial Court from Peking, the division of the city and its spoils among the foreign troops, they were able to make daily trips to parts of Peking which had been hitherto denied to foreigners. The Temple of Heaven, previously a prohibited sight to foreigners, became the headquarters of the British Army and open to sightseers. Many foreigners including Sarah Conger made the most of the first opportunity to visit the Imperial Palace now empty of its royal inhabitants, and what visual feasts met their eyes:

We saw many elegant furnishings of the court: jades, porcelains, brass, ivory, lacquer, bronze, wood carvings, immense mirrors, brilliant decorations, embroidered hangings, fine large rugs and objects of beauty I cannot name. These are collections of the most precious Chinese treasures. New scenes opened our eyes in great surprise. Large generously decorated throne buildings, with their costly thrones and many other buildings with their beautiful valuable treasures were opened to us.

Little did Mrs Conger realise that this informal and surreptitious viewing was to be only the first of a number of visits in which she achieved what she had for long wished – that new doors would be open to her. Diplomatic events following the Boxer Rebellion were to place her in a unique position in relation to the Empress Dowager – and at the centre of international controversy.

The relations between the foreign powers and the Chinese government which had broken down completely during the siege were re-negotiated following the return of the Empress Dowager and her court to Peking in January 1902. That return was very different from her hurried flight from the palace in a cart, clad in the coarse blue clothes of a peasant woman on the arrival of the foreign troops in Peking. Her re-entry into the capital city was carefully planned with more than the usual ceremony, and in the interests of diplomacy, foreign Ministers, their families and their staff were invited to watch the procession of China's high officials, its army and the large imperial escort as they made their way through Peking to the Imperial Palace. One moment in particular impressed the foreign onlookers despite their raw emotions. As the Empress Dowager stepped out of her chair to enter the temple to attend to the rites and ceremonies of homecoming, she paused, looked up at the row of foreigners set apart and against the smoke-blackened walls and 'lifted her closed hands under her chin and made a series of little bows'. As one of those on the ramparts noticed with surprise:

> The effect of this gesture was astonishing. We'd all gone off to the wall in the hopes of catching a glimpse of the terrible Empress, whom the West considered almost an enemy of the human race. . .that little bow, and the graceful gesture of the closed hands took us by surprise. From all along the wall there came an answer of spontaneous burst of applause.

A few days later, six foreign Ministers, among them Mr Conger, had an audience with and presented their credentials to the

Empress Dowager, and for the first time in Chinese history the front gates of the Forbidden City were opened for their entry. It was then the turn of the wives of the diplomatic corps to be received. Mrs Conger was now deemed to be the most senior representative, and as such she played a conspicuous role as go-between in re-establishing diplomatic relations. The very invitation itself had, however, caused something of a stir, and at a preliminary meeting held to discuss what should be the foreign response it was clear that there were several differing opinions. Some of the diplomatic wives wanted to accept the invitation. They had just arrived in Peking and were keen to sample all its delights. On the other hand several others had lived through the siege and lost friends and were therefore very critical of the imperial household for its part in encouraging these terrible events.

As for Sarah Conger, it is clear that she thought that the foreigners should learn from the events of the past, but also put them behind them and concentrate on establishing better future Sino-foreign relations. When the visit did take place this was the gist of her speech made to the Empress on behalf of all the wives of the diplomatic corps:

Your Majesty, the ladies of the diplomatic corps here have responded with pleasure to your kind invitation for this audience; and we most heartily congratulate you and all the Imperial Court that the unfortunate situation which led you to abandon your beautiful capital has been so happily resolved, and that you are now permitted to return to it in freedom and in peace. Your safe return to Peking and to this undestroyed palace, will furnish pages to future history little comprehended at this time.

The events of the past two years must be as painful to you as they are to the rest of the world: but the sting of the sad experience may be eliminated, and we sincerely hope that it will be, through the establishment of better, franker, more trustful, and friendlier relations between China and other peoples of the earth. The world is moving forward. The tide of progress cannot be stayed, and it is to be hoped that China will join the great sisterhood of nations in the grand march. May all the nations united manifest forbearance, respect and goodwill moving on to the mutual good of all.

The women were each presented to the Empress Dowager and the very splendour of the occasion certainly quelled any remaining resentment among the diplomatic wives. After they had been received by high officials, Chinese court women took their arms and a stately procession of beauty and dignity unparalleled in each foreign woman's experience made its way through the courts, up marble steps with wonderfully carved white marble slabs and balustrades and on through brilliantly decorated passageways with their heavy yellow extended tile roofs supported by decorated teak-wood columns all of which can still be seen today. Sarah Conger not usually at a loss for words felt the inadequacy of her pen to describe the pageant. She tried:

> Standing on the broad platform at the top of the white marble steps of the last pavilion in its glow of colourings and decorations were the Princesses of the Court, and, at either side, the high officials. They were all attired in rich, oriental costumes and adornments. Their natural grace of manner and extreme courtesy intensified the beauty of the scene. The picture was a fairy one, and yet the bright sun was shining on a living picture. I never saw its equal in artistic beauty. The Chinese study the effect of colour and the multiplied shades of colour. Never have I more greatly desired the power of innate and cultured art of word and pencil to express what I felt and saw in that native Chinese picture. It stood for far more than extreme beauty.

Sarah Conger found herself as the most senior diplomatic wife and the only one who had been previously presented to the Empress Dowager to be in a privileged position to receive favoured friendship. Indeed, it is still the habit of a host or hostess in China to set great store by previous meetings and immediately to categorise such persons as 'old friends'. Sarah Conger was also one of the few to have been among the besieged, and in acknowledgement of this, the Empress Dowager took Sarah Conger's hands in both of hers and showed much emotion as she expressed her regrets and grief at the grave mistakes to which the late troubles had given rise. After she had promised that there would be no repetition of such events and that China now earnestly sought the friendship of foreigners, Sarah Conger accepted her apologies as sincere and expressed the hope that the two of them would get to know each other better and become friends. Her hostess responded then and there by giving Sarah Conger a very special heavy carved gold ring and engaging in a number of symbolic gestures of friendship including drinking from the other's cup and partaking of the other's biscuit. These gestures were quite unheard of in a palace where nobody was allowed to eat in the Empress Dowager's presence let alone use the same utensils. Thus began an unusual intimacy between the two women.

This intimacy was fostered by a number of subsequent receptions which the Empress Dowager gave for the diplomatic wives at which, as the oldest and most senior, Sarah Conger was singled out for imperial favours. Many of these receptions also took place at the Summer Palace on the outskirts of Peking when the guests would be entertained on the lakes and canals in the lavishly decorated imperial houseboats. Today, even in its state of residual splendour, it is not difficult for visitors to imagine the sight of the many boats with their brilliant colourings and Her Majesty's flags and steamers gliding in and out of the many turnings on the water course under the famed arched white marble bridge to the crystal waters beneath the shining yellow tiled Summer Palace itself. On several subsequent occasions Sarah Conger herself took the initiative and asked for a personal audience with the Empress Dowager so that she might bring other American guests to share in the awe, the splendour and intimacy of these occasions and perhaps to lay public claim to her own personal privileged position within the Imperial Court. Certainly as Alicia Little noted in one of her visits to Peking, Sarah Conger felt the relationship between the two women to be sufficiently intimate for her constantly to refer to 'my friend the Empress Dowager'. It was a friendship however which did not win Sarah Conger universal admiration either in foreign circles in Peking or back home in America.

The controversy which had surrounded the first post-Boxer imperial reception for the diplomatic wives continued unabated. With news of each visit and signs of more intimacies than the niceties of diplomatic contact demanded, the Chinese Christian women in Peking protested bitterly and wept at the thought of their martyred relations murdered at the hands of the Boxers. Their sentiments were shared by the majority of the foreign merchants and journalists resident in Peking and the treaty ports who could not understand how any foreign women could believe her 'honeyed words' or accept presents from the blood-stained hands of the Empress Dowager. Much of the bitterest criticism was directed towards 'nice but gullible' Mrs Conger who was accused of having been taken in. According to some newspaper articles back home in the States the only acceptable explanation for Sarah Conger's intimacies could be that she had her own personal mission which was to convert the Empress Dowager to the Christian Science religion! When as a result of such publicity, Sarah Conger was reminded by Mary Eddy Baker that such a mission might be inappropriate in the circumstances, Sarah Conger rather pointedly retorted that she would consider it a grave breach of etiquette even to mention her own religious affiliation to the Empress or the Court.

After the Boxer siege, the Dowager Empress was variously described as foreign-hating, barbaric, cruel, vindictive and hypocritical. The diplomatic wives were won over by numerous presents including jewellery, jade ornaments, scrolls written in her own hand, fans painted by herself and gifts of flowers, fruitcakes, candies and tea – each exchange of which was frequently construed by others as an extraordinary piece of play-acting designed to seduce the foreigners. Sarah Conger's letters show her to believe that the Empress was sincere and genuine in her wish to make amends for the past and she

expressed some indignation over the 'terrible unjust carica-
tures' of Her Imperial Majesty commonly depicted in illustrated papers; as a letter written in the immediate aftermath
of the Boxer Siege showed she found the Empress Dowager
to be entirely captivating:

> Her manner was thoughtful, serious in every way and
> ever mindful of the comfort and pleasure of her guests.
> Her eyes were bright, keen and watchful that nothing
> may escape her observations. Her face does not show
> marks of cruelty or severity; her voice is low, soft and
> attractive; her touch is gentle and kind.

'To set the record straight', Sarah Conger requested of the
Empress Dowager that Miss Katherine Carl, an American
portrait painter, be permitted to paint her portrait for the
St Louis Exposition in America. She wanted the rest of the
world to see her as she knew her and see for themselves even a
little of the 'true expression and courage of this misrepresented
woman'. This was a matter requiring some delicacy as in China
portraits were normally only painted for memorial purposes
after death; but thanks to Sarah Conger's considerable diplomatic skills Miss Katherine Carl was permitted to take up
residence at the Imperial Court for this purpose. She in turn
also found the Empress Dowager to be totally captivating
in her person, combining as she did a striking combination
of force and charm. Indeed she could not believe that her
young and friendly hostess with so winning a smile could be
the same redoubtable dragon, the bloodthirsty old harridan
and murderess portrayed in the media. At the time she wrote:

> I had heard and read so much of her before I went to
> the palace, and nothing that I heard or read had at all
> prepared me for the reality, so charming, so unreserved
> was her personality, so considerate, so tactful and so
> kind to those around her, she was so full of interest and
> charm, she was a woman of such infinite vanity. . .the
> more I saw of her the more remarkable I found her. . .

It is not only the European participants who have recounted their impressions of court life and its ceremonial receptions. One of the ladies-in-waiting to the Empress Dowager, Princess Der Ling, who married an American and published her court memoirs, has written rather amusingly about the extensive preparations which these foreign visits required. Although the Empress Dowager was very willing to receive the diplomatic wives she was reluctant to reveal any private details about her daily routine. She not only ordered certain personal objects to be put away or substituted for others but on one occasion she even had the colour scheme changed from pink to blue – a colour she loathed! During the ceremonials, the foreign ladies were themselves observed. Indeed according to Princess Der Ling the Empress Dowager and the ladies of the court found it difficult not to take offence at the foreigners' loud comments to each other about the materials of the dress and the costs of the jewellery of the imperial princesses all the while ignoring their wearers as if they were of no account. On another occasion, the Empress Dowager herself was rather taken aback by the behaviour of one American visitor who had the temerity to not only sit upon her throne but also to sit upon her bed! The Empress Dowager thought it showed a want of good manners:

> That was a funny lady: first she sat upon my throne and then upon my bed. Perhaps she does not know what a throne is when she sees one and yet foreigners laugh at us. I am sure that our manners are far superior to this.

Given that the court ladies were frequently assigned to the four corners of the rooms in order to quell the temptation of the foreign visitors to help themselves to small mementoes of their visits, it is not surprising that at court the Empress Dowager and ladies-in-waiting sometimes found foreign manners wanting. If Sarah Conger's interest in and real attempt to follow the rules of etiquette were appreciated, Princess Der Ling also records that the Empress Dowager was always a little nervous at the intentions of Sarah Conger when she asked for a special audience. Usually Mrs Conger just wanted to bring some American friends or visitors to meet her friend who was happy to oblige since she thought Sarah Conger to be 'a very nice lady who both respected and admired Chinese customs and appreciated the importance of good American and Chinese relations'. However the Empress Dowager did dislike the missionaries which Mrs Conger brought with her to act as interpreters. She not only had an innate distrust of missionaries and their interfering ways but also found it very difficult to understand their version of the Chinese language.

It has always been and still is hard for foreigners thrust into positions of privilege in far-away, exotic and closed China not to be seduced by the elaborate rituals and courtesy which emphasise the 'special' relationship. Sarah Conger was no exception in that she like so many others then and since felt herself to be singularly privileged. Although she may have exaggerated the degree of intimacy which she had with the Empress Dowager, she did have unique access to court circles. This seems to have been due not just to her position as senior diplomatic wife but also to her own interest in China, in Chinese custom and in China's women. It was these interests and her concern for the longer-term relations between China and America which led her to single out the Empress Dowager for friendship. As she explained to a sceptical journalist:

> My feelings and actions towards Her Majesty and her people I have reason to believe are well taken. I would not make the breach wider between the Chinese and the foreigners. I should like very much to have the Chinese see the better side of the Christian nations. Would that we had the Christ-spirit so rooted in our hearts that we could forgive and forget!. . . True, the past records dark, awful days in China, but what do we gain by hugging tightly the poisonous thorns of revenge?

Although Sarah Conger herself found it difficult to forgive the Boxers for the loss of missionaries' and Chinese converts' lives, she also had the honesty to admit that perhaps it was not surprising that the Chinese should vent so against foreigners who were frequently severe and exacting in their attitudes and treated the Chinese as though they were inferior beings who had no rights whatsoever. Moreover, she thought the fact remained that China belonged to the Chinese who had never invited or wanted the foreigner upon her soil. Had they not come unbidden and forced themselves, their customs, their habits, their predictions upon China despite a strong protest? Could China therefore be blamed for moving against the foreigner who seemed intent upon undermining the long established custom of an entire civilisation? In these circumstances she had great sympathy for China's wishes to be left alone:

> Poor China! Why cannot foreigners let her alone with her own? China has been wronged and in her desperation she is driven as best she could to stop the inroads, to blot out those already made. My sympathy is with China. A very unpopular thing to say, but it is my honest conclusion honestly uttered!

Sarah Conger also unusually challenged the popular view normally held by foreigners in China and abroad that what China needed most was a clean broom originating in and fashioned by the West to brush away long established customs. Although from the time she had set foot in China she had expressed an interest in learning about Chinese custom it was not until she achieved one of her dearest wishes to visit Chinese women in their own homes that she began to satisfy her curiosity and learn the details of domestic and social rituals and understand their rich symbolism and meanings.

Although it was unique and exciting to visit the Imperial Palace, if Sarah Conger wanted to observe Chinese domestic life she would have to visit the homes of her Chinese friends. With the blessing of the Empress Dowager a new set of relationships with gentry women based on home visits was initiated. It all began with Sarah Conger's invitation to the court princesses to tiffin at the American Legation. The guest list could of course include neither the Empress Dowager nor the Empress, but the adopted niece of the former and the sister of the latter plus other imperial princesses and wives and daughters of high officials were invited to visit the Legation. For the occasion the Conger home was decorated with flowers and potted trees full of red and white buds, blossoms, palms, dwarf flower trees and Chinese embroideries. The tables were laid with flowers with red name cards arranged for all the Chinese visitors, the wives of the American Legation and one Chinese-speaking representative for each of the American missions in Peking. Promptly at lunch-time, a procession made up of the yellow imperial chairs with gold knobs bearing the imperial princesses, red chairs for the other princesses and green chairs for those of lower rank together with their bearers, accompanying eunuchs and minor officials and attendants entered the American compound. It was an impressive and historic moment for all participants including Sarah Conger's head servant who, all smiles, exclaimed that he might 'live for a hundred years and never see the likes of this'. This time it was the Chinese women who were consumed with curiosity. They used knives and forks for the first time and observed closely both the American women and an American home with its peculiar form of home entertainment at the centre of which was the piano. It was this visit by the Chinese to the Conger household which initiated a series of return visits enabling Sarah Conger to realise her long awaited dream and to learn of the home life and customs of the gentry households. She was soon able to write in her letters back home to America that 'the number of homes of Manchu and Chinese ladies of rank receiving us is increasing and many hidden things are revealed to us'.

One of the hidden features of domestic life which most fascinated Sarah Conger, perhaps due to her own age, was the position of the elderly and the rules and customs associated with honouring parents and members of the older generations. She thought this was one of the most interesting discoveries to arise out of her observations of and participation in home festivities, family gatherings and quiet domestic circles. Only then did she realise the extent of 'the respect, tenderness, honour and affection that Chinese parents receive'. What

impressed Sarah Conger was the sense of mutual responsibility
between the young and old which was central to continuing and
strong family relationships through which each generation in
turn cared for the other to the best of its abilities. This reciproc-
ity was extended beyond death. The living cared for and worshipped the ancestors while the ancestors in turn blessed and
assisted to the best of their supernatural abilities. Among the
wealthy the ancestors even had their own hall within the family
courtyards. Sarah Conger felt very privileged when the women
of the household of one high official of imperial descent took
the unusual step and invited her to visit their ancestral hall.
In one of her letters she described how they passed through
outside courts with their pleasure-giving flowers, lakes, summer houses, rustic bridges and gardens until she ascended a
covered walk with balustrades, on each side of which were the
ancestral halls. As soon as the great doors opened they quietly
entered and their hostesses all bowed low. Before them on top
of an elaborately-carved turtle was a miniature and perfect
facsimile of the Imperial Palace with the same yellow tiles,
marble steps, red-lacquered pillars and elaborately carved and
decorated doors and windows which housed the tablet of their
imperial ancestor the Empress Ch'ien Lung. In addition there
were four green- and purple-tiled palaces in each of which was
placed the tablet of the father and mother of each generation.
Before each shrine stood an incense burner, a cup of burning
oil, candles and the various symbols used in worship. On the
floor were satin-covered cushions on which family members
knelt when worshipping the ancestors – who are offered fruits
and cakes and before whom incense is burned. The worship was
concluded with nine prostrations in which the descendants with
the utmost formality lifted the wine cup, each time lowering
their foreheads a little more as a mark of respect. It is in
their presence too, that birthdays, New Year's Day and other
special days are ritually commemorated today.

Sarah Conger was unusually invited to funerals in several
households where she had women friends to witness the
ceremonies whereby the dead were transformed from living
wife or mother into venerable ancestor. One of the most

elaborate in which she participated was a prolonged one for the Dowager Princess Su, the mother of one of the highest ranking princes in China. On one occasion during the funeral ceremonies which lasted many weeks, a modest but cordial invitation was extended to the women of the Conger household to honour them in their sorrow. The day was chosen for them to join the devoted and sorrowing women mourners of the Su family. As they entered the first court servants dressed in white, the colour of mourning in China, received them and escorted the foreigners through a succession of courts, almost noiseless except for the strains of music. Each court seemed to have a greater number of higher-ranking attendants than the preceding one until finally they entered a separate building divided into three rooms. A central room faced the courtyard and was the altar-room with a shrine in front of a large table behind which, curtained from view, was the coffin. At the right of this altar was the room for the sons and grandsons of the deceased; at the left was the room for daughters-in-law and grand-daughters.

Upon the floor of the women's room were large white cushions and upon each cushion facing the altar-room was a mourner arranged according to age and kinship rank. Each was dressed in coarse white cloth and without ornaments or cosmetics of any kind. Their hands were turbaned in white and their features and expressions were absorbed entirely by the ceremony at hand. As the bells rang, cymbals tinkled and uniformed musicians played their wailing music, friends of rank came to pay their respects and bring their 'feasts' which were placed upon the table behind the altar, each to be cleared away to give place to others after special ceremonies. In the court-yard in front of the altar-room lay hundreds and hundreds of gifts each of which bore its special message of sympathy to the bereaved family. There were in addition all imaginary things made of paper or 'papier maché' in imitation of the real that could be of use, comfort or pleasure to the departing ancestor. Long rows of blooming plants which greeted the visitors looked so natural in their pots and stands that they initially believed them to be so. There were trunks filled with rolls of silk and

satins, trunks of jewels, fans, rich ornaments for their hair and
many sorts of toilet articles, outer and under garments, shoes
and stockings. There were servants standing ready to serve,
stable boys, sedan and summer chairs, household chairs, stools,
tables, wardrobes all ready to be burned by fire at their proper
time and place. To Sarah Conger it looked as if everything to
wear or use in a home of wealth and culture was represented in
that court together with many banners, decorations, lanterns,
umbrellas and emblematic animals all to act their symbolic part
when called upon. She thought that no description of the array
of physical objects could do them justice, for there before her
lay all 'the innate adaptability of the Chinese people, their clev-
erness, gentle touch, patience, exactness, ability to reproduce,
keen eye for colours and shades of colour'. It was not just the
physical beauty which entranced her but the realisation that
each object had a significance, each ceremony had a meaning
and each performer a customary role all of which added up to
a whole or completeness which could only be comprehended
in part by the interested foreigner.

Sarah Conger herself described how initially she had been
faced with a Chinese puzzle which at first sight she might have
dismissed as different, obscure or inferior. Just as it took her
some time to decide to taste Chinese food, the delights of
which she soon appreciated, so once she began to realise that
customs and rituals were made up of a rich symbolism with a
depth and continuity of meaning she learned to respect and
enjoy this complexity. She was delighted to receive flowers
from the Empress Dowager to mark her sixtieth birthday and
to learn that each type of flower had a message. The peach
and oleander blossom expressed the wish for 'long life', 'rich
in sustenance and beauty'. The lotus leaf indicated purity and
modesty in that like the lotus 'the superior person, although
coming through mire, is untainted and although bathed in
sparkling water and rising in beauty is without vanity'. The
aster which still appears after frost falls expressed the thought
of unfading beauty and meant 'superior to circumstances'. The
orange marigold, fragrant and brilliant in the declining season,
was 'beautiful in age'. Sarah Conger thought these symbolic

attributes added charm to gifts already beautiful and to antique objects already appreciated. In a letter to a friend, she summed up the prevailing Victorian ignorance of these symbols and their meanings:

> At first as we look we see nothing but confusion; we see no method and everything seems to be done backwards; we see customs without meaning, education without value, religion without a redeeming feature; we are amused at the people, at their style of clothes, of wearing their hair; at the modes of locomotion; the process of tilling the soil; their ancestor worship; their attitude towards women. We ridicule their amusements and doubt their sincerity in all things. In fact we deride, belittle and woefully underrate everything Chinese. We feel that with the banner of progress in our hands, with superior knowledge and wisdom in our minds and dedication in our hearts, a reformation must come to this household that God has foresaken. . . [but China] has conceived, developed and carried into practice, written herself a thoroughly organised and almost unchangeable system of laws and customs that for many years have made her self-sustaining and independent. The object of my letters is to show you something of the thought of this dense population and vast empire as I have seen it. If we can take their line of thought we can better comprehend their actions. Let us be unbiased, charitable and watch to see if we cannot find that which we would assign to the good. As nearly as we can, let us look from their standpoint, as well as from our own.

It was her growing acquaintance with the 'hidden' symbols and meanings which reinforced her sympathy for the China which wished to be left alone and which was observing the erosion of its own philosophies and its own customs. It was for this reason that Sarah Conger forecast that confusion would be the lot of China's younger generations who attended foreign schools and learned of foreign ideas. She came to the conclusion that

China and European cultures were on a collision course, a course which was largely made up of

> a war of ideas in which each is striving to sustain his own. China with her long established wheels within wheels, all working together, does not wish to have the foreign nations touch and disarrange their systematic workings. There is a broad deep gulf between China and other nations. Foreign nations seem determined to change the granite customs of China and China struggles for their preservation. What will the outcome be?

Sarah Conger felt that this question could not be answered or solved by her generation but would continue to be the subject of debate in China and abroad by the next generation. She felt she was privileged to observe at first hand the initial acquaintance of Chinese women with new knowledge and customs. Unlike Alicia Little a few years earlier in isolated western China, Sarah Conger found that the women she talked to had broader interests ranging far beyond their walls. They were greatly interested in new forms of education, political issues and exchanging information on customs in other cultures. Their conversation revealed that they were quietly but surely learning of many things beyond painting, embroidery and calligraphy which commonly constituted the education of gentry daughters. They were interested in the affairs of their own country and had also learned Western geography and read widely the Western newspapers and books introduced into their circles by missionaries. At times Sarah Conger found that they had much information to impart when she solicited their wives on different items and events. She was amused when on one occasion several of her friends visited her shortly after telephones had been installed within their households. The women recounted with keen enjoyment some of the things they had learned through the telephone but Sarah Conger would not write of their secrets! Many of the princesses and ladies of rank were interested in founding schools for girls and were keen to learn of and tell her about their projects.

However Sarah Conger's close acquaintance with the gentry women of the capital city ended in 1905 when Mr Conger sent in his resignation as American Minister in Peking.

Prior to her departure for America, there were many official tributes to the role of Sarah Conger in initiating and maintaining relationships with women of rank and wealth in Peking and with the Empress Dowager herself. On the occasion of her last audience with the Empress Dowager, the formalities completed, the two women sat and talked less formally about the changes in China since Sarah Conger's arrival, the American woman's interest in and views on China, and landmarks in the history of their relationship such as the painting of the portrait of the Empress Dowager. As a mark of the understanding and friendship between the two women, the Empress Dowager bestowed on Sarah Conger an official honour of the highest rank, higher than ever before received by a foreign woman. The Empress Dowager also presented her with many gifts including one of her own good-luck charms designed to protect Mrs Conger on her homeward journey. Sarah Conger was kept very busy right up to the moment of her departure receiving and farewelling her friends who as a parting gesture all arranged to present her with a photograph of themselves. Many of these stately portraits are reproduced in her book based on her letters from China which she collected together on her return to America.

After a brief sojourn in Mexico where Mr Conger had been appointed ambassador, his deteriorating health forced them to return prematurely to California. After the death of her husband in 1907, Sarah Pike Conger remained in their California home where surrounded by her mementoes and active in her continuing interest in China she kept in touch with her Chinese friends. Many were the gifts, messages and letters from her Imperial Majesty, from the princesses, from official wives and daughters, from mission school-girls and from her servants. It was from them that she learned of the further changes affecting the domestic and social lives of her friends and other women in Peking. Within a few years of her departure there were at least seventeen Chinese schools for girls which had been

established by either the imperial or other princesses and
gentry women. Sarah Conger received letters about a new
daily newspaper especially for women which was eagerly and
thoroughly read by large numbers of Chinese women – those
who could not read it had it explained to them by those who
could! As she kept up her long correspondence and interest
in China however, Sarah Conger increasingly found herself
isolated, surrounded by those who subscribed to generally
vague popular ideas about the country and her people which
were largely erroneous and based on ignorance and prejudice.
It was to counter these views, to write of her first-hand intimate
and privileged knowledge and experiences and to end prejudice
that Sarah Conger published her *Letters from Peking* in 1907:

> The object of my letters is to show you something of
> the thought of this dense population and vast empire
> as I have seen it. If we can detect their line of thought,
> we can better comprehend their actions. Let us be
> unbiased, charitable and watch to see if we cannot
> find that which we would assign to the good. As
> nearly as we can, let us look from their standpoint,
> as well as from our own. It may be that we will
> learn lessons of value to our own living. Many books
> record dates and a detailed history of China. My
> letters record little else than my own experiences.

For her times Sarah Conger was unusually curious about
the symbolism and meanings inherent within many of China's social customs and interested in the thought, views and
domestic life of its women. At the turn of the century, to
satisfy her curiosity she had to enter the walled and gated
compounds of the family homesteads. During her first years
in Peking, women were seldom to be seen beyond these walls.
Sarah Conger thought that because she wished to be a friend
and to gain their friendship, doors and walls had been unusually
opened for her. Indeed by the time she left China she had been
rewarded in her greatest aim which had been to learn about the
lives of Chinese mothers, daughters, sisters and wives and draw

attention to their domestic and social accomplishments. In this respect her sentiments anticipate by several decades many of the goals of contemporary feminist ethnographers:

> I have accomplished much of my heart's desire to know the Chinese ladies in their houses: to get nearer to them and to learn of them and perhaps to let them know a little of the heart and ways of foreign ladies. What I have seen and learned and the deep impressions made upon my thought, volumes could not relate. . . To know the man only, exclusive of the woman, we know not one half of a house or of a nation, because we do not see the feminine influences nor the influences of the two combined. The man has his accomplishments, the woman has hers and the two together make up a good whole.

By the time Sarah Conger left China she observed that as the Chinese women of her acquaintance desired to know of more beyond the walls, these walls were beginning to shrink. She forecast that changes the future shape of which might yet be unclear were beginning to take place and were bound intimately to affect women's daily lives, their education and their occupations. Fortunately ten years later another European woman traveller and journalist made it her task to interview Chinese women of a variety of ages and domestic and public roles. In contrast to Sarah Conger's experience, most of Grace Seton Thompson's interviews took place 'outside the walls' and together they constitute a unique record of the changes in the domestic and social lives of Chinese women.

4

Chinese Women Interviewed: *Professional Traveller and 'Lady Journalist', Grace Seton Thompson*

One morning in November 1922 the much travelled American writer, Grace Seton Thompson, was sitting over breakfast coffee in an American hotel when a news item from China caught her attention and imagination. It announced the forthcoming marriage ceremonies and celebrations of China's last boy Emperor who though dethroned and without an empire was to be married at dawn to a bride he had never seen and in full splendour within the Imperial Palace of Peking. So attracted was she by the idea that 'this news caused her to let her coffee grow cold and instead to heat up the telephone wires with the speedy results of railroad and steamer tickets, hotel bills and porters'. Eight hours later she was speeding to a port and on to a steamer bound for China and a journey of which she had long dreamed. What drew her to China was an irresistible combination of the habitual search for adventure and for the unusual and a more serious interest in interviewing women. In contrast to the other five women in this book, Grace Seton Thompson did not reside in China for any length of time. Instead she belonged to the band of inveterate and independent women travellers in the tradition of the better known Isabella Bird. With her husband, the naturalist Ernest Seton Thompson, she developed a taste for long adventurous safaris and journeys to isolated hazardous regions in North

America and later she travelled alone in the Middle and Far East, South America and Southeast Asia. Although she herself was also an interested observer of wild animals in their natural habitats, she was first and foremost a journalist with a professional interest in interviewing 'the new woman' be it in India, Egypt, South America, Indonesia or China. Like Alicia Little and Sarah Pike Conger before her, she sought to learn directly and first-hand from the women themselves in their own homes. Unlike them she was, more than a decade later, able to interview the 'new woman' more easily. By then there was greater access in that she had emerged from behind the 'high walls of her home' and entered into new occupations and public activities. As a result of her several months' stay in China, Grace Seton Thompson was able to bequeath to later generations a set of human documents and photographs published under the title *Chinese Lanterns* which constitutes a unique written and photographic record of the activities and attitudes of the emerging Chinese women of the 1920s.

From a very early age Grace Seton Thompson had been interested in travelling and writing. In 1888 at the age of sixteen during a visit to Paris with her mother she had begun a career in journalism when the first of her many articles were published in San Francisco newspapers under the assumed name of Dorothy Dodge. Thereafter she wrote articles for papers and magazines in Paris, New York and London, and it was while she was on board ship making another trip to Paris in 1894 that she met a young artist and naturalist called Ernest Seton Thompson. They courted in Paris for the next two years and after their return to New York they were married. Ernest Seton Thompson, who had spent his boyhood in the wilds of Canada, wrote and illustrated animal stories for magazines and published many books including his best seller *Wild Animals I Have Known*. He was a founder of modern forms of animal stories which relate in fictional form the free habitat and details of an animal's life and its assumed mode of thought. One of his most famous characters was Lolo the Wolf, and Rudyard Kipling is supposed to have been much influenced by Ernest Seton Thompson's early stories.

Most of the research for his writing and illustrations derived from extensive travels and field expeditions, and on these he was accompanied by his young wife. They were both keen campers, trampers and hunters, and her husband later noted in his autobiography that his wife was a great success as a camper in that she never grumbled at hardships, scolded anyone and she was certainly a dead shot with a rifle, often far ahead of her guides. 'She met all kinds of danger with unflinching reserve and was always calm and clear headed no matter what the circumstances'; and the circumstances were frequently far from ordinary. As Grace Seton Thompson related in her first two books *Nimrod's Wife* and *A Woman Tenderfoot in the Rockies*, many of the tales of her adventures in Canada, the Sierra and the Rockies depicted the deprivations to which intrepid travellers were subject, the portentous yet likely confrontations with wild animals and the numerous funny incidents which are the stuff of memories. The keenness of both husband and wife for camping and the outdoor life caused them to help found several such movements for the young. Ernest Seton Thompson was one of the pioneers and leaders of scouting for boys in America and very appropriately he wrote their first outdoor manual. However, when he disagreed with the increasing militarism incorporated into the scouting movement, he subsequently departed from the scouts and started the Woodcraft League. So as not to leave out the girls, Grace Seton Thompson was among the founders of the Girl Pioneers which later became the Campfire Girls.

At home in Connecticut and between field expeditions, Grace Seton Thompson spent much of the early years of her married life helping her husband catalogue his field reports, drawings and paintings, and in editing his scientific papers and popular books. She spent some time studying book and paper making and printing, and she largely designed the covers, title pages and general appearance of some of her husband's earlier books. She also served as his literary and publicity agent which was no small task as he became more widely known as a popular lecturer and author. She also found time not only to write her own travel books and articles but also to pursue her own interest in women's rights. She lectured on behalf of the Connecticut Women's Suffrage Association, and she recalls with some relish that her lectures were not always as popular as her husband's! Indeed it was not unknown for speakers campaigning for women's suffrage to be pelted with carrots, turnips and rotten eggs. She was by reputation a good organiser and committee person becoming president of a number of associations including Pen and Brush and the Connecticut Women's Suffrage Association. During the First World War she was engaged in relief work raising funds for the purchase, equipping and operation of trucks of the Women's Motor Unit, La Bienêtre du Blessé in France, which she then directed for two years. For this and other of her war services, she received three French decorations. At home in the United States she acquired a reputation as a strong, efficient and interested person, her services much in demand. She served as secretary of the Connecticut Division of the Women's Committee of the Council for National Defense and sold liberty bonds in Washington DC.

After the war both the Seton Thompsons continued to travel widely but increasingly in separate venues: he on his lectures and field investigations into animal lore, and she further afield to Asia, Africa and Latin America where one of her primary aims was to interview the women. In 1922 Grace Seton Thompson undertook her first extended trip to Egypt which was designed to combine travel and adventure with a specific brief to study the complex roles of women in the rapidly changing times. There she had adventure aplenty and became accustomed to all modes of travel including camel and elephant caravan which were at common risk, when wandering lonely across the desert, from thieves and assaulters. When not travelling, she interviewed prominent women in unusual public and official roles, working women and Bedouin women. They included numbers of 'new' women who were emerging to take a leading role in political movements boycotting the British presence, new women's rights movements and philanthropic organisations undertaking social welfare work for the advancement of women. She was mainly interested in studying the complexities of the relationships between old customs and new practices, and with this aim in mind she interviewed numerous women about their occupations, their thoughts and aspirations and the patterns of their daily lives. As a worker for women's rights in America, she seems rapidly to have gained the respect and confidence of her informants with the result that they seem to have told her their stories or life histories in some detail. She was quite surprisingly permitted to take and publish photographs of the Moslem women who, eager to join with women of other nations and take their rightful place in the world, were pleased to have their stories and activities published. She wrote up her Egyptian experiences and interviews in a book called *A Woman Tenderfoot in Egypt* which was published in 1923. Given that it is a unique record based on the interviews and photographs with a cross section of Egyptian women of that time, it is not surprising that it was included in several lists of 'best books' written by American women. Sometime before its publication, Grace Seton Thompson had set sail for China.

Although Grace Seton Thompson spent the first few weeks after her arrival in China entering into the social life of the capital city and the ceremonials leading up to the young Emperor's wedding, her more serious aim in travelling to China was to meet and interview women of varying ages, social background and occupations. As she herself said, although as a journalist she 'might toy for a time with emperors and presidents, politicians and revolutions, the deeper and underlying aim and intent of her travels was to study the condition of Chinese women'. She had set out to explore a little the happenings of the 'dark places' or the 'women's quarters', and what she found was a self-styled generation of new women, who had benefited from the abolition of footbinding, the establishment of new schools for girls and new opportunities to take up occupations outside the home. The speed of change had been so rapid that neither Alicia Little nor Sarah Conger would have recognised the new woman in China. First and foremost she was the product of missionary and government schools for girls.

The new century had been marked by the increasing popularity among gentry and merchant households of educating their daughters. Mission schools for girls, first established several decades into the nineteenth century, began to expand and multiply. After a long struggle to establish the credibility and respectability of their schools, missionaries no longer had to provide incentives to encourage pupils to attend. Indeed with their Western curriculum and foreign equipment they were now seen to provide the most advanced educational courses for daughters. Other more conservative officials and gentry, unwilling that the education of their daughters be left entirely in foreign hands, began themselves to sponsor the private establishments of girls' schools. Although girls had initially been excluded from the new government system of education, a few years later in 1907 a new code provided for the establishment of government schools for girls. According to the *Peking Gazette* in 1917, girls' schools, normal and primary, were to be found in most of the provincial capitals and main cities and by the 1920s the number of government, private and mission schools for girls had increased so rapidly that a new generation of girls from gentry and merchant families had had the advantage of an education combining a Chinese and Western curriculum.

Among the gentry and merchants an education for daughters had been primarily viewed as a means towards a very desirable end: the strengthening of the female half of the population in order that they had the ability and skills to educate their sons. As one of the early magazines for girls explained:

> A good girl makes a good wife; a good wife makes a good mother; a good mother makes good sons. If the mothers have not been trained from childhood where are we to find the strong men of our nation? If then we say as China has said for so long: Let the men be educated and the women remain ignorant, half at least of the nation cannot be as useful as it should.

However, although the initial aims of the new girls' schools might be officially circumscribed and there was to be no intended change in their role and status, education in the new schools inadvertently opened up new occupational, public and domestic roles for the younger generation of Chinese women.

The establishment of the schools for girls – be they mission, gentry or government sponsored – provided for the first time a new environment which had the potential to influence girls against the more discriminating of family customs. For both teachers and pupils, the schools provided opportunities to escape from intolerable domestic circumstances and to acquire an occupation and some mode of economic independence. There are numerous accounts of girl students who refused to accept arranged marriages, who were encouraged to take up teaching, missionary and medical occupations or to go abroad for further education. The schools not only took women teachers out of the confines of the homes but also introduced them to a new learning, a new literature, new institutions and public activities. These new interests were generated by the May Fourth Movement, a literary movement aiming to discredit the old Confucian ideals and social institutions and introduce new social values largely derived from Europe and North America. One component of this new cultural movement was the 'Woman Question' as the issues surrounding the role and status of women were collectively referred to. Old practices such as the seclusion of women, arranged marriages, concubinage or the taking of additional wives, the double standard of morality for women and men and footbinding were severely criticised, while the new forms of education appropriate for women, romantic love, birth control and ideal family relations were widely discussed, often advocated and sometimes practised by the educated young. Most of the early magazines for women were published by school teachers and students who aimed to raise the consciousness of women to an awareness of their existing position in domestic affairs and to educate and mobilise them to participate in public affairs, The schools became centres of political, patriotic and revolutionary activities at a time when no question was deemed so urgent as the threatened autonomy of China and the encroachment of the foreign powers scrambling for their share of the country. In the new school-centred patriotic associations, public meetings and political demonstrations, many of the young girl students were inspired by the example of their teachers to acquire both a degree of personal independence and contribute to the country's political and nationalist needs.

Unlike Sarah Conger who at the turn of the century thought the absence of women to be a conspicuous feature of city life, twenty years later for Grace Seton Thompson the most noticeable characteristic was the number of women of all ages, no longer domestically secluded, who had emerged to undertake public and occupational roles hitherto denied them. Although as in Egypt she was very excited by much of the novelty of what she learnt from her informants in short interviews, she was also aware of the limitations of this method of obtaining information of a more sustained and intimate nature. What she set out to do was to obtain a snapshot in time of the range of experiences and expectations of Chinese women as they emerged from the women's quarters and acquired new public roles which characterised and demarcated the new woman in China. Although they still constituted a small urban minority, they were important in the vocal support for the new, the modern and the Western in the early 1920s. Grace Seton Thompson thought that the very range of attitudes and experiences of women of all ages which she encountered in her travels reflected the rapidity with which political, social and economic changes were taking place at this time. At one extreme lay the women of an urban official's household who had never seen a foreign woman. Although the official excused them from meeting her on the grounds that they would be afraid of her, it was perhaps more to the point that he also added that he himself did not want her to become acquainted with them and communicate her own attitude towards Chinese customs, and especially women's and public roles. Others were reluctant to meet Grace Seton Thompson and were suspicious of her motives, largely because any previous contact with foreigners had taught them how seldom they as Chinese were valued for their worth or credited with any learning or depth of character. At the other extreme were those who thought that if an attitude, attribute or article was of foreign origin, then it must be good, modern and progressive. As a result of her suffrage campaigns in the United States, Grace Seton Thompson was particularly interested in the younger generation of women whose experience was so different from that of their mothers.

This was the age when European ideas, literature and dress enjoyed a certain popularity among the modern educated young. Grace Seton Thompson's own photographs of members of this younger generation show them to be clad in Western fashions, to have adopted Western names and to be sophisticated in their bearing. Their hair was bobbed and waved and they had a gay social life quite in line with the smart sets of New York and London. Grace Seton Thompson thought Rose T. Hsiung to be the best example of the 'flapper type' that she met in Peking. Her hair, bobbed and waved, crowned a piquant face alive with vitality and charm. Her gown was very French and very chic, and her English was excellent largely because she had had an American college education. She and her sister were frequently to be found at the dances held at the big hotels where much of the social life of the 'advanced set' was centred, as it still is today. She even skated and rode in the company of young men which was very avant-garde for young unmarried girls. Indeed the activities of the younger set who enjoyed a giddy whirl of teas and dances provided a never-ending source of gossip among the more conservative.

Although older women were more likely to fall into the category of 'conservative', some of their number had also travelled abroad and adopted the ways of their foreign counterparts. One very enterprising and adventurous older woman, as soon as her children were launched, had taken herself off on a much longed-for trip to America where 'she visited all the larger cities and met all kinds of people'. She told Grace Seton Thompson that she had learned more during that visit abroad than she could have in several years of study at home. Many an old-fashioned mother who was not especially interested in or informed about the outside world was pulled into its affairs by the education or travels of her husband or her children. Several of the older women interviewed by Grace Seton Thompson spoke no English and had never been abroad yet their children were either studying in Europe and North America or preparing to do so. Some had spent all but the last few years of their lives in the seclusion of their homes. Now, because of their husbands' occupations, they were expected to accompany them and meet and talk with foreigners, make speeches and play independent public roles of their own. They had found this abrupt transition from a domestic to a public role very hard and were sometimes not even sure that they approved of the new trends which their own activities represented.

Grace Seton Thompson had not expected to find such a range of publicly active women in politics and philanthropy or in new professional and commercial occupations. Of all the women acquiring new public roles, it was the thirty to forty or so female physicians and surgeons who alike excited the most attention and interest from foreign and Chinese observers. Traditional Chinese doctors had been male and the rules of seclusion were such that they had no direct contact with female patients. At the most the doctor could feel the patient's pulse through the protecting curtain and usually he could only identify the location of the patient's ailment by examining a holed porcelain figurine into which the patient had placed a skewer at the spot corresponding to the pain in her own body. Although the young foreign-trained Chinese doctors and their missionary mentors were very excited by the idea of Chinese woman doctors improving the health of their sisters, there was considerable prejudice against both foreign medicine and its practitioners. Frequently they were consulted as a last resort and then blamed for the death of their patient. Although the woman pioneers in medicine and surgery interviewed by Grace Seton Thompson had a difficult time in establishing their hospitals and clinics for women, they were all committed to this profession and had strong views about the status of women in their country.

Of the pioneering half-dozen or so women doctors, the best known was Dr Mary Stone. Like the others of this first generation, she had received her initial training in one of the many mission hospitals established in China from the middle of the

nineteenth century, and afterwards in hospitals abroad. Like
the other first woman doctors, she was determined to improve
the health of Chinese women by establishing hospitals especially for women and children. However as Mary Stone told
Grace Seton Thompson this aim was not easily achieved. For
instance after raising the funds for supplies and equipment
she had returned to her birth place on the Yangtze River
to establish a Women's Hospital. When she had all ready
and in place, the mission group responsible for the hospital
refused to allow her to head it. Very much hurt, she moved
to Shanghai where she began all over again. She returned
to the United States to procure the surgical instruments and
apparatus necessary for a modern hospital which she purchased
with the help of American Christian well-wishers. In Shanghai
she converted an old house that had belonged to a foreign
Minister and in which no one would stay because it was
'inhabited by ghosts and rats' and because the pool, which had
once been part of an ornamental garden, bred mosquitoes and
pestilence. Despite these unpromising beginnings, Dr Mary
Stone achieved her goal and opened both a Women's Clinic and
Dispensary to which women travelled from afar by sampan,
cart and foot, and a modern school for the training of Chinese
girls in Western medicine. Her example had been followed by
most of the pioneer women doctors so that by the time of Grace
Thompson's visit she was able to interview some of the younger
second-generation women medically trained within China.

Outside of the main cities these young women doctors found
it difficult, associated as they were with foreign medicine, to
persuade patients that they were not the bearers of foreign
magic. The health of women had largely lain in the hands
of old-style doctors and midwives, who though they might
have had a full and extensive knowledge of curative herbs
and other indigenous practices, had little knowledge of the
importance of hygiene or sterile conditions the lack of which
were responsible for the very high mortality rate in childbirth
and childhood. Dr Emma Dau told Grace Seton Thompson
about her experience in the countryside as a young doctor
trained in foreign medicine where she encountered ancient

superstitious beliefs and prejudices. The worst case she could remember involved a young woman who had been in childbirth for three days some fifty miles from the hospital. By taking the hospital launch Dr Dau made the first thirty miles in four hours or so; the next lap of ten miles had been in a bullock cart and taken three hours and finally the last ten were travelled either on foot or in a wheelbarrow. She had expected to find the woman dead when she finally did arrive at the poor, small, rear lean-to of a home where to avoid 'polluting' the household the woman had been consigned. She described the scene to Grace Thompson: the unfortunate woman was lying on a box bed made of wooden planks, a filthy comforter was her sole covering beside the wadded rags she wore, and the dirt floor was littered with insanitary objects. An antagonistic midwife stood by helpless now that her 'well-meaning butchery' had only worsened the situation. This was not the view of the woman's family although the condition of that child and mother was such that the only thing the young doctor could do was to give morphine and assist her to die in peace. She told Grace Seton Thompson:

> The only thing I got for those twenty-four hours of hard travel was a summons to appear before the head of that woman's family and explain why I should not be prosecuted for practising 'foreign-devil medicine' on his kinswoman and her child which had resulted in the death of both!

Despite such experiences, Emma Dau told Grace Thompson that she loved her work and her commitment was such that she vowed that if she ever married she would certainly not give it up.

Grace Seton Thompson was impressed by the quiet strength and determined confidence of the young women doctors not only to reduce the suffering of women but also to overcome the prejudice and discrimination which they themselves experienced. Another young doctor, who equipped and managed a large hospital for women and children in Canton city, had not found it so difficult to gain the confidence of the authorities

or the patients. She had dedicated herself to the improvement
of the condition of Chinese women and told Grace Thompson
that women had suffered for so long that if this were to change
'they must have power. They must be in the Courts and public
affairs. They must be educated and know how to stand up
for themselves.' Another group of professional women also
aiming to provide an unusual service to improve the condition
of women were those who had taken up banking. The women
bankers whom Grace Seton Thompson met had established
separate banks or departments of banks for the exclusive
use of women. It was not only a professional interest but
their wider concern for the future of Chinese women which
motivated them in their new endeavours.

Grace Seton Thompson, greatly intrigued by what she had
heard about the women's banks, visited the Women's Department of the First Citizens' Bank in Peking. She found its
suite of offices to be 'well-equipped, well-lit and commodi-
ous'. The reception room for clients was furnished with a
number of writing desks supplied with 'convenient' blotters,
ink, pens and stationery while a settee, some easy chairs, a
good Chinese rug and a teak table gave the room charm. The
window curtains were of blue silk and several banners with
large Chinese characters wishing good luck for the enterprise,
gifts of co-operating friends, hung upon the wall. Mrs Chen,
its founder and manager, told Grace Seton Thompson how
she had set about establishing and extending the bank. To
extend its working capital, she and a staff of canvassers
called upon wealthy women in their homes to explain the
principles of banking and to reassure them of their rights to
the control of and the safeguards surrounding their savings.
These visits had apparently set many women thinking and
the list of bank depositors had grown and was still growing
rapidly. Mrs Chen told Grace Seton Thompson that one of
the advantages of the bank was that it safeguarded a woman's
dowry or savings against the claims of other family members.
Previously such savings had frequently dwindled to nothing
in the force of such claims. Only a few days before Grace
Seton Thompson's visit, a woman had come to the bank to

ask if they could 'fix it' so that she could not draw out of her account for a while. A feckless brother-in-law needed money and the family was making her life miserable to supply it. While Grace Seton Thompson was visiting the bank, one women client banked a deposit of a goodly sum which she had received as rent for houses she owned in Peking. She also arranged for a temporary loan to be made to a relative presently in need of $200. Although most of the depositors had so far come from wealthy homes, Mrs Chen aimed to establish in the near future a savings department for those with lesser incomes. She had a double aim: to make the bank pay and at the same time to educate women along progressive lines. She described for Grace Seton Thompson the other women's banks in Peking, Shanghai and Tientsin and the special schools which had been established in these cities to train women for a career in banking. Mrs Chen stressed that in all the banks it was not only the commercial side that interested them but the general opportunity they gave to help women to become independent.

Grace Seton Thompson found that almost without exception women with professional skills were mindful of the condition and needs of Chinese women less fortunate than themselves and that this concern was shared by a number of older gentry women who without the benefit of a modern education made a profession of philanthropy or charitable works. This interest in social welfare had initially been fostered by missionary schools and organisations, educational institutions and new women's clubs or associations. The Chinese National Association for the Advancement of Education emphasised that women with a modern education and training had a special role to play in improving society:

> Women's contribution in the world of thought and deed
> will be incalculable in building up China's new social
> structure. Such problems as child labour, women's
> employment, long hours and low wages and poor
> working conditions should be analysed and, if possible,
> solved. To meet such needs schools, colleges and

universities should offer girls and women courses in theoretical and applied. . .techniques of social service. In the community, the improvement of housing, diet and public health should engage the most serious attention of social workers.

Most of the social projects to improve the lot of poor girls and women were undertaken by clubs or organisations for women. Many students, returned students, professional and business women joined Women's and Business Women's Clubs, the Young Women's Christian Association, the Women's Social League or the National Council for Women. Like their American counterparts on which they were very much modelled, one of their main interests was social welfare. The founder of the first of one of these clubs to appear in China, the Chinese Women's Club of Shanghai, had been most impressed by the growth of such clubs in America:

> This is the first women's club that has been formed in China of the same nature as those in America. When we think of the early days there, not so very long ago, when the first women's club emerged out of the sewing-circle, and now when we read of the conference recently held by the American Federation of Women's Clubs, we feel encouraged and know that we too have made our humble beginning.

In China such clubs aimed to promote social welfare and charitable activities to provide for the education and economic independence of poorer unskilled women. Grace Seton Thompson interviewed a number of their members including some of the wealthy patrons.

Perhaps the most prominent woman Grace Thompson met was Madam Hsiang Hsi-Ling, the wife of the ex-Prime Minister. Madam Hsiang was the energetic president of several societies and described as an indefatigable committee member of many more, all concerned with welfare and ranging from hospitals, homes for destitute women and orphanages to schools and training centres for girls. She took Grace

Thompson to see two of her projects located in the pictur-esque Western Hills near Peking. One was a modern Red Cross hospital set upon a hill at the back of an old temple which had been founded by Madam Hsiang herself. She had raised the money personally and supervised the construction of the building where hundreds of eye and tubercular patients had already received free treatment and breathed the pure air of the former Imperial Hunting Park. Nearby, nestling in the hills, was the children's home of which Madam Hsiang was the director. The new buildings were solidly constructed and served many purposes, some for dormitories and schools and others to house the many industries taught there such as dyeing, weaving, basketry, carpentry, cobbling, machinery castings, lace-making, photography, modelling and silk culture. These all formed part of an educational experiment designed to equip and train the resident 1200 children of all ages. The objects made by the students were sold in a co-operative store and the proceeds deposited by the matron in their own savings-bank accounts. Madam Hsiang explained to Grace Thompson that the children were all poor though many were from 'good' families, and the aim was to make 'better citizens' of them. For example, to teach them the use of money and encourage them to be thrifty, they were given a monthly allowance out of which they had to buy their supplies and if they should accumulate any savings, they were encouraged to deposit them in the savings-bank. All kinds of animals were kept to teach the children how to care for and be humane towards them. Responsibility for younger children was delegated to students, some of whom were selected to act as 'prefects-cum-police'. Madam Hsiang, who could not walk easily because of her once-bound feet, was earnest in her wish to develop a better citizen for China.

Grace Thompson visited many such charitable enterprises designed to help girls not only acquire a skill but manage their skills. Another Peking matron, Mrs Sia, had established a school for knitting and crocheting work and placed it on a partially paying basis to encourage the girls to become self-supporting and independent. As she wished to supervise the school personally, she had it constructed in a secluded corner of the family compound. She had begun her experiment for 'social betterment' with just three girls; it had since developed into a class of twenty girls varying in ages between fourteen and twenty-five years. They remained in school long enough to learn how to knit and crochet and, once proficient, they undertook special orders for knitted goods, sweaters, bootees and caps of special designs which came pouring in from interested patrons. All the raw materials were furnished free and the proceeds of the sale of this work was paid into a fund which was used to pay the wages of the girls and for the development of the project. Six days a week Mrs Sia gave her personal attention to the enterprise ensuring that the girls had nourishing meals, paper serviettes as handkerchiefs and acquired a sense of personal neatness. She herself was a Christian and placed a great emphasis on social manners. She described herself as 'hardworking, paying first attention to cleanliness; unlike most society women, always rising early and supervising the routine work of domestic servants'. Unusually, she also liked tennis and other open-air exertions, bridge, mah-jong and she enjoyed a sentimental movie and a good play.

Mrs Liza Hardom of Shanghai was altogether of a more serious disposition and combined her interest in promoting the welfare of children with writing, translating and interpreting Buddhist texts. She described a typical day to Grace Thompson. For the past eleven years she had risen at five in the morning to write and had produced one book of 440 volumes, each a huge tome and which altogether occupied a whole bookcase. At one o'clock she had lunch with her husband, a very wealthy banker and merchant from Baghdad, after which she supervised the teachers, the courses of study, the dormitories and the diet of her schools, one for 370 boys, another for 205 girls and yet another for fifty musicians. Another pet project, also in the gardens of her Shanghai mansion, was an orphanage for over 100 babies and small children all of whom she had adopted! She had been an orphan herself and was determined to give the advantages of personal interest and wealth to her charges. Grace Seton Thompson wondered at her capacity to organise her time and deal with the infinite problems and interests which both her hundreds of children and hundreds of volumes demanded of her.

There were not only many women of the older generation who were involved in the development of welfare work, trade schools, kindergartens, hygiene, hospitals and orphanages but some of the younger social set had also been persuaded to add a dash of charity to their social activities. Twenty-year old Shirley T. C. Chow who hosted a dinner party for Grace Thompson in Peking was an example of the younger generation who was interested in fashion, the movies, theatre, riding, skating and 'limousining' but who was also a director of a school for poor children. Others were Christians and less interested in such amusements. They worked mainly with the YWCA or YMCA which were important bodies in introducing the young to charitable work and social welfare. These organisations became particularly concerned with the conditions of work within the factories of the largest cities.

The growth of the manufacturing industries in China from around the turn of the century had drawn numbers of women from peasant and handicraft artisan households into the new factories, many of which were foreign-owned and took advantage of the country's cheap raw materials and low labour costs. Since textile production formed the main component of the new industrial complexes much of the new factory labour force was composed of girls and women. In the busy silk villages and cotton mills of Shanghai, Tientsin and Canton, women worked on a twelve-hour daily shift for seven days a week earning low wages ranging from 12 to 15 pence per day. There was little escape for the female labourers from these conditions for the work force of the cotton mills in particular was largely made up of indentured labour. Poor peasant families, desperate for cash and the promise of a portion of their daughters' wages, contracted out their girls to the owners of the factories who in turn advanced their fares to the factory and undertook to provide board and lodging of a sort. At the time of Grace Thompson's visit to China, the YWCA published a column in the leading Chinese daily newspaper in Shanghai publicising the low pay, the cramped working conditions and the neglect of welfare and safety standards in the factories employing women and children. As a consequence a joint committee of representatives from Chinese and foreign ladies' clubs was set up in Shanghai to study factory conditions. Its First Secretary was Soong Mei-Ling, later to become Madam Chiang Kai-Shek or 'the first lady' of China, and it was she and her famous sister Rosalind, the widow of Sun Yat-sen, who accompanied Grace Seton Thompson to the factories so that she might see for herself the condition of women workers.

When Grace Seton Thompson was taken to a silk filature factory in Shanghai, she was at a loss to describe the toil of the silk workers that went into the production of a hank of silk: 'What shall I say about the silk filature where women and little girl children wear out their lives that some of us must be clothed in silk and others may profit out of their life force.' She couldn't get over how stifling and vitiated were the thick steamy vapoured rooms of the factory. The closest parallel she could think of was the hot room of a Turkish bath, only here it was like a bad dream where long rows of raggedly-dressed women could be dimly discerned. Each was seated before a metal bowl of steaming water, on the surface of which a half-hundred cocoons bobbed a merry dance as the precious filaments of which they were composed unwound themselves and converged to a common centre some eighteen inches above them, where the delicate threads so fine as to be scarcely visible were being wound again upon a large bobbin. In front of each girl or woman there was yet another small metal basin, presided over by small girls or 'feeders' dressed in rags of garments, some of whom were so tiny as to require stands to perform their labours. These consisted of soaking and manipulating the cocoon with a forked stick in boiling water until the silk filatures were loosened and the loose end from which the whole web of silk could be unravelled was found:

> Hour after hour, all through the long working day of twelve to fourteen hours, these small girls stood, their little arms in constant motion, their little fingers getting many a burn from careless contact with the boiling water or the heated metal of the container.

On the floor behind the spinners Grace Thompson spied two or three babies rolling about on the floor. Their presence was only suffered because the mothers had no place to leave their children and there were no facilities such as a rest room, a lunch room or even stools for the feeders so that they might sit for a period and so ease the conditions of toil.

However there were signs that the women who worked in these mills were far from satisfied and had begun to agitate for better conditions. Just before Grace Seton's visits in August 1922, Shanghai had seen its first widespread strike of women in the silk industry when 60,000 women employed in seventy factories demanded higher wages and shorter working hours. The strike had been organised by the Society for Promoting the Welfare of Working Women when the mill-owners extended the number of working hours in response to America's increasing demand for silk. Processions of women workers with banners held aloft demanded a reduction of four hours to a ten-hour working day, an increase of five cents in wages, one day of rest every two weeks and the respect of their society. The mill-owners at once closed the factories, although the necessity for the daily bean curd soon forced the strikers back to work. They felt however that they had at least let the world know of their harsh conditions and, although inexperience and lack of organisation, co-ordination and funding had rendered the strike unsuccessful, the lessons of the strike were not lost on worker or employer. As the Shanghai newspaper, the *North China Herald*, pointed out at the time:

That a number of women, and those of the poorer and most ignorant class should challenge the powers of such an extremely wealthy organisation as the silk field indicates a consciousness of their own importance and determination to assert their rights. . .We call attention to this strike merely to indicate that a new phase in the women's rights movements is opening in China.

One factory which Grace Seton Thompson visited was exceptional and proved to be a pleasant contrast to the cotton and silk filature mills. This was the Commercial Press in Shanghai which had been founded in 1896 by three Chinese Christians. It was housed in large and modern buildings well-equipped for printing and publishing books and papers which it did for all the new educational institutions and educated persons all of whom demanded 'new learning'. It was designed to serve as a model for other factories in that it had established a nine-hour day and a dining room where the employees took their meals provided free by the company. Their lodgings were free and the factory had a roof garden for recreation and a club house for classes, a library, shops and bars, and it had a hospital and dispensary attached to it. It was thus very much ahead of its times in terms and welfare rules. A pregnant woman working in the factory was allowed to retain her position up to seven months, after which she was permitted to have two months at home before and after the birth. Nursing infants were allowed to be fed by their mothers during working hours and the press itself had a primary school of 1000 students. There was a retirement and pension scheme and a fund for helping employees in extreme need, the costs of which were all met from the profits of the company. As Grace Seton Thompson noted, there could not have been a greater contrast between conditions here and in the mills and other factories of Shanghai.

While in China, Grace Thompson had the imagination to investigate the production of the ubiquitous hair net without which a European woman's attire was not complete. She wondered if American women had ever thought where the hair net came from or whose hands had shaped the delicate article with its tiny strands so neatly knotted? At the height of the fashion for hair nets some millions of dollars worth were exported annually from Chinese ports. In some northern provinces nearly every family compound employed its men, women and children to make this toilet adjunct for their Western sisters. They each patiently tied hairs on a board of 18 by 12 inches which had steel pins driven into it to shape the outside net to form the crescent. The hair was then woven in meshes over the steel pins and tied whenever the strands of hair met. Skilled workers could certainly expect to earn more than servants and for women it had the added advantage that it was a convenient way of augmenting the family income at home.

Thousands of young women were also employed in the mending and sorting factories at which the hair nets produced in individual households were collected, sorted, repaired and stacked. In Shanghai, also, there were 10,000 - 15,000 women and children employed just mending the nets. Nets frequently had to be repaired with new hair threaded on net needles and any streaks of hair of different shades had to be removed and the proper shade put in their place. Nets of the same colours had also to be sorted and packed for posting to their American destinations. The American visitor was intrigued to learn that such is the distribution of Western hair shades that of every 100 nets cleaned, treated and coloured, the range of demand was such that 30 per cent were dark brown, 25 per cent medium brown, 30 per cent light brown, 9 per cent black-haired, and 8 per cent each were auburn and blonde. Many of the users of the blonde net were grey; grey nets were always scarce since most Chinese donors had died before their black hair turned grey. She thought that the best feature of the industry in China was the opportunities it had given to Chinese women to earn relatively high wages in an occupation which was lighter in its physical demands than most. The very rapidity of its expansion and demand for labour had pushed wages up and created a higher standard of living. As the use of the hair net was on the increase in Europe, Grace Seton Thompson thought this an interesting example of the way supply and demand for a commodity linked women on opposite sides of the world. It was these links, unguessed at by the millions involved, which she was keen to highlight in her book.

Another group of women workers who laboured in their homes were the weavers of silk. Grace Seton Thompson could not believe that out of the dark and humble farmers' mud or cement stone huts where two to three looms might be hidden away emerged the most wonderfully rich and exquisitely intricate and colourful fabrics, mingling the finest woven gold or silver brocade, stiff with silk and bullin and also the marvellous uncut velvet produced in designs of lions and elephants, phoenixes and dragons as well as gold-scaled fishes and silver pagodas. Several houses she visited had a loom in each of their three rooms which also contained a wilderness of ropes and pulleys, of hanging silk, wound bobbins, metal weights and modern contraptions among which was the usual small boy hanging in mid-air in the rigging of this exhausting machine. The loom was placed directly on the brown dirt floor with barely enough space to walk around it, while behind it was a narrow kang or platform where the family all slept. A small boy perched on top of the loom and rhythmically pulled certain threads, while the weaver used the many foot treadles to put the threads in position and manipulated a long metal shuttle carrying gold thread with skilled accuracy and according to an intricate pattern of which there seemed to be no visible guide. In one very dark room Grace Seton Thompson's attempt to photograph a bright-faced girl in striped wadded trousers weaving the narrow silk braid used for tying round the ankle required a three-minute exposure. Despite the poor working conditions and the minimal returns of these home workers, she thought that they were more fortunate than those who laboured in the mills or in the fields.

Grace Seton Thompson like most European women rarely had the opportunity to converse with peasant women and satisfy her curiosity as to the details of their daily lives. However she was interested to observe that although the national image of Chinese women was one of bound feet, dainty demeanour and seclusion, this did not apply to peasant women who made up nearly 80 per cent of the female population. Many of these peasant women, in the south of China particularly, were no strangers either to heavy manual labour of a kind that would shock women from Europe and North America, as it still does today. There Grace Thompson observed the great variety of loads, heavy trunks, bags of food, cement and coal that were carried by 'slim, erect but muscular Amazons', all identified by their cotton trousers swishing above their trim ankles and their trim loose coats of coolie cloth, whether they be stone breakers, builders, roadmenders or transporters of goods. In the rice paddy fields the labour was not so heavy but was never-ending. Grace Seton Thompson watched, as others before and after her, the slow meticulous lifting of the water by two persons, as often as not women, by means of a small round basket swinging on ropes dripping between the river and specially constructed mud basins. She estimated that not more than two quarts of water came up at a time with perhaps six motions a minute, so that it took hour after hour first to fill the basin and then to carry those driblets of water onto the fields or to fill the irrigation ditches to flood the paddy fields.

On the inland waters, women were to be observed every-where taking their share in the life of the river: at the oar equally with the men and in the culinary and domestic pursuits necessary to sustain the family in their floating homes where babies, children, dogs, cats, singing birds all lived together in one confined space. Grace Thompson observed that although some of them were buxom and young, most of them were sturdy and scrawny with little more than muscle and skin and, unusually for Chinese women, looked old before their time with prematurely shrivelled faces. Dressed in the universal blue cotton garment of working China, Grace Seton Thompson thought their work was physically extremely demanding. She watched one older woman hang her entire weight upon the direction rope placed at the end of the big and clumsy oar which was often worked by several at a time. The woman hung upon the oar every half minute; Grace Thompson calculated that she performed this violent gymnastic exercise one, two or three times an hour, and hour after hour, day after day it went on. . .even to think of it made Grace Thompson tired.

Like other visitors to Shanghai, famous for its night-life, Grace Thompson could not help but notice the numbers of prostitutes on the city streets. She saw girls of fourteen and fifteen years riding about in rickshaws – two together on a seat made for one. The length and cut of their tight fitting and short jackets, the wide, short silk trousers, the colours they wore, the style of hairdressing with a braid bound with a silk cord and their ornaments were all very distinctive and 'signalled business'. She likened them to gay little birds, always very young with snapping black eyes and conversation which revealed little or no education but much native wit and shrewdness. At the time of her visit, the ultra-smart garb for a girl of pleasure was a man's foreign sports cap, a mannish tweed coat and a fancy vest, linen collar, a short skirt and high-heeled slippers. In this costume she swaggers about, cigarette in mouth and gives every evidence of feeling herself very 'high collar'. Rarely to be seen on the streets were the very highly skilled entertainers who were hired by tea houses and clubs to entertain their clients with music, poetry and conversation. As in other parts of Asia it was the custom for men to entertain and for business to be conducted at a tea or sing-song house in the presence of entertainers who were frequently also prostitutes. Many of the younger generation of new women indicated to Grace Thompson their dislike of these establishments and the role they played in the social life of men, although they felt bound to accept them so long as wives, mothers and daughters were denied a free social life in the company of both sexes.

Grace Seton Thompson thought it was hard for a foreigner to ascertain the exact status of women within Chinese households. In her interviews and talks with Chinese women, two topics dominated the conversation when it turned to discussing domestic life. The first, and the one that was treated with the greatest sensibility and aroused the greatest passion among women, was the age-old custom of husbands taking a concubine or an additional wife or wives. Although law and custom only allowed one principal wife, husbands were generally permitted

to take secondary wives ostensibly for the purpose of providing
them with sons. In practice, and limited only by their preferences and financial circumstances, this custom licensed the men
of the household to enjoy the romance and companionship that
might be missing from an arranged marriage. Concubines were
often attractive girls from poorer families or were courtesans
skilled in the arts of music, dancing and conversation who had
attracted the attention of their suitors at the local tea houses
or restaurants. Some wives, especially if they were childless,
co-operated with their husbands in the choice of a second wife,
while others felt very threatened by their arrival. It was said
that the presence of several women competing for the same
favours of the one male often caused intrigue, rivalry and
jealousy in larger wealthy households. Very revealing is the
word for 'peace' in the Chinese language which denotes 'one
woman under one roof' and there was also a common saying
which similarly suggested that: 'Do you ever see two spoons in
the same bowl that do not work against each other?' Although
once taken into the household the concubine was guaranteed
long security, many were reluctant to become concubines for
not only might they become the focus of aggression and jealousy but no formal ceremony marked their entrance into the
household. Just as 'a hall was not a room' the concubine was
never accorded full membership in the family unit.

At the time of Grace Seton Thompson's visits many women
had begun to take up the cause of the concubine although it
must be said largely in their own interests as wives! These
interests were very much inspired by the Western ideas of
monogamy and in deference to these ideas Grace Seton
Thompson suspected that some of the 'cousins' she met were
in fact secondary wives. In some households she visited, the
point was emphasised that no concubines were present and
this was very much taken as a sign of its modernity or of its
progressive attributes. There was also much discussion among
the women she met about the rules of a new Chinese Wom-
en's Patriotic Association established in Tientsin city which
had recently announced that one of its aims, in addition to
arousing women to play a greater role in the public life of their

country, was to abolish concubinage because it was 'degrading to the individual women and lowered their overall status in society'. To further this aim, no concubine was to be eligible for membership of the Society. Interestingly it was not so much the platform that was contentious as the decision to prohibit concubines from becoming members. This caused much hard feeling especially among concubines who felt marginalised and discriminated against by the members who were very often also their personal friends or relatives.

Another cause on which there was more agreement was the plight of young girls adopted into their husbands' families as potential daughters-in-law. Poor parents of daughters often felt they had no choice but to shed the burden of an additional female child, while for the husband's family the custom had the advantage of avoiding the crippling expenses associated with marriage and early initiating the girl into the customs of the household. What bothered the women Grace Seton Thompson met was that the girls were sold and that there was no law to protect them so that their wellbeing was entirely dependent on the temper and the favours of individual households. For some, status might be said to be nearer to that of a slave and many were the stories of abuse and even death. On the other hand the women critics were also aware that if the system were to be abolished there was still so much poverty that such girls might well be forced to become 'mere' servants or even prostitutes. It had to be recognised that in the China of the 1920s girls with any form of family support were better off than those without. Conversations with Grace Thompson generally revealed that while the modern generation might question particular family customs which seemed especially detrimental to women, only a very few questioned or campaigned against the concept of the family and its ideals.

The most radical in their approach to these questions were the young women writers who were highly articulate in their rejection of the patriarchal family whose members were ranked by age and sex. The writings of young women authors revealed the contempt for the Confucian ideology which they held responsible for the subordination of Chinese women and a persistent obstacle to any form of change in the pursuit of equality. Confucian sayings such as 'women and villains are the only people who are difficult to deal with' and 'women are of no account' were all cited to illustrate his contempt for women, important only as mothers of sons or commodities to be bought and sold in marriage.

Perhaps the most compelling contemporary family concern of the articulate young was with arranged marriage which gave them no voice in the selection of their marriage partner. Some of the rebellious young now had the temerity to arrange their own marriages or alternatively some of the more radical of women vowed to avoid marriage altogether. According to young women writers an increasing number of women who had some form of occupation or economic independence were able to choose celibacy rather than marriage which had been well-nigh the universal fate of women in the past. Although they thought that celibacy might not be the most desirable answer to women's problems, it did, in the words of one young woman writer, show their

> awakening to the horror and undesirability of their social and family life . . . it shows their reaction to the age-long oppression by men. It expresses their discontent with the present family system. It is a sign of their progress in thought and in ideals of life.

Grace Seton Thompson came to the conclusion that the power of the pen had been added to the cause of women's emancipation in China and that it was with no pale ink that the women writers took their pioneering responsibilities. One of their number added her pen to the cause in the manner typical of her contemporaries:

> Now is the time to call the attention of Chinese women to the gloomy and unwholesome ethics of their social life. They should immediately be brought to the full realisation that they constitute a nucleus of society and that as such they should co-operate and insist on their

right of co-operation with men for the advancement of the general social welfare. It is only through a diffusion of new learning and new knowledge, accompanied by an elevation of their thoughts and the enlightenment of their views on life, that they can be awakened to the fullest sense of their responsibility.

The awakening of other Chinese women to a sense of their past and present subordination and future potential was a common goal among educated, radical and professional women, and an increasing number had come to the conclusion that unless Chinese women were able to acquire a number of public rights and some measure of participation in the newly established democratic political institutions they would never be able to take their rightful place in society. The new political institutions were founded in the wake of the collapse of the Ching dynasty in 1911 and were composed of national and provincial assemblies to which the first women's rights' organisations had claimed rights of representation and franchise. Many, inspired by the example of their Western contemporaries, had incorporated the term 'suffragette' into their association names. One of the first, the Chinese Women's Co-operative Association, based at a Shanghai school had closely modelled itself on suffragette associations in England and North America. It had published a monthly magazine almost entirely devoted to translations of foreign articles and views of Western suffragettes. One American who visited a number of schools in Peking shortly after 1911 reported that the first question he met with was invariably 'Tell us about the suffragettes in England'. This would be followed by particular questions which revealed the acquaintance of the questioners with the militant hunger strikes, demonstrations and the firing of letter boxes. They themselves were not strangers to such activities; several times their organisations had stormed the legislature to put their case forcibly before those who perpetually ignored their cause. Although they were successful in procuring the right to vote in many of the provincial legislatures, by the time of Grace Seton Thompson's visit they had not yet succeeded in securing new political rights in Peking.

In Peking, Grace Thompson visited a number of schools and colleges in order to interview the leaders of the suffragette movement. At one school she found the leaders of the new Chinese Women's League for Political Participation to be 'up-to-date young women, alert, capable and intelligent, sparkling with wit and bristling with questions about the status of Western women'. At the Peking Women's College she interviewed Miss Alice Chou, the leader of the Women's Equal Rights' Association. Grace Seton Thompson found it difficult to believe that the tiny shy demure women before her, dressed in a grey satin fur-lined gown and black silk jacket with brushed wool scarf and muff, was the same person who had two months earlier, and with three other valiant women, taken a petition to Parliament. It had been signed by 500 women of all classes and had urged certain reforms for women. They were given a hearing in which they freely expressed their ideas and presented their Seven Demands which together, as the copy given to Grace Seton Thompson shows, embraced a wide range of potential changes:

1 The opening up of all educational institutions in the country to women.
2 Adoption of universal suffrage and the granting to women of all constitutional rights and privileges given to men.
3 Revision, in accordance with the principle of equality, of those provisions in the Chinese Civil Code pertaining to relations between husband and wife, and mother and son, and to property rights, disposing capacity, and the right of succession of women.
4 The drafting of regulations giving equal rights to women in matters of marriage.
5 Prohibition of licensed prostitution, girl slavery and footbinding.
6 Addition of a new provision to the Criminal Code to the effect that anyone who keeps a concubine shall be considered guilty of bigamy.
7 Enactment of a law governing the protection of female

labour in accordance with the principles of 'Equal work, equal pay' and 'A woman is entitled to full pay during the time that she is unable to work owing to childbirth'.

Alice Chou and her friends had had no immediate effect on the audience, although two months afterwards two members of the upper and lower houses of Parliament were persuaded to visit the women's college where, in response to incessant pressures from their audience, the members had no choice but to make promises to see what could be done. The demand for the vote was to become increasingly irrelevant, however, as the national and provincial assemblies were themselves relegated to the sidelines of Chinese politics. China had dethroned an Emperor and the once powerful centralised kingdom was fast degenerating into an area for competing warlords and foreign powers as they scrambled for political spoils and a guaranteed share of the Chinese market. Grace Seton Thompson thought there was nothing extraordinary about the suffragette leader Alice Chou except that she had the extra initiative to organise a determined effort to bring about quick results for Chinese women. Indeed she had found that there were dozens, hundreds, like her in China who were 'Amiable, efficient, well-educated, refined, eager to help along her country and her sisters'.

Again and again Grace Seton commented on the activities and attitudes of the women she met and interviewed with respect and admiration, amounting almost to a reverence when she thought about the depressing socio-economic conditions and problems of China. Like other visitors at that time, she was at once both spell-bound by the tradition, customs and aesthetics and repelled by the poverty, lack of hygiene and inability of the government to govern. It was against these latter characteristics that she marvelled at and measured the magnitude of the task these women had set themselves. Her own contribution to the cause was to return to America and write of their endeavours so that they might take their place in the world-wide records of women who sought simultaneously to improve their own lives and the socio-economic and political environments in which they lived.

Grace Seton Thompson returned to America where she spent the next six months writing up her travels and interviews in China. In writing her book, she likened herself to a Chinese lantern. Indeed, she entitled her book *Chinese Lanterns* because she thought that the

> heart and imagination of any traveller in China could not help but be captured by the glittering, gleaming, dancing light-givers fashioned of paper or bamboo, of horn, wood or stone, of silk or lacquer, and printed, embroidered, carved or bejewelled, which adorned every temple, shrine, shop or dwelling from the merest hovel to the Imperial Palace and without which no festival, pilgrimage, wedding or funeral was complete.

Not only did they light the way for the guest or visitor, but their very mission in life was to direct light and show the way. In the same manner Grace Thompson hoped to take her own lantern, alias pen, and cast a clear light on the China of her travels and especially on the lives and conditions of women. When her book was published in 1924 it was well received and widely read but by that time Grace Seton Thompson was continuing her travels, this time to India.

Grace Seton Thompson travelled widely in India, and though as in China she met many public spirited women devoting their lives to welfare and service, she also succumbed much more to the mystery and romance of India, spending much of her time away from the cities and hunting and tracking wild animals. The same was true of her subsequent travels in South America where she accompanied a scientific expedition in the interior of Brazil thus resuming her interest in the tracking, measuring and studying of wild animals which she had once shared with her now estranged husband. A photograph of the time shows her looking very much at home in the saddle with a hat, jacket, riding boots, swag bag and rifle. However she shed these to contact the Women's Suffrage Party in Peru. Once again it was her interest in women's power and status which finally took her to Cambodia on a search for a society that was matriarchal.

She had already come into contact with such societies among the North American Indians, on the west coast of India and in the Andes, and she hoped that among the Mois of Cambodia she would find that women enjoyed a social status which for all their rights to vote, the women of North America or Europe did not have. Sadly after her travels and observations of village life there, she came to the conclusion that her preconceived ideas of women under a matriarchal system must be modified. She found no complete reversal of customs. Indeed, although women might be the owners of property, proprietors of their children and the custodians of tribal authority, they were less authoritative or respected than the older women in China. She concluded that nowhere did mother-right underwrite female dominance albeit that father-right underlay male dominance. This was the last of her major journeys and travels to far-flung and unusual places in search of new and powerful women.

In America, when not away on trips, Grace Thompson continued to lead a life remarkably similar to that of many of the energetic and public-spirited women she had met on her travels. As she had travelled and developed her own interests, she had become increasingly independent of her husband, and some time later they both decided that they were happier apart. Her husband then married his research assistant who had collaborated with him for many years and they continued to collect data on animals which they incorporated into the Ernest Seton Thompson Library and Museum in Santa Fe, New Mexico. Meanwhile Grace Seton Thompson continued to write and work for the many councils and committees of which she was a member. Her interests remained wide, but most continued to centre around geography, travel, writing and the status of women. She was the secretary of Women Geographers, The Pen, and the Society of Women Writers. She was an active Republican and sat on many national committees to improve the status of women both within the Republican Party and for the country as a whole. She was selected as a member of several delegations to represent American women at international conferences and meetings. In 1933 she combined her interest in writing and women's issues by organising an international conference of women writers, and in conjunction with this she collected and arranged an exhibition of some 3000 books written by women in thirty-seven countries as part of the Century of Progress Exposition. This collection later became the core of the Biblioteca of Feminism at Northwestern University's During Library.

Travel remained one of her first loves and towards the end of her life she looked fondly back to evenings spent in her hotel rooms when after an exhausting but interesting day she had donned her loose silk dressing gown and with her hair 'non too-tidy' had scribbled hastily away on the day's happenings – ink on her fingers. Not for nothing was she dubbed 'The Lady Journalist' and she would have been pleased with the headlines of her obituary in the *New York Times* on 20 March 1959 which styled her as a 'Writer, Journalist and Feminist'. As a writer and journalist she felt that she had succeeded in her aims if she questioned the common stereotypes, understood complex customs and shed her own Western standards in writing of other societies. She hoped her writing would reduce ignorance and provide a better understanding of other cultures. Indeed for China, later students are indebted to her for some of the clearest portraits, both visual and verbal, of a generation of women of all social and economic classes, ages and political persuasions who played an important part in the rapidly changing society of the early 1920s. She captured the mood of this generation of women caught as they were between the old and the new, between tradition and modernity and between Chinese and Western ways. The tension and the conflict between these two poles for supremacy would continue to be the subject of debate among the younger and older generations both within and outside of China. A number of European writers on China, including Alice Tisdale Hobart, were to make it an important theme in their best-selling novels.

5

Homesteading in China: *'Company Wife' and Best-Selling Novelist, Alice Tisdale Hobart*

Chicago-born Alice Tisdale Hobart, a proud descendant of Rebecca Nourse, victim of the Salem Witchcraft trials, settled in China as the young bride of an American engineer working in the Standard Oil Company. She spent the first few years of her married life in the isolated and desolate far northwestern provinces where she alternated between transforming a succession of makeshift company houses into an American home and by travels in the frozen north. In the beginning and to dull the pain of her isolation she had conceived of herself as a pioneering wife on one of America's new frontiers of trade very much in the tradition of the homesteading of the first European settler wives in America and the prairie wives of the old American western provincial frontiers. In China though, homesteading had a quality of exile about it and it was to help reconcile herself to this exile that Alice Tisdale Hobart turned to writing. She first wrote of her travels, her homesteading experiences and of Europeans in China in what virtually amounted to a manual for European company wives in China. Long before the term 'company wife' gained international currency, Alice Tisdale Hobart drew attention to the importance of her loyal support for the success of the company man and therefore of the company itself. She subsequently wrote several novels set in China including a trilogy which thoughtfully explored the form, the content and the quandaries of individuals mediating Chinese and European trade, commerce or religion. Unexpectedly one of these novels, *Oil for the Lamps of China*, became a best seller and the subject of a film which for weeks attracted packed houses on Broadway.

Alice Beaman Nourse was born in 1882 and lived most of her early life in a poor Chicago household. A happy and carefree childhood was cut short by two tragic happenings. First, she contracted meningitis, which was to render her flat on her back and physically helpless for long periods, and shortly afterwards her beloved mother who had nursed her through the illness died. She was to feel for the rest of her life that she had been early deprived of someone warm and loving or a gay companion in whose presence 'everything had seemed possible'. She was brought up by her father and sister who were both teachers. Her father, a poor but dedicated teacher, early implanted the ideal of service for and responsibility in society which set her on a determined bid for a satisfactory education and a first career in the Young Women's Christian Association before she followed in her sister's footsteps by entering the teaching profession. In 1909 she travelled to Hangchow in China for a vacation with her sister Mary, who was already teaching there in a mission school for girls. Her first impressions of China were of the stark contrast between the misty beauty, the rich velvety shadows or the lively or boisterous sounds of the streets and the dirt, poverty and illness, only thinly veiled even for the foreigner, of a China poor beyond belief. Soon her enjoyment of the beauty and her sense of adventure as a sightseer wore thin and she began to teach in her sister's school where the task of educating and guiding the lives of young girls newly released from the confinement of the women's quarters and locked in the dramatic struggles between old and new customs, was daily challenging and engrossing. She had anticipated that her stay in China would be a temporary sojourn but a chance meeting with a young New England businessman also in Hangchow led to marriage and a much longer stay.

Earl Tisdale Hobart, a graduate in engineering from Cornell University, escaped the confines of the Bostonian world in

which he had been born and bred by travelling to China
where he first taught electrical engineering in Peking. There
he had also undertaken some serious study of the Chinese
language and culture, and it was this interest which had
caused the American Minister in Peking to persuade him
that such skills and knowledge could better serve the new
commercial relationships between America and China. He
joined the Standard Oil Company which had its headquarters
in New York and his career with it began with a posting
to Hangchow where he met his future wife. Normally the
chances of their meeting would have been slim for there was
little contact between the mission and business worlds even
within the smaller foreign communities. By chance however,
Earl's sister, an Episcopalian, was staying with him and it
was she who had made contact with the two Nourse sisters.
The slender, reasonably tall and fine-featured young junior
executive who had already seriously attempted to understand
Chinese cultural traditions and had evolved very definite ideas
on how business between Americans and Chinese ought to be
conducted, impressed the young teacher and, although he was
soon sent to far and northern Manchuria, they corresponded
until their marriage two years later. Thus began Alice Tisdale
Hobart's years of homesteading as a young peripatetic company wife.

The conditions in which she lived the first few years as a company wife in China were harsher than most. On her marriage
she joined her husband in Newchang, a strange bleak town in
the far northeastern province of Manchuria where there was a
total of some eighty foreign residents. Shortly afterwards Earl
Hobart was posted to Antang, an even more remote town
on China's frontier with Korea where there were but two
or three other foreign households. As the long, cold frozen
winter which lasted a good portion of the year closed in, the
rivers, the main communication channels, were ice bound and
frozen many feet deep so that there were no steamers or junks
for many months and overland sledges were the main form of
travel. The temperatures fell below zero for months, and the
wind, the flying snow and the dust of the winter storms were

a permanent accompaniment to their lives. There were few fresh vegetables and fruit so that salads and fresh fruit salad became the stuff of mirages and dreams. There were some compensating factors in the short summer and autumn with the memorable and vibrant changes of colour with the setting of the sun on the far horizon over the red-golden fields, and the clear distant views extending for miles. But for most of the year, Alice Tisdale Hobart felt it was a bleak enough place to test the courage of any company bride.

The Company was only a little more accommodating than the climate, for Alice Hobart, like other new brides, was not welcomed into it with any grace. The Company, preferring its men to remain single, had introduced a company rule forbidding its employees to marry within the first two years of their service. Given a choice, the China manager preferred his men to remain single. If wives there had to be, they should make few demands on the Company and be ready to put its interests first at all times. Alice Tisdale Hobart was fortunate in that their local manager in Newchang accepted wives although he would not 'coddle' them! He set out to test her resolve. He allowed Earl two weeks in which to settle his new bride into Newchang and sent him off again on his travels into the cold frozen northeast. As the circles drawn around the days in her husband's pocket calendar showed, he was away from home for a total of 245 days of the first year of their married life. Disliking the separations as they did, they both knew it was part of the company test to see if they, and she in particular, could withstand a long separation, the harsh conditions and the Company's prior demands on her husband. Alice Tisdale Hobart soon realised that she was destined to play a part mapped out for her by the Company which was essentially a man's world in which her presence was merely tolerated. She set out to make her presence as unobtrusive as possible.

In Newchang there was a small ready-made foreign community made up of an unusual number of retired sea captains who had sailed their own vessels in and out of China's ports as they had one by one been opened to foreign trade. They were pilots versed in the law of the China coast, men who had made and lost fortunes in straw braid and treaty port property and men, like the company boss, who had gone to China as boys and never returned home. The men's wives were sturdy women who had accompanied their husbands and seen through both danger and hardship. They had had their babies at sea without the benefit of help and been parted from them almost as soon as they were born, for that kind of life was not for the children they would soon only know through photograph and letter. They had spent long years away from their homes and they now looked upon Newchang as their hard-won bit of the universe and were inclined to exercise their power accordingly. In the intricate social hierarchy that was English-influenced, each person had her or his place and was not expected to cross the carefully constructed barriers. Alice Tisdale Hobart along with other beginners, the office juniors and 'those engaged in retail and outdoor work', held no social rank to compare with that of the managers and the 'Taipans'. At the apex of the social hierarchy was the English Commissioner of Customs and his wife whose house reflected another world of 'bright chintzes', shining silver, its napkins stiffly starched and fluted and place names'. The dinner guests wore evening suits and long low-neck gowns and were watched from around the rooms by pictures of charming English children at school. Alice Tisdale Hobart herself was particularly sensitive to the personal and national jealousies exaggerated by the isolation of the meagre village and she found herself in an anomalous position not only ostracised because of rank but also as an American. She was thought to be strange in her speech and her ways and on no occasion more so than when she quite innocently had the temerity to serve ice cream in November. Fortunately, in a world of quick acquaintances and rapid intimacies, an English manager's wife befriended her as a kindred soul 'so simply, naturally and freely' that she did not again think quite so often of the social barriers that had been created by others of British and European origins.

In the frontier town of Antung where they were next posted it was all very different, for there was only one other young wife, busy with her new baby, at the other end of the settlement. Altogether there were only two other European residents, the Commissioner of Customs and the American Consul. Among the Chinese too, this was regarded as a man's town where men and boys spent their days and nights in Chinese business houses leaving their wives and children elsewhere – normally in the safety of their ancestral family homes. Here, left much more to her own devices by the Company, Alice Tisdale Hobart went with her husband on several of his long trips into the northern interior. Amid the seasons of the red plumes of the giant Sorghum which stretched as far as the eye could see or the snow and cold of the relentless winter, they would walk and climb in the mountainous territory where the temperature was 30 degrees below zero. On one occasion when she stood in front of her house ready to depart 300 miles up the Yalu River, she noted that she was wearing two suits of flannel underwear, a flannel shirt, fur-lined trousers, a sweater, a stout leather fur-lined coat, fur cap, muff, heavy shoes and sheepskin-lined outer coat which was so thick that she could scarcely move of her own accord, and last of all Chinese felt mocassins over her shoes. They travelled in two springless carts covered with heavy blue cloth to protect the latticed wood and lined with fur to keep out the intense cold. On one of these clandestine trips she nursed her feverish husband back to health fearful all the time that she would need help and so have to admit her guilty presence to the Company!

It was in these circumstances that she, like women the world over, immersed herself in creating a succession of homes both to retain and express a little piece of her individual self and to provide a 'mantle' for her soul. Creating such a mantle kept her fully occupied, for the first eight years of Alice Tisdale Hobart's married life were punctuated by seven moves to seven different houses. For the wife of the frontier businessman not only was the mantle forever changing; it took the form of a ready-made garment, the company house. Even the furniture belonged to the Company, the pieces of which were standardised according to the rank of the occupant and were numbered on an inventory which was checked twice yearly. As to the houses themselves, they could still only be secured according to the haphazard treaty laws of China and ranged from a Chinese palace to a Chinese warehouse, to a vacated sing-song house, an English terraced house or a thatched roofed half-Chinese mission house to a Chinese junk. The location too had to be accepted with equanimity. Alice Tisdale Hobart thought that this also was in the hands of erratic gods for there were company houses standing grandly and forlornly alone, alongside their neighbours on a river or busy sidewalk, or hunched immediately next to Chinese fish markets or weavers' workshops. Such constant and haphazard changes made an existence that fluctuated between the grand, the rich, the poor or even beggar-like. Alice Tisdale Hobart learned that like the vagabond or tramp, women and men of the Company at the frontiers of trade had to accept philosophically 'a life of fun, fast or famine'; she herself experienced all three in close succession.

In Newchang on the tide-washed delta of the Liao River, her first home was a small English bow-windowed terraced house which once entered was passed through with almost absurd rapidity. At first sight she had immediately likened the front four rooms with their tall windows admitting the golden sunlight to a stage. The house was served by dingy dark wings from behind, while in front, the edge of the settlement and the half-tamed frontier served as a foreshortened dress circle of the theatre. She discovered later that this analogy was apt for she and her husband did seem to be centre stage in those front rooms where all the show and ceremony of their days went on. In contrast 'all the business and commotion of their living went scurrying up and down those dark passageways as does the business of a play through the wings of the stage'. The soup arrived by way of this wing as did the entrée and the joint for their formal dinner. They were prepared and served by the stage hands who rarely appeared on the stage proper for it was the houseboy as the stage manager who directed the play with precision and formality. The furniture too seemed simply part of the act. The chest of drawers in the bedroom was number 608 which meant it was one of the latest models; the dining room table on the other hand was number 56, a type long discarded. Throughout the first year of her married life she felt she occupied these front rooms like an actress with lines, and only a move to a second home with a large rambling garden enabled her to shape a house more to her liking.

The second house was of an unusual design. Its second storey had been burned off years before and above the first floor a makeshift tin roof leaked like a sieve in the rainy season. Underneath the floor lay a brick-lined cellar cunningly devised to house the tides which in the summer came boldly up the river and along the streets to flow into this receptacle from which they had to be bailed out through a trap door. To her advantage, Alice Tisdale Hobart could sit in her living room and look through the entrance door down the long hall and out across the neglected garden to see the large brown sails of the junks going by on the Liao River. The river was on the other side of the street and hidden from view by the boundary wall and a castle-like warehouse so that, seemingly detached, the sails would poise framed in the doorways like enormous butterflies with folded wings before gliding majestically away. She had just settled in and was taking full charge of the house itself when her husband arrived home early from work one day and announced their imminent departure for the frontier town of Antang on the Korean border where he was to open a new sub-station and she was to feel more isolated than ever.

There were no Chinese houses in Antang to rent, for in this frontier town the people were still suspicious of foreigners and negotiating the opening of foreign business offices and residences was fraught with many problems and delays. For the first few weeks they resided in the one foreign hotel managed by a Japanese keeper in the main street which, as a ghost of a European world, was imposing, pretentious, empty and cold. Her husband could not explain to his Company that the hotel bill at the end of the month did not leave them sufficient funds to even pay for their washing. As a junior he was still on trial and it was part of his 'test' not to appear to be complaining or to let on that wives were an expensive affair. After some weeks they managed to rent the edge of a sugar warehouse and with every bit of her energy, she 'fought that sugar warehouse to make it a home'. On one memorable day she felt she had succeeded. She had just unpacked her china and had arranged it in the kitchen on shelves which lacking all other alternative fixtures were fastened with heavy wires to the beams above. She was proud of the shelves as she was of everything else in the house which was a makeshift and an ingenious contrivance of her own. To celebrate this auspicious moment, she had the cook bake cookies for tea and for the first time the smell of spice actually transcended the sweet sickish odour of sugar in the warehouse. Her feelings of achievement and contentment were shattered by the sudden crash of the shelves which lay in a heap with their loaded dishes on the dirty floor. Just then her husband arrived home announcing excitedly that they could now move to another empty sugar warehouse! She burst into tears. Their new home was not unlike their present one and the whole move smacked too much of a repetition of the arduous labours she had just completed.

On reflection however her new home did have three advantages. They would have it all to themselves; it would have wooden floors; and they would forgo the too-close companionship of sugar. The rooms however were arranged on four sides of the courtyard and entering anyone involved a quick dash across this courtyard which in temperatures often ten below zero meant donning a fur coat, storm boots and a fur hat. Nor was there any other way to hide the cobwebs and dirt of time but by papering the partitions and the red roof beams and once more Alice Hobart set to work to create a home. Cave-like in its light and shape, it was sandwiched between the tower of a bean mill and a colony of weavers whose machines 'clink-clanked' through the day and far into each night. Against this background of 'Chinese noise and activity', Alice Tisdale Hobart fought to maintain the 'American quality of their home' which she felt must be kept inviolate at all costs. In their improvised American home high ceremony existed. Their Chinese servant, who had previously served in the house of the British representative in Harbin city, brought with him a keen sense of ceremony, and the cook, who had formerly been an actor, had a dramatic touch. Between the two of them, they saw that her husband did not lose face as 'the manager' despite the fact that he was the lone representative in his Company. At home, when they sat down to tiffin, there was a servant to stand behind each of their chairs, and as for tea, Alice Tisdale Hobart thought that the pomp and ceremony of the service was at least worthy of an ambassador. Indeed she never expected to approach anything like this inflated status again. At first it made her a bit dizzy to jump from the hard struggles of the day's dirt and inconvenience to the afternoon and evening ceremonies, but she also recognised that this very juxtaposition was a hallmark of Chinese custom in which pomp and not comfort were the attributes of high estate.

Eventually however the desire for some comfort and peace got the better of them, and they very fortunately found a small piece of land on a hillside outside the city which one elderly woman was willing to lease to them. It was just big enough for a Chinese house which Alice Tisdale Hobart had built to her specifications. On its completion, she felt that she had acquired the nearest to her dream home that she was ever likely to come – perhaps because she knew every mud brick that veneered its surface. It was certainly not because of its perfection, for its walls were decidedly out of plumb, the steep slope of the hillside governed its incline and the approaching gully washed out by the rains was so steep that it was impossible even to pull a rickshaw to its front door. Sadly illness and a long sojourn in a Shanghai hospital followed by another posting elsewhere in China cut short her time in that dream house. For a long time afterwards nothing was ever to shake her faith in that little house, not even when she heard of the rebellion of another company woman who came later and thought it 'just too impossible'. The latter had come to it as a bride by way of the comforts of America; Alice Tisdale Hobart had come to it by way of the sugar godown and the cave.

Bleak and lonely though these experiences and expeditions in the northeast seemed at times, it was not all hardship for she had adventure aplenty and created a partnership and a pleasure in the company of her husband which she might not have had in other more sociable circumstances. It was also during the long periods of loneliness in Antang while her husband was away that she developed an interest in writing. The initial impetus which caused her first to put pen to paper in any serious way came with the visit of her mother-in-law to stay with the young couple for several weeks. Her husband's mother disapproved strongly of her son's absence in China, of her son's career, of her son's wife and of the house into which his wife had poured such energy. As her mother-in-law set out to weave her own ties of exclusivity around her son, the isolation of the outpost bound the three of them into a new and frightening triangle the only relief from which was escape. Alice Tisdale Hobart temporarily left her home, and in her painful separation from her husband she wrote out in all its vividness the hardships and the pleasures of her married life thus far. To her surprise she found that through writing she could shift herself into another world and that there within herself lay her help. As she later recalled, she inadvertently had come upon the knowledge that writing could be for her a door through which she could leave pain and disaster behind. Month after month she wrote, seeking to create an experience which could be passed on to others and be worthy of publication. Her first articles, 'Leaves for a Manchurian Diary', which related her experiences in the northeast, were first published in *The Atlantic Monthly* and later put into book form, *Pioneering Where the World Is Old*.

It was an apt title for in much of her married life in the far north, she had drawn on and found inspiration in the parallels between her own life and the American traditions of pioneering and homesteading. The frontiers might be different but the experiences were similar. During the long absences of her husband, she had to find a growing capacity for solitude, and for help and inspiration she turned to the heritage given to her by the pioneering women of America. They had homesteaded from Massachusetts to California, they had lived solitary lives in isolated cabins and looked out upon great new stretches of American prairie as she now looked out upon the Asian plains. She thought of these forebears of hers a great deal and drew some comfort and pride in the fact that she could take her place in the procession of American women from the *Mayflower*, the covered wagon to the Empire. The distance from homes, the uncharted land, the hostile environment and the unknown dangers were the same, although, except in the southern plantations, those other women had not known the soft luxury of being waited on hand and foot. Thus pioneering took on a new form once the American boundaries had moved from the internal to the far-off frontiers of trade. Across the seas she thought that pioneering women and men were different in that they were no longer individualists or their own masters, but rather part of a large business corporation which required that they blend the fearlessness of the pioneering tradition with the subtle and exacting discipline of new corporate institutions. Drawing on her own experience Alice Tisdale Hobart thought that the novel demands on the women of the new commercial frontiers were as exacting as those on the men and that indeed women might have a special role to play.

There were times when Alice Tisdale Hobart thought that as a young company wife this new type of pioneering life was both demanding and exciting in that at one and the same time she felt herself to be part of a large business empire helping to extend the frontiers of American trade in the East and yet also bound to its policies, its priorities and its *esprit de corps*. It was an old trick of hers in times of trouble to conjure up the tall building with the rounded side in New York whose portrait hung in each large and small office in the Company, in each large and small port and in all the saloons of its large tankers and small riverboats. In unanchored moments of uncertainty and depression she liked to think of it as the castle of a twentieth-century empire with herself and her husband playing their small parts in turning night into day by furnishing the oil for the lamps of China. It fitted the vagaries of her personal life into a larger pattern of American life and gave its isolation additional meaning if she thought of herself as one of a long line of women and men extending the old trade routes and new commercial frontiers of America, helping to create wealth for that country. It was this thought which brought her an undisputed sense of usefulness and importance in China so that it was always with some pain that she experienced a loss of importance on returning home to America. There it seemed so very much a letdown to have their pioneering thought of merely as a curious or picturesque way of life!

Alice Tisdale Hobart often pondered the role of the wives. She frequently wondered if the personnel at American company headquarters in New York ever thought of the role of the wives they liked to have hidden away in so inconspicuous a part of their empire. Did they not owe a peculiar debt to these women who travelled abroad and set about homesteading in the interests of the oil business and were expected at the same time to mould themselves to the demands of the Company of their husbands? Did they realise that the women were by their very presence and contributions also members of staff, and that it was very often within their power to make or break the dedication of their men? She wanted the Company to recognise both its demands and also its debt to these women. It was particularly to explore the role and to draw attention to the importance of the company wife that she compiled a record of her own domestic and social life long before sociologists devised the term 'the corporation wife'.

She began writing *By the City of the Long Sand* shortly after their arrival in Changsha. In Changsha after serving her apprenticeship in homesteading, she was thrust into the elegance of a prize company house on an island across from the long sand. She also had graduated to being the wife of the manager of an American oil company and the circumstances in which she lived her life became more generally typical of those experienced by treaty port women in China. Instead of having to create a home from the raw beginnings she inherited a large and gracious company house with eight large rooms, seventeen-foot high ceilings, fine white-tiled bathrooms, a garden, a tennis court and an ice plant. In this, the seventh cycle of homesteading in as many years, she had but to arrange their belongings in order to personalise the rooms and discard the company image. It was a new experience for her to have a house with a history although at first she had rebelled against the stamp of former occupants: the chipped tables, the castorless bed, the blurred and blotched mirror and other discarded and dull things. She soon delighted however in the fact that woven into the history of the house were portions of every company-family and that, like others, she and her husband would leave a little of themselves behind.

The first occupant, who had had the house built to specification ten years before, had fashioned for himself some of the pomp and splendour of the English aristocracy. The dining room was large enough for dances and for balls, and all the bedrooms had adjoining, white-tiled bathrooms while the full-length French doors looked out upon the garden and tennis court. The next occupants, an American couple, had had the large English dining room divided into two by sliding doors of pine and had inserted an airtight stove into the large fireplace to create a cosy corner in the great towering house. A 'small master' and 'missy' were born to them within the house giving it the happy laughter of childhood. The house had also witnessed the suffering of bad news on the occasion of an upcountry death when a bride of one year had looked out from the bedroom window and over the river watching endlessly for the company launch which would bring her young husband back from an upcountry trip. On his death, their place had been taken by a large Dutch bachelor from whom, as the last occupant before her arrival, she had inherited aplenty bachelor possessions lightly acquired and lightly discarded in the moment of leave-taking. Still in evidence on their arrival had been the cigars, glasses and other accompaniments of his home-leaving party. The house had finally become hers for ready and easy homemaking and safekeeping.

The demands of homemaking in Changsha were so considerably reduced during her three years' residency that she had much time for her writing, and in *By the City of the Long Sand* she gives a very detailed picture of treaty port community life. In Changsha, she found she had not only adopted a ready-made house but also a ready-made community. In describing a treaty port community for her American readers she suggests that they imagine an American Vermont or prairie town usually located on a waterfront and reduce the number of houses to a dozen or so with each or two or three having a high surrounding stone wall or strong fence. Then subtract from the American equivalent the churches and the schools so that there is only one public building in the main street – the club. Take away the stores, for the residents are so few that they rely instead on Chinese merchants and Montgomery Ward boxes from home. Take away all the necessities of life and in their places substitute the luxuries of life including any number of servants, ceramics, handmade silks, satins and other material objects such as only the rich aspire to in America. In contrast, plumbing and steam heat are luxuries, and in all her ten years in China she had never lived nearer than a day's journey to a package of hairpins. Children might not blink at the sight of caravans and camels yet a car ride or the freedom to walk alone without the watchful eye of an *amah* would be an adventure for them.

Alice Tisdale Hobart thought that there were other more fundamental differences between a town in America and an American town in China. In an American town in China there were no young girls going to their first party with their first boyfriends, and no young boys with changing voices and undecided futures. Children in China must be sent home to America to be educated or it was thought they would grow up without a country. Subtract too from an American town all the elderly women and men. Never are the words 'grandmother' or 'grandfather' heard in the main street! Such are the cycles of transfers and home-leaves that there are few if any long-time citizens to give stability and permanence to a settlement. Mobility was such that two years in a place might confer the title of the 'oldest resident'. Sometimes in a spring or autumn, the best migrating seasons, every house in one of the little towns would change hands so that one minute it was full of the wary and sober-minded who had lost their initial zest for pioneering, while in the next six months it might turn itself inside out and become an outrageously gay little place with a bride and groom in every house. Alice Tisdale

Hobart thought of these 'queer little fly-by-night community settlements as 'America's hidden towns, unknown and unsung', but nevertheless belonging not the least in the minds of the company men and women.

In Changsha, Alice Tisdale Hobart, as the wife of the oil manager and the mistress of the largest dining room in the community, was no longer the young bride relegated to the margins of treaty port life. Their arrival had been eagerly awaited as it was of some importance to all the community that the new occupants of the company house be sociable, outgoing and of benefit to the community. The sociable of the community would like to have claimed their company at least five evenings a week in mah-jong, bridge and dinners. Such were the rituals of social life that London and Washington could not outdo them in creating and attaching significance to social hierarchies and the nuances of social rituals. In any gathering each foreign resident was reminded of position and rank. Nevertheless tension between individuals and nationalities, only half-disguised by tea, small talk and leisure interests of ordinary times, could flair up suddenly with an intensity that quite shocked the participants. All the members of the foreign community normally came together at the club on occasions such as Christmas when there was general feasting and gaiety in order that nobody was left out. But however noble and splendid the occasion, it was also fraught with danger for, like other small isolated communities shut away from the rest of the world, there were 'wheels within wheels' and it was quite common to wake up one morning and find the community in the throws of a port 'scrap' which at intervals would tear the main street to shreds.

On one Christmas occasion recounted by Alice Tisdale Hobart in her book, the party started badly for it had been prepared by two 'lesser ladies' rather than the 'number one ladies' of the port, and whoever had heard of any great event going forth without being conceived and sponsored by 'the great'? The committee moreover consisted of three Americans and one British which had almost caused a diplomatic offence given the number of British residents. In ordinary times Alice Tisdale Hobart thought that the port 'boiled like a tightly cramped kettle' which indeed it resembled and on this Christmas occasion it was the difficulties over the menu which caused it to 'boil over'. Each nation insisted on the inclusion of its own Christmas dishes. The British feared the Americans would insist on ice cream, and the Americans were outraged by the British insistence that the turkey could only be served after it was properly announced by soup, fish and roast beef to which no vegetables other than boiled potatoes were to be attached. The British retorted that the dinner could be foreshortened by leaving out the salad which was anyway wholly American and not part of a truly 'proper' dinner in which three meat courses were followed by a meat salad and some pudding. The Americans, dreaming of something fresh and green, suddenly denounced cranberry sauce without which no Englishman could consider a Christmas dinner to be correct. As Alice Tisdale Hobart remarked, the port scrap with its wooing of networks of support had little to do with those culinary preferences or even nationality; such things occured when residents had grown tired of seeing the same thirty or forty faces at the bridge and poker tables as they looked upon the length and breadth of the island days without number, walked uncounted miles on the long sand and talked of the same topics for weeks. On this and other like occasions the air was cleared and the atmosphere calmed down almost as suddenly as the argument had erupted – in some ways she thought that the feud had even had an enjoyment of its own for mixed with the Christmas preparations was the joy of battle. Everyone had something new to talk about and on familiar faces there was a zest of uncertainty so that a smile or stare took on added meaning. When it had all blown over and everything was arranged amicably, community friends were all the more appreciated. Hence on Christmas night, the L-shaped table gay with crackers and crystal bowls of holly and with covers for fifty persons groaned with the delicacies of every nationality who were to sit around it: 'There were Sakouskas for the Russians, roast beef for the Englishmen and ice cream for the Americans and something else for the French.'

Of all the community residents it was the women who, without enough occupations of their own, were thrown together and drawn into the life of the treaty port settlement. As such they shared a common fate, although as Alice Tisdale Hobart noted each also had her own private or in some cases not so private life. For the wife of the Commissioner of Customs, for example, every public appearance was a humiliation for was she not a former lady-in-waiting to the Queen? Pictures of the royal family on her table and piano verified her past glory, but now on all public occasions she was out-ranked by the wife of the British Resident Commissioner who was but a commoner. Her only comfort was that nobody from her past life was there to witness her humiliation; in contrast for the wife of the British Resident Commissioner every social event was an occasion to remember. Did not a former lady-in-waiting to the Queen and all the island wait upon her entrances and exits? She was astute enough to know that this island community in far China afforded her a position she would not have otherwise received. For another of the women the pull of home and the pain of separation were especially hard and each evening at her young children's former bedtime hour she set aside the time to try eagerly and hopelessly to make so vivid her written word that their simple baby minds would feel the imprint of her presence when, a month later in England, they read these letters. Childless herself Alice Tisdale Hobart sympathised, for to be pulled two ways at once – either to be with her children or to be with her husband – was the mother's central dilemma at the frontier of trade.

Alice Tisdale Hobart as the senior company wife on the island was also responsible for the welfare of other company wives. This responsibility turned out to be both more eventful and taxing than she might have anticipated. First there was the wife that shouldn't have been a wife. The Company had very strict rules that each young man recruited to its staff should spend the first three years in an unencumbered bachelor state free to learn the ropes, free to travel and free to give the Company all his energies and attention. Disgrace, dismissal and return to America was the fate awaiting any transgressor as the young man in Changsha who secretly married his companion of the voyage out to China knew well. How they managed to keep their guilty secret even for a few weeks was a source of amazement and wonder to Alice Tisdale Hobart who had inadvertently stumbled on the truth of their liaison. She stayed silent, but it was only a matter of time till they were found out and he was ousted from job and community. Nor were all young brides as ready as Alice Tisdale Hobart had been to accept the dominant rule of the Company in influencing and shaping their lives. One young wife rebelled against her exile to an upcountry posting. On her arrival in Changsha she had given but one searching glance at the company house and settlement where she was to live and for which her beautiful clothes, her parents' home and her former entertainments had barely prepared her. She had brought with her a vision of her first home: ivory wicker, blue and rose cushions, hardwood floors, blue Chinese rugs, blue and white kitchen and, of course, white-tiled bathrooms. Neither her husband, the Company, her Chinese servants nor China escaped a share of her resentment. She refused to let her husband travel into the interior which was an essential component of his work, she pleaded for a better posting and house and eventually her resentment and yearnings for the gaiety of a better life combined to force him to resign and depart from Changsha for an unknown and uncertain American destination.

One of the ways the Company retained its control and power was to foster the myth of uncertainty and failure outside its paternalistic boundaries. It was commonly said among company staff that the Company looked after its staff as if in a family, and that the common fate of those who broke ranks and left or had to leave the Company was that none of them would ever make good again. Whether it was because nobody had ever heard of anyone who had made good outside of the Company's employ or whether this mechanism softened the unquestioned demand for obedience and compliance posed an interesting question to Alice Tisdale Hobart who herself likened its policy, its postings and its patriarchy to any rich

Chinese family household. To her, a burgeoning feminist, the island which bound her own and the other women's lives seemed symbolic of the fate of the Company women – leisured and powerless in the river of men's activities. In giving voice to women's experience and women's emotions she found herself gradually living two lives: one of the Company and island woman of whom she wrote and the other of her own secret creative self whose thoughts and writing were extending far beyond the island and the Company to China itself.

It was while Alice Tisdale Hobart was in Changsha that she became much more interested and increasingly concerned about the China in which she resided. Although her husband had long studied the language, customs and institutions such as the guilds and clan groups. Alice Tisdale Hobart had been more affected by the physical landscape of China in her first few years in the northeast. She thought this was probably because of the climatic and physical extremes of the northeast, the intense light and long stretches of apparently quite uninhabited land and the intense cold. Moreover in the northeast she largely dwelled in settlements that were themselves on the frontier and outside of the mainstream of events and movements. Changsha, the capital of Hunan province, on the other hand, was at the turbulent centre of a turbulent age and foreign residents were much more likely to be caught up in the events of the Chinese Revolution that were taking place on their doorstep. It is perhaps not surprising that Alice Tisdale Hobart found that the balance of her interests in writing altered during this time as she became increasingly aware that her homesteading and community life took place against a much larger and richer tapestry – that of China and its revolution.

For the first time, and from her own balcony, Alice Tisdale Hobart watched many of the anti-foreign demonstrations of the early 1920s, the competition between warlords and bandit groups for hegemony in the absence of any strong and central national and provincial government and the perpetual devastation wrought by flood, famine and drought. Observations of these she also wove into her book *By the City of the*

Long Sand. She sensed and watched the growing want when week after week for all winter, spring and early summer it seemed as if the rain would never stop and the waters broke through the inadequate dykes, flooding the rice paddies and destroying the year's crop of rice. Unlike the Emperors and the imperial governments of old, landowners now sold and shipped away the previous year's reserves of rice leaving the inhabitants vulnerable to famine. Alice Tisdale Hobart watched as silently the people worked to rescue their pitifully few possessions from their huts. Rafts were manoeuvred across the once-green paddies laden with pots and pans and the family pigs. Sampans were moored on the eaves of thatched roofs just showing above swift moving water. In the dim depths of one hut, just discernible were trestles on the top of which were perched the household possessions and persons. Wherever Alice Tisdale Hobart looked there was water and only when it seemed as if the floods had taunted enough did they recede. A year later the rice crop which had been destroyed by flood the year before was now threatened by drought. All watched as the squares of young rice plants which should have been soggy with water became dry and parched. Even behind her walls Alice Tisdale Hobart herself could increasingly feel once more the growing despair of the peasants as vainly they strove to appease the wrath of the gods. The lucky ones who were near the river trod all day and night prising the river water into their fields, but for the rest it was to the temples that they went to pay and offer incense to unresponsive gods. To make them more responsive the peasants took the gods out to look at the sky so that they would see how bare it was of rain. Each night now, round and round the island moved the gods, borne on their chairs and carried on the shoulders of men and accompanied by the bang of the tom-toms. Little by little, the gods answered their cries and this time the rains came. The jubilation of the peasants was great but only afterwards did Alice Tisdale Hobart realise that not once during any of the disasters that had befallen them had she heard any cry or form of protest from the people in the little straw huts which surrounded the foreign settlement.

The foreign community also witnessed at first hand the warring between warlords and bandit factions, and indeed at times only the Hobart's sand-bagged house stood between the two. In the absence of a single strong cental government, China had become an arena for competing warlords, and in Hunan the governor and one of his men were locked up in combat over the revenue of the illegitimate opium trade. Every evening, the guns of the two armies who fought for dollars and cents were fixed and each time there was the fear that if one of the leaders were defeated the soldiers might break what discipline there was and begin looting and killing. Traditionally soldiers were feared in China and all in Changsha avoided the officers who walked or rode through the streets with the power of life and death in their hands. On several occasions the besieged Hobart house looked vault-like and grey behind its barricaded windows; it smelt of the damp and the musty hemp of the gummy sacks which had been stacked high in front of the windows to protect its inhabitants from chance shots – many of which had already hit the trees in the garden and the pillars of the veranda. There were sometimes long days of waiting, as for weeks the armies attempted to attack and take the island and city in a battle which settled once and for all the victor and vanquished. To the foreign onlookers, it made little difference which was which for like the people around them they had grown used to the fact warlords waxed strong to put new and unlawful taxes on foodstuff and coal, demand under threat of death large sums of money from individual cities and issue their own currencies which they forced the people to exchange for silver. With these resources in hand, they then fought amongst themselves for supremacy. Like the people around them, the small foreign community had no choice but to hope to go about its self-appointed tasks with as little interference as possible.

In the early 1920s not only was there much internal unrest and in-fighting, but the anti-foreign demonstrations which earlier European residents in China had found so threatening in 1900 and 1910 reappeared. Now many of the students and the young declared the birth of a new order in the country in which all that was old and all that was Western was banished from

their shops and from their beliefs. At first it was Japan that was
singled out in the demonstrations and boycotts largely because
of 'The Twenty-one Demands' that it had made in China at the
Treaty of Versailles following the First World War. From her
balcony again, Alice Tisdale Hobart watched the processions
of white-clad students meet the Japanese ships at the wharf in
order to dump their cargoes. On one occasion with the aid of
binoculars she and her servants watched the Japanese retreat
and kill one of the student protestors who swarmed on to the
wharf. This act brought all students, from high schools to primary schools, onto the streets of Changsha in protest. A few
months later anti-foreign feeling, with placards and pamphlets
denouncing all 'white' men, was again so high that it needed but
one incident – the shooting of Chinese students in Shanghai by
the police – for it to ignite and spread in Changsha where as in
many other cities Europeans were killed and houses wrecked.
From her terrace, again Alice Tisdale Hobart watched the
great masses of white-clad Chinese moving along the bund
with floating red banners on which was written 'Kill the white
man!' 'Down with imperialism!' 'Down with Christians!' 'China
for the Chinese!' She heard the volume of noise rising from
the crowds over the city and felt the surge of hatred against
the foreigner. It was a terrible sensation to know that even
on the lips of children her nationality was a by-word for evil
and her presence an anathema. Even for those with whom
they had co-existed and worked for years, their presence
was ambiguous and threatening. This time, fortunately for
the foreign community, it was protected by the governor of
the province who brought out his soldiers and placed the city
under martial law to contain the violence and hold quiet the
city.

Alice Tisdale Hobart, like others, felt that although on this
occasion they had passed unscathed, it would be only a matter
of time before the battle of the conflicting forces within China
was played out and that this battle was bound not only to
set the course of China's own history but also the shape of
future relations between China and European nations. She
was fascinated by the curious mingling of Eastern and Western

customs in a town like Changsha where old and new, East and West juxtaposed in the minds of the elderly and the young. In her first book-length manuscript written in Changsha, she noted the contrasts: the new schools on European lines, the nearby tinker's village, the conservative bandit, the illiterate soldier, the boatman living as his ancestors did without a single mechanical aide, and the progressive patriotic student. She thought the contrast of the dim peanut oil and smoky lamps with the new and brighter oil lamps or even electricity to be symbolic of the dualism of opposites she observed around her. Alongside the old industrial and business Hunan with its ancient bills hundreds of years old stood modern business Hunan doing trade with the great corporations of the West. The astute, blue-gowned Chinese gentleman of business with his old-world sense of honour was still as much a part of Hunan as was the new-style office man who wore a natty suit and straw hat from Japan (when there was no boycott) and called himself George Washington or Longfellow Yeh.

Once she had completed *By the City of the Long Sands*, the manuscript was sent off to several publishers the first two of whom rejected it on the grounds that it portrayed a too realistic view of life in China with its wars and famine and was not what an American audience in the carefree years following 1926 wanted to read. They preferred, it was pointed out to the author, another storybook China with its romance, mystery, intrigue and fortune. On her third attempt the manuscript was accepted and published by Macmillan who liked the book and encouraged her to continue to write and to turn her pen to fiction. Thinking that she could only write out of her personal experience, she decided to write a trilogy of novels portraying the lives, ideals and dilemmas of Europeans in China. As she had observed the increasing anti-foreign sentiment which characterised events and demonstrations in Changsha and elsewhere in China, she had often thought back with some sadness to that long line of persons from both China and Europe who had given of their best to establish a new commerce, education and religion in China. It seemed very hard for them to stand by and watch it all destroyed. It was of such individual relationships represented in fiction form but depicting China and symbolic of East-West relations that she wrote.

Alice Tisdale Hobart's first novel, *Pidgin Cargo*, is set on the Yangtze River, the same river that had run beneath the willows along the bottom steps of her garden embankment in Changsha for much of the year from each spring, when it ended the isolation of the little foreign settlement and linked it to the great trade routes of the world. She used to imagine how it flowed from Changsha into the Tungting Lake and from there on to the main Yangtze channel and out to sea, carrying the products of 200 million people of the Yangtze Valley to the great trade routes of the world. From her window she had seen the tall masts of passing junks propelled by their sails and long poles which half-naked sailors stuck into her garden embankment. She had liked to imagine that under the rounded-matting tops of their holds were calicoes from English mills, boxes full of cigarettes from Virginia, bales of cotton from Georgia and American copper or oil. In the opposite direction going downriver, rafts of wood logs, government salt junks, and sampans loaded with rice, opium, firecrackers, linen or zinc were all part of the trade of the world on the river at her gate: 'of America and England giving, China receiving, China giving and America and China receiving'. From Alice Tisdale Hobart's front door it seemed as if all movement and all life on the Yangtze River hung on the whim of the rapids and rocks of its gorges.

The novel is about the power of the Yangtze and the threat of the new European steamers to the livelihoods of the river's junkmen and traders, of European to Chinese custom and of European men to their women. It was on this giant river that Western man had challenged nature with his machinery, challenged 50,000 junkmen who, with the help of prayers and blood offerings, had for thousands of years battled with the river and strained on the ropes to pull the junks through the rapids. She had her hero Eban Hawley settle in Ichang at the entrance to the upper Yangtze and fight long and hard to navigate the gorges of the upper river with his specially designed steamers. Interestingly into this novel she wrote an idealistic dreamer, a Mr Archibald Little, and had him inspire and advise Eban Hawley in his struggle to conquer the river. Despite constant setbacks, Eban Hawley had remained personally convinced that with his machinery he could conquer the turbulent and virulent river which had always defeated the cajoling junkmen, traders and labourers although in the end, after a lifetime in Ichang and in service to the river and its trade, his steamer lay smashed, his life ended and his family in flight from the anti-foreign terrors. Alice Tisdale Hobart conceived of Eban's struggle against nature and the river and its traders and junkmen as representing the struggle between East and West on several different levels. Western man with his all conquering machinery was pitted against the Eastern man with only his body, primitive skills and physical strength. The turbulent and sometimes violent politics of China swallowed up the small white man who was at once powerless to influence events and whose own influence could be instantly obliterated without a trace – even after a lifetime of effort. The question behind her story was were the rewards of the Industrial Revolution in the West appropriate to the East with its wealth of labour power and was the ensuing dislocation of Chinese socio-economic structures and institutions worth the gains?

Another theme in the novel was the resignation of Eban Hawley's wife who pleaded with her husband to give up, so sure was she that nature, the river and China were more powerful than they and would defeat them in the end. She lived for most of her life in a lonely, isolated outpost where she early lost her bloom and vitality. With little to occupy her, she had a habit of standing at the window looking downriver with a kind of frozen expression yearning for both her former life in Shanghai and an American life of which she could but dream. Briefly she regained her vitality and vibrancy when she realised that she too could create life. At once she set about building for herself and her child a home where her son would know a little of her own American heritage and culture as well as things Chinese. Soon however to protect

him from the river, cholera and anti-foreign terror and to give
her son an American education, she had him sent back home.
She herself remained to spend twenty-five years in the house
overlooking the river and in the end she had to ask herself if
it had all been worthwhile. When her son returned to Ichang
with his new American wife, the mother suddenly saw herself
through the younger woman's eyes: wan, passive and wasted.

It was not until she completed the book that Alice Tisdale
Hobart realised that inherent within it lay a pessimism about
the relations between woman and man, person and nature, the
assertive progress so liked by Europeans and the passivity or
fate of the Chinese. Her publishers, Macmillan, didn't much
like 'River Supreme' and finally Century Publishers agreed to
accept it but with major revisions and a new title, *Pidgin Cargo*,
which referred to the illicit cargoes of opium. Moreover when it
did come out, the book set in China and written by an unknown
author attracted very little attention. As small compensation
a rather dejected author received a few letters mostly from
retired sea captains who said how they had read it with both
pleasure and nostalgia!

Although Alice Tisdale Hobart could not help but mourn
the stillbirth of her first novel, she did not allow it to deter
her from writing the second volume in her planned trilogy. In
this next novel she returned to the theme of the corporation
and the part it played in American trade in China and in the
lives of its employees. It is the most autobiographical of her
novels. It was only written however after her husband had
left the oil company, they had returned to America and there
had been time to take a sufficiently detached view of their
misfortunes during the last months in China. In *Oil for the
Lamps of China*, Stephen Chase works for a large corporation
selling oil in China and with his wife Hester their story closely
follows that of the Hobarts. After his apprenticeship in the
northeast, Stephen becomes the manager in Changsha where
he is constantly beset by the worries of organising a large staff
and fulfilling the Company's orders in a China characterised
by the increasing anti-foreign sentiments and violence of the
mid-1920s. After Changsha, Stephen, again like Earl Hobart,

was transferred to Nanking to manage the company office in the old capital high on the banks of the Yangtze River. From there his wife and he were forced to flee and join the growing number of refugees in Shanghai, whereupon the Company was forced to abandon many of its stations and contract its staff. In the fierce competition among the many experienced men for the few top positions in Shanghai, Stephen's loyalty to the Company and his protection of its interests in times of unrest and trouble count for little. In the final competition Stephen Chase, like Earl Hobart, became one of the unlucky ones, losing out, resigning and returning to the unknown in America.

The book incorporates an action packed plot, rounded characters and authentic and informative descriptions of life in and for a Company, in a foreign community and in a variety of regions and circumstances of China earlier this century. The author however is no longer the same company wife who wrote *City by the Long Sand*, and in this second novel she had her main characters become increasingly ambiguous in their relation to the controls, authority and power of the Company over their lives. In the early days of his career, Stephen Chase had, like Earl Hobart, determined to live up to the expectations of the Company. He put its interests before his own and his wife's; indeed he presumed that the Company's interests were synonymous with his own and his wife's. Did not the Company always look after its men even in times of uncertainty? Did anyone ever hear of any of its employees faring as well as he would have done if he had not left the Company? No opportunity was lost to play on the fears and stresses of life outside the Company, and mere talk of the misfortunes of those so short-sighted as to have left its secure employ was enough to bind them to the Company by injecting into them the fear of the unknown and the uncharted – for such had America now become to them. For managers, the code of conduct was even more strenuous, based on service that asked nothing for extra hours or long periods of strain, and responsibility that involved subordination at all times to the whim of the Company. Dramatically and rapidly, however, unease and the contraction of the China operations conspired to show just how little the individual meant to the Company. Stephen, like Earl Hobart before him, was gradually but ruthlessly demoted and posted to uncertain, unsettled and dangerous locations until finally he was squeezed out and forced to resign his job, his pension, his income and his way of life. True to its reputation the Company never fired him; it made the conditions of employment so intolerable that he had to fire himself.

Hester too had her own personal struggles. In the first years of her married life when Hester, like the author, had realised rapidly that she had married the Company as well as a husband, she was determined that she would be equal to any test the corporation put to them and that the Company should never find any weaknesses in her to use against Stephen and detract from his performance in the Company. Like Alice Tisdale Hobart, Hester found it a constant challenge to retain her sense of self and control within her household. The servants who had long served her husband were determined that his new bride should not appropriate undue power within the household and all but effaced her very presence by a variety of time-honoured practical and symbolic gestures. Outside of the home, she had few ready neighbours or friends and her efforts to become acquainted with the few Chinese women either socially or by teaching them English were unsuccessful. This was because either few Chinese men were accompanied by their wives or in the anti-foreign mood of Changsha and Nanjing, sustained contacts with any Chinese women were almost impossible. She defied the Company by asserting a little of her own individuality albeit often secretly. Therein lay the clue to her own preoccupation with homesteading or the subordination of the company house to her own will and stamp; and in defence of her own self Hester, like the author, secretly transported herself to another world. Music not writing was her secret weapon:

> Often with her violin under her chin she stood between the fireplace and Russian stove playing the fire music motif from the Valkyrie. She and fire

music in league against the conformity of chairs, tables, bookcases done in the Company pattern, against the [oil] tanks leaning over her, shadowing her, shadowing Stephen as they shadowed her house.

Mirroring the experience of her creator Hester too acquired confidence in her own self as she became more concerned with events outside her cocooned homestead and less dependent on her husband for information and interpretation of outside events. Hester's struggles closely reflect the search of the author for a personal identity within the relationship with her husband and his Company. However much the Company might struggle to detract from her individuality and however important this individuality was, Alice Hobart was also convinced that her own support and stamina were necessary to her husband's success. Indeed the title of her book *Oil for the Lamps of China* was chosen with care. Symbolically it likened women to the oil, the life force directed and constrained by, but also feeding and nurturing, their menfolk, the vessels.

Oil also represents Western knowledge and technology leading to progress and modernisation, and in this second novel the author focuses on the relationship between the Western men of commerce and the Eastern merchant. In their early years in China, Stephen and Hester had commonly thought of themselves as instruments bringing the light to China and that their presence in China had a far larger purpose than just their own careers and the fortunes of the Company. They were located at a new frontier where East not only met West but West was helping modernise and improve East. Stephen initially thought of the oil, his oil, as a means by which to alter the East but over time he became less sure of this purpose, the role of his Company and of notions of progress and modernisation. As he once prophesied in a conversation with Hester:

I used to think of the west coming to China as light illuminating darkness. It's not going to be like that. It's going to be hard travail to get the West born in the East, if it ever is.

Through his rare friendship with a Chinese agent steeped in Eastern ways and methods, Stephen came to understand the complexity and importance of the relationship and networks of responsibilities which tie each Chinese merchant and agent to the centuries-old intricate ways of the family, guild and religion inherited from his fathers, and fathers' fathers – indeed not unlike the respect, personal honour and obligation due from the European to his Company. However the long and developing friendship between the two men which helped each to smooth the path of the other and mediate cultural and commercial differences was doomed for it was not 'large enough' to bridge the chasms generated by the anti-foreign movement in the 1920s. During these Stephen was wounded and evacuated and Ho was murdered at the hands of the mob largely because of his relationship with and protection of the foreigner. As in the first novel, relationships and friendships based on mutual regard and respect between individuals from East and West had ended in conflict, violence and tragedy.

It took Alice Tisdale Hobart two years, mostly lying flat on her back, and several drafts to shape the novel to her satisfaction. Fortunately on this occasion the publishers Bobbs Merill immediately accepted the novel and in contrast to her first book, *Oil for the Lamps of China* became a best seller. If it had been published earlier during a period of security and wealth then the book might have had less impact, but coming as it did during the depths of the Depression, its readers were much more inclined, as they too became unemployed after years of faithful service, to identify themselves with Hester and Stephen Chase. Alice Tisdale Hobart received letters from readers in America, South America and Europe all saying 'If you change the name to mine it would be my story.' Warner Brothers made a film of the novel which was shown to packed houses from Broadway to small provincial towns. Interestingly Alice Tisdale Hobart did not see the film for quite some time as her husband, although wanting success for her, did not want her to be spoilt by it. She felt that he feared relegation to a subsidiary and secondary role in her life: did he have so little trust in her that he assumed she would be spoiled? As she embarked increasingly on a new and absorbing life which was exclusively of her own making, she knew that they had reached a turning point in their relationship. In the future her husband would have to recognise that her scribbling had turned into a profession. She also thought that although her writing would take her on her own separate path it need not split them if they learned to combine their different lives. Alice Tisdale Hobart continued to write even though at times this meant putting herself and her writing before her husband's needs and demands; on his part her husband had to accept a new professional woman with her own needs and demands as a more equal partner in marriage.

The popularity of her second novel encouraged Alice Tisdale Hobart to a third on the onslaught of aggressive Western modes of thinking upon the quietude, fatalism and acquiescence of Eastern philosophy. In a foreword to this book, she wrote that 'to those of us who have watched it, the impact of West upon East has been tragic, beautiful and terrible all at the same time'. This time the story focused on the story of European missionary teachers and doctors in China. In particular she chose the true story of an American doctor who, in the interests of investigating the endemic and debilitating disease caused by snails – schistomiosis – took the parasite into his own body in order to examine its effects at close quarters. Surely such a person could in his own person reconcile East and West in the interests of friendship and understanding, harmony and eventual reconciliation that would not end in separation, exploitation and conflict. She called the book *Yang and Yin* which is based on the symbolic circle in which each of the two interlocked halves is shaped to the other and contains within it the essence of the other. This symbol incorporated the dualism of Chinese philosophy which simultaneously divided but united women and men, passivity and activity, darkness and light, inertia and energy, spirituality and materialism. In her title however she has reversed the usual order by placing the passive 'yin' second and active 'yang' first thus representing the Western reversal of the ordering of the terms.

One of the most difficult Chinese characteristics for the young American doctor Peter Fryer to come to terms with was the passivity, acceptance and fatalism with which accidents and troubles, be they sickness or illness or flood or drought, were accepted even if they could have been avoided. In a mission hospital compound in an inland China town he works all hours, day and night, to raise funds to establish medical and hygienic facilities, train staff and to cure the sick. All the time he was aware that if he was to continue his work and service, he couldn't afford to have many failures. Sometimes he felt like a man trying to stem the tide of a vast ocean of sickness and wondered why it was that he should have felt so propelled by his religion to spend his life in such circumstances where the loss of a patient could generate ugly rumours questioning the true purpose of his and other foreign doctors' stay in China and where sickness and death were accepted as part of a pre-ordained life-course. Why did he continue to strive so and to stretch his will and body to unbelievably weary limits? In periods of self-doubt he wondered if this philosophic acceptance of circumstances was not a bedrock of strength. While Peter is so convinced of the importance of identifying the life-cycle of the parasite that he takes it into his own body, to his young Chinese student Sen Ho-shih, the parasite is not necessarily a menace and is simply 'one of the ten thousand things of the universe'. The relationship between the two men each steeped in his own philosophy is slow to develop, for the young Chinese at first found the doctor's aggressive fighting spirit difficult to understand and was even more than a little scared of it. Once convinced, however, the young Chinese assistant is awakened to the possibility of scientific enquiry and its potential in reducing suffering. He goes on to qualify in Western medicine but in so doing becomes convinced that it is necessary to eliminate the foreigner from all hospitals and schools if China is to develop and modernise in her own way. He thus eventually ousts Peter from the hospital and his lifetime's work. Neither the doctor nor his school-teacher wife Diana had foreseen how their school and hospital might bring about a change in their pupil's attitude towards his European mentors.

Peter's wife Diana was a young mission school teacher who had been convinced of her vocation to provide support for her schoolgirl pupils in their rejection of some of the age-old customs of the Chinese family which she perceived to be detrimental to the development of young Chinese women. Once she had tried to save a favourite student from having to return to the life-long confines of her dead husband's family. After her own marriage to Peter however and the birth of her three children her loyalties are divided between China and the mission school on the one hand and her own children and their American heritage on the other. The sudden death of two of her children from cholera swiftly decides her priorities. In the case of Diana, Chinese colleagues and friends found it difficult to understand her prolonged and fierce resentment of her children's deaths which surely had been their fate and should be accepted as such. Diana, in her grief, could 'hardly remember the woman she had once been who had dreamed and planned for the women of China', now that her self seemed merely a garment which had been rent asunder from shoulder to hem revealing a woman fiercely maternal and protective of her only surviving child from the sickness and harm that seemed to be China. This experience also separated her from her husband who continued to give all his energy to his Chinese patients while she and her daughter returned to America. Just when she thought Peter had joined them to resume family life there she finds that he has brought within him the deadly parasite. She interpreted this gesture as the ultimate rejection of herself, family and things American.

Peter, after a lifetime of service in China, had not only alienated his wife and family but was in turn rejected by both. He was left with the question of whether he had been presumptuous during his long stay in the country of his friend in pressing his Western ways? Depressing as this conclusion was, and given that it was not really what an American audience wanted to hear, this third novel was still widely and popularly read. Alice Tisdale Hobart herself increasingly feared that there could be little meeting ground or point of contact between the two philosophies, peoples and countries. She had felt for some time that China was entering a tumultuous period that would be characterised by struggle, conflict and violence in which those who had helped to bring about this situation would themselves be caught up in it. As part of the research for this book, she had returned to visit China where she found hatred and avoidance of all things American, European and Western. The vocal younger generation seemed intent on building a new China where there would be no room for co-operation or friendship with foreigners and indeed no foreign presence at all.

Alice Tisdale Hobart was to return to these themes once she had written a number of novels about the relationships of individuals, often women, to groups, often families, in a variety of settings including Mexico and the Californian grape country where she lived in the last decades of her life. In her final Chinese novels she was again sensitive to the fate of the young sympathetic foreigner in China's modernisation and revolution. She continued to be especially interested in the motivations and experiences of young professional Americans who, going to China with the aim of helping it into the modern technical age, subsequently found themselves questioning their role of assured superiority when they knew so little about the history and cultural and philosophical heritage of those whom they were teaching. She continued to be especially sensitive to the ambivalent motivations and experience of young European women who had quite a different experience of China once they were mothers. In one of the novels, *Venture into Darkness*, a young wife at first saw only beauty in the curve of roofs, the proportions and balance of the architecture and in the delicacies of embroidery, Chinese paintings and chrysanthemums. After the birth of her children, this sense of excitement and adventure turned to ambivalence and fears that the poverty, disease and anti-foreign sentiments which seemed to surround them on all sides would take her children from her. She feared that the child would never know its American heritage. Moreover what kind of future would these children ever have in China given the country's new determination to develop in her own way and without the intervention of foreigners? Her last book placed these questions at the heart of a Chinese-European family in which a European mother and Chinese father, who married in 1912, confidently dreamed that they would one day build a new kind of family, by combining traditional and foreign customs, and a new democratic China, by combining all that was best from East and West. In the turbulent years that followed however they found it difficult to substitute new customs for old let alone reconcile East and West in their own Eurasian family in which each member came to inhabit a different China. The struggle within this family became symbolic of the much greater struggle to bring about the China of their dreams.

Although Alice Tisdale Hobart primarily sympathised with Europeans in China, her explanation of the relationship between the two cultures was frequently more complex and sensitive than those of other observers of the time. She felt that she understood and sympathised with America in its experiences of China and she had felt herself to be a part of these. In addition she felt she both understood and supported the aims and aspirations of a new generation of younger Chinese women and men whom she observed to be very much caught between the influence of the old and the new and between China and Europe. She remained interested in these themes and in events in China until her death in 1950. Although she had inherent within her some of the American prejudices of the time, she was one of the first seriously to question in fiction form and for a wider audience the assumed superiority of what America and Europe had to offer China. One of her great regrets was that circumstances in China were such that she felt that she was a member of a disadvantaged generation of Europeans there who had never really been able to get to know as friends the young Chinese women and men who were re-making the country. However, unbeknown to her, at the same time as she was in Changsha writing her experiences for Americans in China and back home, another young American woman was having the unique experience of living as an 'adopted daughter' within a Chinese household.

6

A Chinese Noble Household: 'Daughter by Affection' and Writer, Nora Waln

In 1920 at the age of twenty-five, a young American woman student from Philadelphia, Nora Waln, had the rare opportunity to live within the courtyard walls of a Chinese household as an 'adopted daughter' in a large gentry family. It was made up of a total of six generations with eighty-three men, women and children. As a result of her privileged intimacy, of which the other women writers in this study could only imagine or dream, she acquired a unique knowledge of daily life within a gentry household. At first she found it all so strange that she likened herself to Lewis Carroll's Alice: 'From the moment of my arrival in China, it was as though, like Alice, I had stepped through a looking-glass into another world.' It was this world which she sought to portray in her book *House of Exile*, and as a domestic and social record of everyday life in China it has been described as a classic, admitting its readers to an unusual and authentic intimacy. Certainly her adopted family were so convinced of the accuracy of the details that they insisted on some disguise, given that the use of their real name in so intimate a history would 'raze the privacy of their courtyard walls'. The circumstances surrounding Nora Waln's adoption into a wealthy Chinese household came about as a result of old trading links which dated back to the early nineteenth century between the Walns, an old Quaker Philadelphia family of sea-faring merchants, and the Lin family, well-established Cantonese merchants.

In far-off China in the ancestral hall of the Lin household, it was recorded in the family history how in the late eighteenth century Lin Yan-ken went to Canton to join his maternal uncle, the famed Houqua, who was one of the thirteen men appointed by the Emperor of all China to trade with foreigners in Canton. There it was one of his tasks to select merchandise for foreign merchants which might include such exotic items as amber, beeswax, cinnabar, Chinaware, ivory chess men, embroidered fans, earthen ginger pots, hemp and indigo, jute, musk, medicinal rhubarb, umbrellas, vases, wallpapers and writer's ink. One of the foreign merchants for whom he selected this merchandise was a Philadelphia Quaker merchant named J. S. Waln who was pleased with this service. One of the valued mementoes safely stored in an ivory box in a green lacquer cabinet within the Lin household was a yellowed envelope containing a letter in both Chinese and English from J. S. Waln which had been entrusted to Captain Blackinson of the ship *Perseverance* and was dated the tenth day of the sixth month 1804. Addressed to Lin Yan-ken, it expressed satisfaction at the knowledge that 'any packet with his seal did not need examination to assure the receiver that its contents were of the promised quality'. Its American writer went on to express regrets that conditions of the era did not permit the exchange of other than material goods and ended with the hope that in later generations, 'when suspicions between peoples must certainly disappear', members of the Lin and Waln families might exchange visits. On special occasions, when the letter was taken out of its ivory box and passed around and read, succeeding generations of the Lin family were reminded of their historical trading with the Philadelphian J. S. Waln and of his hope for further contact.

More than a century later, members of the Lin family did travel abroad to America and made contact with the descendants of J. S. Waln of Philadelphia. Nora Waln was then an undergraduate student of Chinese at Swarthmore College, Pennsylvania. Nora Waln had first become interested in China when as a little girl she had discovered various family records in the attic of her grandparents' house in the Grampian Hills of Pennsylvania. Years later she could remember the exact day on which she had first become aware of her family's connection with China, Canton and the Lin family. It was raining, and since she had a hole in her rubber boots she had been prohibited from leaving the house. Rebellious Nora had fled to the orchard only to be returned to her grandmother with soaked black slippers, mud-stained white stockings and the starch of her grey chambray dress limped by tall, wet grass. Told by her grandmother to go to her room, she hid in the attic where in a chest under the eaves, used to keep moths from the wedding dress of a slim-waisted Quaker bride, she found old and yellowed copies of the *United States Gazette*. There the name Waln featured in the columns of marine notices announcing the berthing of vessels, the lists of their merchandise and the consignee for whom delivery was designed. It was the lists of exotic goods assigned to Waln and brought to Philadelphia by brig, sloop, schooner, frigate and ship that captured her imagination and from that time on Canton in southern China became her favourite port of dreams. In later years, this early and romantic acquaintance with her own family and their early China connections developed into a more serious interest in their activities and into her own academic studies.

One of her forebears, Robert Waln Jr, has been called America's 'first Sinologist' because of the research he conducted while trading in China in 1819–20. His extensive writings have been seen as among the most forceful early American assertions of the positive features of Chinese society and the most earnest early American effort to eradicate an anti-Chinese bias. Waln asserted that accounts by European Catholic missionaries in particular were 'so confused by the credulity and superstitions of the narrators it would be almost impracticable to obtain from them a proper insight into the character and condition of the Chinese nation'. He had been especially incensed by their accounts of infanticide which he felt to be exaggerated and based on hearsay. He argued that while the Chinese might practise infanticide during conditions of extreme hardship, such as famine, the practice occurred with no greater frequency than under similarly harsh conditions in other societies. He suggested that the omission of positive features of Chinese society from missionary accounts, such as the government-funded foundling hospitals which he had personally observed in Canton, reflected a deliberate intent to depict Chinese culture as a particularly self-serving version of heathen barbarism designed to elicit support for their cause.

Years later, influenced by these writings, young Nora Waln came to possess her own bookshelf of Chinese histories and her own Chinese dictionaries. Like students of Chinese today she became acquainted with the classics of Chinese literature, the philosophies of Lao Tze, Mencius and Mo Tzu and she committed to memory some of the works of Confucius. She added translated volumes of the classics to the maps, log books and old letters which she had inherited and collected from her relatives. The last boy Emperor of China, Pu Yi, captured her imagination and she wrote a sad ballad about the 'last little son of Heaven' which was printed in a magazine. One memorable day while a student at Swarthmore College she received a telephone call from a woman member of the Lin family who, on a tour of America with her husband and desiring to meet a member of the Waln family featured in the yellowed letter of the green lacquer box in the ancestral hall of her husband, had located the name of Nora Waln in the records of the Society of Friends' schools. So Nora Waln was invited to visit the House of Lin in China when she finished her studies. In 1920, at the age of twenty-five, she set sail for China and a new life as the 'adopted daughter' in the House of Lin.

That the Lin household was located on the Grand Canal in Hebei province in northern China was no accident, for six and a half centuries earlier the founder of the House of Exile, a skilled engineer named Lin Fu-yi had travelled from the southern province of Guangdong to assist in the extension of the Grand Canal to Peking in order that southern foods and riches might be transported to the capital. Famed and honoured, Lin Fu-yi built a courtyarded dwelling for his 'green skirt' mate, and though she could never officially take the place of his wife left behind in Guangdong, they founded the House of Exile, the sons of which had ever since been closely associated with the upkeep and maintenance of the Grand Canal. It was perhaps fitting that the first major journey that Nora Waln took within China was on the Grand Canal between Peking and the Lin homestead. Her observant eye for detail gave a wonderfully vibrant picture of the ice-sealed canal and its immediate environs. After a one-hour train journey from Peking and accompanied by her adopted mother Shun-ko, Shun-ko's husband, her husband's elder brother and his wife and daughter, Nora Waln boarded the Lin family boat waiting to take them on the one-day journey to the House of Exile.

The boat was fitted with sledge runners and a sail for use when the wind was favourable. Three boatmen worked in single shifts measured by the burning incense stick set before the image of the Dragon Goddess who 'ever listened to the prayers of mortals who pass over water'. On board were enough provisions for two weeks even 'so as not to be fretted if there is delay' though the expected length of the journey was only one day. The boat had two compartments, the fore for the men and the aft for the women whose travel was made comfortable by snug red mattresses, fox-fur rugs, back-rests padded with camel's wool and silk quilts of duck down, and charcoal foot braziers. In a nest of soft fur and gay quilts, Nora was made cosy between her adopted mother Shun-ko and her adopted sister Mai-da who each held one of her hands beneath the coverlets. Propelled forward with a long metal-tipped staff the boat left the canal side and turned south on the ice, narrowly avoiding the similar sledge boats that 'careered by in like manner'.

The Grand Canal being one of the main thoroughfares of persons and produce between north and south China, the Lin boat passed a continuous line of boat sledges piled high with country produce. Crates of chickens, yellow-billed white geese, brown ducks, demure grey pigeons in wicker hampers, rabbits contentedly nibbling at greens, squeaking black pigs protesting raucously against carriage, and broad-tailed fat sheep were all seen and heard. Foodstuffs included heaps of eggs, bushels of hulled rice, red corn, golden millet, reed containers of celery, lettuce and beetroot. Packed amid their produce were farmers and their wives and children en route to town for market day and all dressed in clean starched long blue gowns over wadded coats and trousers, their cheeks like rosy pippins, their dark eyes sparkling and their jolly faces quick to smile on this day of leisure. Young girls and boys darted through this more serious traffic on small sledge boats pushed forward in the same manner, miraculously escaping accident by fractions of an inch. Individual skaters pursuing earnest errands glided swiftly up and down the frozen highway; the leisured amused themselves by skating fancy figures in wayside bays.

Men cut ice and buried it in the canal-side earth mounds for summer use exactly as their forebears had done for thirty centuries. Women wheeled hamper barrows down to the open water and exchanged banter with the ice cutters as they let their ducks and geese out for swims. All along the frozen road, fishers made round holes and squatted over them with nets waiting for inquisitive fish. As the boat slid under frequent, high arched stone bridges, some humped and some in the shape of the perfect granite half-circle, the Lin men recorded the ice level against each bridge. They told their foreign visitor how the Grand Canal, carefully tended for generations, was like a dragon sprawling through the provinces whose enormous strength required correct and careful attention. When neglected it could be of 'dangerous temper' sweeping out in time of melting snow or summer rain devastating fields and cities, taking heavy tribute of human life and leaving folk who survived to face famine. Now what they feared was such a time, and they themselves had personally reported to the government on the tilted channels and weakened dykes.

From her vantage-point among the quilts, Nora Waln surveyed the new and unfamiliar beige and barren landscape here and there indented by rice paddies and roughened by dead stubble. At intervals there were patches of sparse winter wheat in which cattle pastured. Along the way she saw no isolated farmsteads; rather worn paths went up from the canal side to

walled villages, radiated from the fields to the walled villages
and from walled village to walled village. Each village had its
gates hostile to travellers and its 'asking protection' shrine by
the canal, and the people had built their homes well away
from the water 'because it is wiser to carry needed water up
and to take the washing down than to dwell where all sorts
of people pass'. Women and men rode over the countryside
paths, straddling wooden saddles perched high on the backs of
little donkeys with scarlet collars and tinkling bells. Other folks
were reclined in comfortable-looking litters swung between
shaggy ponies. A few travelled in gaily coloured sedan chairs
– green, scarlet or blue – and a goodly number of riders sat
in high wooden-wheeled mule carts. Pedestrians peopled the
paths carrying sometimes a rooster, a paper image to burn at
the family grave, perhaps returning a cooling pot to the next
village after a celebration or apparently just strolling along.
Most had shoulder poles loaded with looped-up clouds of
threadklike spaghetti or tissue-thin mooncakes of gelatine,
the twin staples of the district.

A stop for lunch took the 'lazily lulled' travellers to the
shadow of the east wall of the City of Noon-Day Rest which
rose in perpendicular height from the canal. There on the
waterside a merry throng of idle sedan chairs and boatmen
from craft at anchor had gathered. Young girls, carrying
kettles of steaming water, soap, soft towels and blue basins,
called 'Wash your face for a penny!' Barbers had set down
their portable barbers shops to trim the cropped heads of
the modern and to comb the queues of the old fashioned.
Letter writers under the shade of thin, oak-stemmed oil-paper
umbrellas brushed letters for 'those who have no leisure to
write for themselves'. Here two itinerant cooks wheeled their
barrows built to combine portable work-board and stove, and
as they worked they advertised the quality of their foods – thick
meat and vegetable soup, piping hot! crispy golden doormat
twists! sweet steamed yams! flaky white rice! roasted chestnuts!
pork dumplings! buns of light steamed bread! grain porridge!
candied red apples! nougat stuffed dates! fried noodles! bean-
curd of rich brownness'.

Once disembarked, the travellers were conveyed by sedan chair up steep narrow streets inside the town to a luncheon inn where after a meal of five dishes they were served clean bowls of steaming rice and fragrant tea made in a squat brown pot. It was explained to Nora that all good restaurants and careful homes had teapots for different needs. The inn host had never seen a foreign girl before and on learning that 'she was to visit the Lin homestead' had suggested tea from 'the pot which prevents misunderstanding'. Back outside on the canal however, the afternoon's journey was very different.

An intimation of events had been suggested by the intrusive presence at lunch of an insolent, ill-kept and ill-clad but armed soldier whose every whim had been satisfied by the elegantly-gowned innkeeper himself – even when the soldier paid for his meal in worthless money and had demanded change in worthwhile silver! Now after lunch they passed sledge boats overloaded with soldiers and propelled by frightened boatmen. They had ruthlessly pushed about an old farmer and his 'lily-foot' wife, scattering their produce on the ice. One had speared the old lady's rooster with his bayonet and held him high while the others applauded. When she struggled to help the dying bird, the officer clouted her on the head. Half a mile on, the travellers heard a shout and saw a child fall; she had been reluctant to give up the donkey hitched to the mill where she was grinding flour. The Lin family made plans to continue their journey overland in order to avoid trouble but it proved difficult to secure assistance in any of the villages. There had been no soldiers in the district for the previous five months so that the mid-morning foraging raid had come as a complete surprise at the time when the gates were open and the folk scattered. Villagers had lost carts, animals, food, winter clothing and all their sons between the ages of twelve and sixteen years – excepting those who had quickly and shrewdly hidden. Now they were busy tightening walls and gates, taking their saddles, sedan chairs and carts to hide the pieces separately, driving their cattle in and sharpening kitchen knives and farm tools as weapons. 'No', her companions told Nora, it was not war – just one of those intermittent periods of unrest lasting sixty to a hundred years, which linked dynasty to dynasty and was to be borne stoically and philosophically.

After sledging on routes away from the main canal, the travellers reached the Lin homestead city long after sunset when the great gates had been sealed. It was a sign of the times that although the gateman knew the persons in the boat, had known them since childhood and knew that they had gone to meet the foreigner in Peking and could also recognise the voices, he would not open the gate till the appointed time at sunrise. At last a messenger was prevailed upon to bring to the gate a Lin family elder who took it upon himself to open the gate and, closing it again, secure its locks and paste a fresh strip of paper bearing his name across the crevices where the two halves of the gate met. He had brought sedan chairs in which the travellers followed through narrow passageways between grey walls, broken at intervals by closed vermilion gates to a broader street with a scarlet gate in which a peephole was slid open at the sound of their coming. Camel-back, the Lin gateman, recognised his 'family', opened the To and From the World Gate and smilingly welcomed the travellers home. So Nora entered the closed, secluded and 'real' world of the Lin household which was to make the world she had left behind seem like a 'dim fantastic dream'.

The Lin homestead was composed of sufficient courts to house comfortably the six generations of the Lin family now living. The eighty-three men, women and children dwelt in one-storey high single-room houses which had been built four-square about a series of paved courtyards. The roofs extended well over the pillared verandas which finished at the front of each house so that one could get into a sedan chair in rainy weather without exposure to the wet; after this utilitarian duty was done they tilted upwards in easy curves displaying fairy scenes and fabulous creatures painted gaily under the eaves. Adjoining courtyards were connected by gateways cut in the courtyard walls, often in the shape of a flower, a fan, a vase or a full moon. The courts with their dwelling rooms for the living clustered around the higher double-roofed Hall of the Ancestors which sheltered the life-tablets of the twenty-nine generations of Lins and their wives who had 'plucked the flower of life'. Over the centuries the household had expanded to meet the needs and accommodate the multifarious interests of family members. A library had been built and the collection of ancient manuscripts begun; the azalea terraces were grown; a school-room court for the children at lessons was constructed; a main garden of rocks, pools, pavilions and bamboos was provided by a favourite son for his mother; a pavilion in the garden was erected by a loving husband for his poetess wife; while a Lin wife who loved birds had constructed a courtyard where carved feeding-boards held scattered rice, baskets held suet in zero temperature weather, stuffs for nest-making in the mating season, and sand and water baths.

To accommodate the succeeding generations, the high grey walls which surrounded the homestead – six-foot thick and four times a man's height – did not run in straight lines but had instead been stretched to surround whatever land could be secured to provide new dwelling-space. There were but two openings in the wall connecting with the outside world: the Gate of Compassion, a small window cut in the north wall where charity was given to the needy, and the To and From the World Gate, a door of solid planks large enough for a horse and carriage to be driven through into the entrance court. Even the entrance view at the To and From the World Gate was closed by a screen of porcelain tiles, featuring a gorgeous green dragon rising over a blue sea and after a scarlet ball of life, which was an arm's length thick, twice as wide as the gate and as high as the homestead wall.

The first stone laid in the building of the original Eastern courtyards bore the following words:

> Glazed brick, white mortar and blue roof tiles do not make a house beautiful; carved rosewood, gold cloth and clear green jade do not furnish a house with grace; a man of cultivated mind makes a house of mud and wattle beautiful; a woman, even with a pock-marked face, if refined of heart, fills a house with grace.

Within the dwelling, housing a continuous succession of many generations, the Lins had evolved like other old and established families complex sets of customs, rules, legends and beliefs which defined the behaviour of its members. Each courtyard within the walls was inhabited by a person entering the family by birth or marriage in accord with the customs that had grown into the family regulations with the generations. In this and many other respects, the arrival of Nora had posed a problem. She had no place either by birth or marriage, she was the first unmarried woman guest without the chaperonage of her mother and she was the first foreigner even to enter the homestead. After the family council puzzled for two moons, it had been decided that since she was a young girl of marriageable age she be assigned to the most carefully guarded court of the homestead, the Springtime Bower. The reason given was that it was the 'only safe place in a Chinese homestead' for a 'maiden of marriageable age'. However within the Lin household, the Springtime Bower had only three houses. One was for the twins Ching-mei and La-mei. The second belonged to the absent Su-ling, another daughter of marriageable age who was away studying in France. Her room could not even be borrowed for according to the rules of the household each daughter's house was absolutely hers until she acquired by marriage a house in another homestead. The third house was occupied by Mai-da, who was willing fortunately to share with Nora. Once it was ascertained that the two girls' horoscopes recording the month, day and hour of their birth matched, in that a period of tranquil weather and a good piece of good fortune in the repayment of a loan occurred while the two horoscopes lay on the family altar, the co-residence of the girls was deemed to be auspicious. Although Nora was already in residence she could not formally become a member of the homestead until she had been presented to and received by the First Woman and each other woman of the household.

On the day she was to be officially welcomed and assigned her place within the household, the serving matron of the wife of the Family Elder and Lady of First Authority brought word that if she was ready the Orchid Door would receive her. Her confidante and guide in the ways of the household, Shun-ko, explained that this was a command for her now to make a formal call in each house of the women's quarters. She rehearsed her how to accept a tea-cup into the palms of both hands and to walk backwards slowly and gracefully when taking leave. They first went to the Garden of Children where the nine little boys and girls in residence were solemnly ceremonious. When they had exchanged bows, the eldest of the girls poured tea into rose-patterned cups and the eldest boys passed it with sugared dates. The Springtime Bower to which the girls graduated from the Garden of Children came next. There Mai-da received her formally into the house she shared with her and then accompanied her to the house of each of the thirty-six women married to Lin males. Each woman had her own house furnished and decorated according to her tastes and dowry although in all other respects the age and position of husbands dictated the place of women in the household hierarchy. In the ceremonial of her reception, Nora noticed that Shun-ko was careful to have her stay just as long in the houses of the women who wore the 'green skirt' or the concubines as in those of the wives. With the exception of one woman, all her hostesses, whether they were of serious or gay temperament, made her feel most welcome and glad that she had come. The exception was Sung-li who at seven years old had seen her mother raped by a foreign soldier in the days of terror following the siege of Peking in 1900. Hating and fearing all foreigners, she had protested in the family council against Nora's presence in the household. Although this one dissenting voice was not sufficient to dent the feeling of elation which Nora experienced, the afternoon did not end so well. The First Lady of Authority dismissed Nora prematurely when she addressed her in Chinese and Nora replied in English. She was only to be brought into her presence again when she was 'sufficiently civilised to hear and to speak in Chinese'. From that day on no member of the household was permitted to speak to Nora except in Chinese, and only after she had passed her oral test with the First Lady was she pronounced civilised enough to be presented to the ancestors. In the Hall of Ancestors the family gathered within the circle of generations and the elder told the ancestors of her residence and status within the household. As a sign of her acceptance Nora then lit a candle before each tablet of which there was one for each woman and man whose earthly life was woven into the household history. The morning after this ceremony, she was told that she was henceforth and forever 'daughter by affection' to the entire clan of Lin.

As a daughter of the house she was able to observe the intimate details of the lives of the wives, daughters, mothers and grandmothers of the household and was herself incorporated into a new and entirely absorbing set of daily and annual rituals and routines which punctuated the days and years in the Lin household. On her first day, the nightly and early morning routine was set for the months to come. The night of her arrival, the serving maid assigned to her, Bold-the-Third, set up a bust-high screen and pushed her behind it to undress. She reached around the screen as Nora shed each of her garments and then helped her mistress into an earthen jar half-filled with hot water. Once Nora was in, Bold-the-Third poured more and hotter water until the bunch of herbs she had added floated just under her chin. The earthen jar was of a size that she could just sit in, with her feet tucked under her. The maid kept her soaking until supper when dried in warm towels and folded up in a nest of quilts upon the brick bed she was served three dishes: breasts of chicken, red cabbage and green pepper, and tenderloin of pork and chestnuts, each cooked in such a different and delicious sauce that she was eager to possess the recipes to send home to her sisters. Fish soup, plain rice, hard white winter pears and jasmin tea followed. After discarding the wooden log which she should have tucked under her neck as a pillow, she went to sleep to the merry sound of the crackling flames in the 'stomach' of the heated kang or brick bed which touched three walls and occupied three-quarters of the floor space. It was used for sleeping at night and as a sofa in the daytime when the folded quilts were stacked to one side making bright layers of scarlet, gold, leaf green, lavender and sapphire.

Wakened in the morning with hot rice water, she dressed for the day after the style of her Chinese sister, Mai-da. First she wound herself from her armpits to her hip points with a tight bias binding of strong fish-coloured silk. Then she put on pyjamas of peach silk with trousers that wrapped over in pleats at back and front, over which she put on a second suit cut to the same pattern, but of heliotrope satin lined with white rabbit fur. Next she pulled on white socks, tucked the legs of the two pairs of trousers neatly into them, wrapped her ankles in puttees of apple-green satin and donned black velvet boots lined with red fox fur. After this she had a third pyjama suit fashioned exactly as the first two but of wine-red brocade warmed with an inner lining of grey squirrel fur. She felt stiff in all her winter layers, but she did look like a fairer version of her 'sister' Mai-da. Much was the sadness among the serving maids that Nora's hair was the colour of the yellow gentian of misfortune although she did wear it in the style of Mai-da – gummed smooth, parted in the middle, pulled back behind her ears and braided at the nape of her neck into a pigtail that reached her knees. Dressed for the day, Nora was ready to participate in the rituals of the daily household routine.

The day itself was measured by a time stick in the form of a long spiral burning before a bronze 'bird of dawn'. Each day, Camel-back, the gateman, made the spiral of well-mixed sawdust and clay which he then lit by the stars as had his fathers for eleven generations before him. The Lins had never found it more than a quarter of an hour wrong and now they even regulated their Western-made watches by this time stick. There were twelve carved divisions on the spiral of the time stick, each of which represented two hours of Western time and the hours were named in the same sequence as the years: rat, ox, tiger, rabbit, dragon, snake, horse, sheep, monkey, cock, dog and pig. Except for Camel-back himself, who carried his lanterns through the courtyards sounding his 'I am here robbers' rattle, all members of the household usually slept between the hour of the pig to the rising hour of the dragon. Then, after rice water and sweet cake, the children went to their studies, the men to their duties and the women to household tasks which they shared in rotation until a gong announced the morning meal in the hour of the snake which they usually took in the company of small courtyard groups. The afternoon passed according to age, necessity and inclination until the evening meal in the hour of the cock. Then after a restful digestion each one was occupied until sleep. It was a busy household in which it was frequently said that idleness brought ruin to a home and to make a family prosper was like digging clay with a needle so that each member had to do her or his share.

Most of the women had a quarter month at kitchen service and a turn at washing, bluing and bleaching the family wash with only a break after sun-up for a brief basket lunch at midday. Shun-ko kept the family records and Nora was often assigned to help her prepare and pound the paints in a small mortar and pestle in order that she could compile the weather records kept to help with garden and farm work. At the beginning of each season, Shun-ko drew a plum tree of nine branches to each of which was added nine twigs. After shading the tree forks and branches realistically and the leaf buds with care in browns, greens and silvers, she put in the shadow of a pink blossom on each of the eighty-one twigs. Thereafter each day she painted the petals of a single blossom in a particular manner according to whether the day was cold or mild, cloudy or fair, windy and rainy, or sunny. It was the custom for the wife resident in The Second House of the White Rabbit to keep these records as they were started twenty-two generations previously by the wife for whom that house had been designed. Already a pair of cabinets in Shun-ko's room contained fifty silk scrolls on each of which was painted the weather reports in the form of a plum tree with eighty-one blossoms no two of which had shapes and arrangements that were exactly alike. On another set of fifty scrolls could be read the harvest of fifty seasons and the yields of the summer and autumn crops from the farms and the Lin garden.

Back home in America, Nora had always had difficulty in keeping to any time schedule which meant that her relaxed temperament adjusted more easily to 'time's easy flow' than most. She soon observed that the very concept of time had no sense of immediacy as it had in America. For instance the swift passage of a lifetime was accepted as naturally as the fall of a flower or leaf and this parallel signalled a philosophic acceptance of the individual life as part of something much larger or even limitless. A century past or a century in the future was not considered far off in a language that has no tense and which, in ordinary speech, could tell of an event centuries ago as casually as an incident within the very hour. Only with time and experience had she been able to distinguish between the two and then only with difficulty.

A rickshaw runner explained as he pulled her to market one morning:

> Events that happen are not put away in books. That would not be fair. Only a few folk have the leisure to read and history belongs to everyone. It flows in every mother's milk and is digested by every babe. Thus it becomes a part of everyone's experience to use when needed. That which happens is not past. It is all part of our now.

In a farm household hours, days, weeks and months glided smoothly by in a cycle of seasons timed by the Farmers' Calendar. Although there had been nine official calendars since the Dynasty that produced the Farmers' Calendar, crops had continued through the centuries to be planted, tilled and reaped according to its ancient wisdom. The Farmers' Calendar was a sun calendar which traced the sun's pattern across the heavens by twelve stars and divided the sun's journey into four sections or the four seasons, which were further divided into periods called Rain Water, Get-up Insects, Time of Clear and Bright Air or some other such allusive and picturesque title. On the eve of each new phase, all the members of the household were called together while the Elder read aloud of the rituals and tasks appropriate to the new season from the Farmers' Calendar.

Spring was welcomed by a procession in which the torches were lit with fire drawn from the sun with the aid of a concave mirror. Seeds of each crop the House intended to plant were wrapped on blue-green or vermilion silk, carried to and watered on the earth altar with dew previously collected in a white jade bottle. A craftsman brought a life-sized papier maché water buffalo and buffalo driver to chase winter away and drum-beats were used to call the patrons of the soil, water, fields, mountains and sky to smile harmoniously on humanity and nature. Finally the singers in glad chorus announced that spring had arrived and all listened to the Elder's oration, a combination of rhetorical welcome to spring and prudent advice to the farmers. Later in the spring, on the first few days of Spring Divided in the Middle, the Elder put on the ceremonial ploughing coat and opened the ploughing season by cutting three furrows across the eastern fields. Then generation by generation in orderly succession according to birth, each son of the house ploughed three furrows. Next, in precedence determined by length of service to the family, each labourer opened three furrows. After days of earth ploughing without cessation and on the evening of the Time of Clear and Bright Air, the Elder read to all the family from the Farmers' Calendar.

> All the ploughing, harrowing and rolling that has tortured the Earth since the vernal equinox shall now stop for three days that the Earth may be rested by undisturbed enjoyment of the Sun's caresses. All the beasts shall have three days to relax their muscles and no person shall even hitch an animal to a light pleasure cart. For three days all the Families must cease to give thought to material gain. Tools must be laid down. Shops shuttered. Offices closed. Men, women and children must now lift their spirits above mundane concerns and make merry in appreciation of all that the gods give them free.

Thus began the spring celebrations during which women and men, and girls and boys wearing clothes and shoes of springtime silk in blossom colours set out to tidy and sweep the graves of their ancestors. While the musicians of the family piped airs on reed flutes for the pleasure of the 'souls', food and tea were put down on embroidered cloths beside each grave. The family bowed and knelt at each grave to show respect for their forebears and to show their gratitude for the establishment and continuance of the family, the present members of which then sat on crimson cushions and picnicked off the food that had been ceremoniously offered at the graves. It was a happy occasion for all the descendants among whom there was no mourning for they had come in happiness to put in order as an act of remembrance the mounds where the earthly bodies of their predecessors had been laid. They also spoke of and measured the exact places where they hoped their bodies would be placed and they talked calmly of their descendants a hundred years in the future. The children of the household were given baskets filled with pigeon, hen, duck and turkey eggs and packets of bright dye. Assisted by their nurses, they coloured the eggs by boiling them in the dyes over the elm-wood fire, and when the eggs were cool they polished them with sweet perfumed oil, arranged them in woven nests and presented some to each adult member of the family. After much fun and sport, work began again. The House of Exile sowed in accord with an ancient system of crop rotation which it trusted would keep the soil enriched. Shun-ko, who kept the crop records was kept busy verifying statements as to what was grown in each ground plot last year and several years back.

There were no ceremonies to welcome summer, as the vermilion bird who came from the south and ruled the agricultural year from the arrival of summer until the beginning of autumn would be angered if folk stopped their work. The rice plants, then five inches tall, were transplanted into the mud in terraced fields prepared for flooding. Peanuts were hoed in. The sprouted sweet potato tubers were cut into small pieces and planted in sandy soil. Peas were brushed so that they could climb up towards the sun; gourds poled. Cucumbers and melons were moved into sets of four and covered with bamboo frames that had coarsely woven cloth stretched across them to keep out melon bugs. Turnips, leeks, carrots, onions, parsnips, chilli peppers, celery, cabbage, lettuce, ginger and artichokes were thinned and the plucked-out seedlings were planted in other places. Beets and eggplants were sown.

In the 'small fullness' that followed, men's backs were bent to weeding in every field. With fine one-toothed hoes, soil was loosened around each stalk of the winter wheat now heavy with swelling grain. Unfortunately, the ripened crops of the district were so abundant that few could be sold in the local market place. The profit in red cherries was too small to warrant their travelling and what cherries could not be eaten were made into cherry vinegar, compotes and jellies. Soon all the members of the household, including the children and their tutors, were released from other duties to gather in the fruits. Nine boatloads of strawberries packed in leaf-lined trays were despatched to the Peking market 'for the foreigners who liked strawberries'. Raspberries ripened, black beans were gathered, rosy-cheeked golden apricots were carefully picked so as not to bruise them and placed in frayed baskets; ripe chilli peppers and capsicums were pulled, dried, roasted and ground to a fine spice. Millet and oats were reaped, sweet potatoes taken up and soya beans gathered. The corn was cut, the ears stripped from the stalks and the stalks laid away for fuel; the earth sheaths were turned back to expose the kernels and the cobs suspended in rows of orange, red and yellow under the eaves of the courtyard. Harvest had called home every available Lin man and daily they visited the village threshing-floors to measure the harvest of the tenant farmers. The Lin women, since women were considered the most capable in material matters, supervised the division of the crops between tenant and landlord.

The House of Exile was the second largest landowner in the district and possessed the 'red-card' title to a total of 1,563 acres or the right to use this land which it leased from the government in whom actual ownership was vested. They farmed ten acres themselves and the rest was divided between some 600 tenant farmers some of whom had farmed the same land for generations. Under the Lin management, the tenant provided all the farm implements, the animals, the labour power and, with the exception of rice, the seed. In turn, the House of Exile paid all government taxes, was responsible for the maintenance of the irrigation system and controlled the principal crops grown. In addition to the principal crops, divided between tenant and landlord, the tenants produced subsidiary crops which belonged entirely to them so long as they did not encroach upon the principal crop. If the agreed principal crop was a fruit or vegetable, it was gathered by the tenants and divided in the village market place. If the crop was a grain it was threshed on the village threshing-floor by the tenant in the presence of a Lin family member who supervised the measures of the grain. The crop was then divided to settle a year's rent; the advantage of this was that the tenant never fell into arrears of rent payment, and landlord and tenant shared in subsequent good and bad seasons.

During the Thank the Harvest celebrations all work stopped for three days. The store houses were already filled, and field and orchard still held the promise of further abundance. At dawn on the first morning of the festival, the men, women and children of the House of Exile met the tenant farmers at the Temple of Agriculture and together they went to the eastern fields. To the accompaniment of music 'played for the Earth Mother's delight', they offered a part from each crop and burned yellow scrolls in which they had written their prayers of gratitude. At the hillside spring, the procession knelt in a circle of thanks to water for nourishing this seed. Then came three days of 'pleasuring' during which the village Elders boasted that there was not one empty food basin in the village. There were feasts and banquets, theatrical entertainments and sporting competitions between rival troupes of lion dancers and stilt walkers and the exchange of gifts. But the young wives, maids and the girl children were sulky. The village was in carnival but they were forbidden by the First Lady of Authority from joining in the festivities. Girls of marriageable age were especially constrained in their activities; they were not expected to see or be seen by young men. Nora received some hint of the seclusion which was awaiting her as a young woman of marriageable age within the House of Exile on her very first trip on the Grand Canal. Then by accident two oranges from the family basket of foodstuffs had rolled over the ice crossing the path of a tall skater dressed in a claret silk gown who with admirable grace returned them with a polite bow and a short exchange of words with the men of the family. As he skated east and the boat sledged west, Shun-ko strongly reprimanded Nora and Mai-da with the words:

> Girls of marriageable age are as dangerous to the people of the family as smuggled salt. Don't ever again while under my chaperonage, look at a man. Direct your gaze modestly to the ground when he is in front of you.

Once inside the House of Exile, they had few opportunities to direct their gaze at strange men secluded as they were within the central courtyards of the household. The younger women were subject to the authority of the senior women of the household before whom they knelt as 'flowers bent by the nourishing rain' which was the name of the salute due from daughters to house mother. In the House of Exile, the First Lady of Authority was stricter than in some neighbouring households. Maids under her protection did not join in any festival procession which included men – except the procession which led directly to the bridegroom's door. During the Welcome the Spring Procession, Nora and other maids were left within the household. The First Lady of Authority locked the To and From the World Gate with the special key she used for such occasions. The envy of those girls and wives who were permitted to go out was such that maids were said to be in a hurry to marry so that they might have a wife's right to ride in the nicest procession of the year. Not even girls or wives however were allowed to join in the harvest celebrations during which they were all forbidden to leave the women's quarters of the household. Not only was the village out of bounds, but even the masculine side of the household was said to be 'rowdy with too much barley wine'. Despite close chaperonage and arranged marriages, however, girls of marriageable age in the Lin household seemed to find their own ways of arranging a secret correspondence or tryst.

While Nora was resident within the House of Exile, there were four women of the household who married, each in very different circumstances. Mai-da, Nora's close confidante and friend was the first, and her wedding was the most conventional even if it had been unusually delayed. The Family Elder who had only recently returned home after sixty years in government service felt very sorry for anyone who had to leave home, and sad to break the family circle. So thinking, he was slow to complete the marriage contracts for the family daughters. He had to be reminded that it was years past the time at which Mai-da should have married. For a while it looked as if Mai-da had been about to take matters into her own hands. Secretly she had arranged to meet a young Mandarin prince on the Lantern Festival's eve. Secretly at his request she had made a pearly fairy costume in order to attend a street masquerade to match his disguise as a fisherman's son. At the appointed hour a fisherman's son kept tryst with her and flirted in a dance all down the mystic lantern-decorated streets, returning her frolic with quick response. Unbeknown to her however, the gay companion of her escapade was not the Mandarin prince but her favourite uncle. An itinerant priest had seen Mai-da put the secret letter under the shrine in the Street of the Purple Bamboo, secured it, followed her home and sat down at the To and From the World Gate to sell it to the first man of the family who came out. He demanded 600 dollars, her uncle had got it for 300 and sealed the priest's lips against gossiping Mai-da's name all along the route of his next holy pilgrimage!

Perhaps it was no coincidence that two days later the Family Elder called Mai-da into the library where five cards proposing marriage were laid down on his writing table. Thus Mai-da who over a period of years had managed to avoid betrothal, selected her husband, and the Family Elder was saved from making a choice for her beyond giving his sanction to the Family Council's decision that any of the five were suitable. From that fateful moment Nora watched Mai-da, who had already given her heart to another but bred of centuries of folk who conceive of marriage not as a relation for personal pleasure so much as a duty and a contract involving the ancestors, the descendants and property, accept her fate philosophically and without undue curiosity concerning her future husband. After the betrothal she would be subject to much teasing about him as she was laughingly told that he had flat feet, a terrible temper, a pock-marked face, a beard, untidy habits, a finicky appetite, a weak digestion, the body of a giant and the mind of a simpleton. She met this jesting with admirable self-control, perhaps because she had already bartered away her birthday camera to her boy cousin in return for snapshots of her betrothed. Thus she had satisfied herself that he was not only whole but also the same young man she had seen two years previously worshipping the God of Knowledge at the city temple.

To test the 'rightness' of the match, two red cards containing a record of the year, month, day and hour of the birth of both prospective bride and groom were laid on the altars in both the households. Three days later because there had been harmony, peace and no ill omens in both households, the family of the prospective groom presented a betrothal contract signed by the Family Elder and four heirs in succession to the Family Elder-ship who were 'united in eagerness to welcome the daughter of Lin'. Betrothal gifts were exchanged between the two houses, the wedding date announced and sweet cookies called phoenix and dragon cakes with the wedding date stamped on them with red sugar were wrapped in wedding paper, sealed up in lacquer wedding-cake boxes and sent to all the proposed guest house-holds. These homesteads responded with gifts appropriate to the bride's dowry such as garments for the trousseau, house-hold furniture, bedding, crockery, silverware, kitchen utensils and jewellery. The bridegroom's family presented Mai-da with jewellery and with gowns, one for each season, in which every woman in the homestead had put stitches of welcome.

Meanwhile Mai-da's household busily prepared to receive the marriage guests. The gardeners were busy in the courtyard and garden coaxing the peonies in order that the showing of flowers and buds be perfect as they rose on glazed-tile terraces in a luxurious hill of colour shading through dark plum, wine red, sunset rose, sunrise pink, apple bloom and cloud white over the pond and wistaria arbour. Red awnings were put up to shade the courts and crimson carpets laid in brilliant patterns on the tiles. The house pillars were wrapped in bindings of silks and vermilion court curtains were hung in doorways. All the decorative treasures of ivory, porcelain, bronze and jade were brought from chests and set where their antiquity best showed. Scrolls of red and gold were posted on either side of the To and From the World Gate announcing to all who passed that Mai-da, daughter of the House of Lin, would go out to complete the House of Tsang as wife of Tsang Huai-ching on the birthday of the Protectress of Blossoms. There was a continuous bustle and stir in the kitchens which hummed with activity as delicacy after delicacy was prepared for the round of feasting. A delightful confusion of servants bore gifts of wine, cakes, roast geese, braised duck, pickled pork, spiced mutton, sugared nuts, candied fruit and sweetmeats between the two house, in itself a source of happiness as they were tipped each time they delivered a basket.

A marriage within a household was an occasion to reinforce family and kinship relationships and advertise its harmony and status to the outside world. Four days before the wedding day, friends from a distance and women relatives and friends who desired to assist in the preparations began to arrive, and one day before, bearers in brilliant wedding garments carried Mai-da's dowry to her new home. Musicians played wind, string and hand instruments at the front and rear of the procession which coming from a rich land-owning gentry household was ninety-one carrying poles long. The large pieces of furniture were wrapped in red covers and the smaller articles and clothes packed in chests. In pride of place, a Swiss clock with a bird that sang the hour was carried uncovered so that all the village might enjoy it.

On the marriage eve, the 'Maid's Feast' was held in the Hall of Hospitality which was decorated with the symbols of happiness and illuminated with scarlet candles. Mai-da's mother presided and Mai-da came to the hall when the first course had been served and poured wine into each guest's cup. She was dressed, for the last time, in the costume and thick plait of girlhood. She, as was the custom, dined alone with the First Lady of Authority and burned the incense of farewell in the Hall of Ancestors before being sent to bed. At sunrise on the wedding itself, the bridal chair arrived accompanied by the groom's musicians who played 'Call for the Bride'. Meanwhile Mai-da, bathed, painted and dressed by her mother and servants in lotus-perfumed undergarments and wedding dress and admired by all the women and children of the household, took leave of all that was familiar and dear to her. Her mother hid her emotions by scolding daughter and servant alike, and Mai-da, quiet and calm up to this moment, suddenly broke into shrill hysterical laughter. Quietened by her mother and by lute lullabies played by her favourite uncle she made ready to bow to the guests and kneel in farewell to the elders and to her parents. Her father fastened the groom's cloak about her shoulders. Her mother dropped his handkerchief as a veil over her face. The family cried their last wishes for good fortune and crackers were fired in loud explosion as Mai-da was lifted into the bride's chair which was closed and fastened with sealing papers signed by the First Lady of Authority. To the accompaniment of drums, cymbals and flutes playing the 'Wail of Departure' the lifting poles creaked and the bride's procession passed out of the House of her girlhood. The To and From the World Gate was locked behind her and henceforth she as a member of another household could only return as a guest.

What a contrast the second wedding in the Lin household was when several months later a thirty-six year old widow in the household wished to marry the proprietor of a local restaurant. The Family Elder's wife showed her disapproval of this step by hiring craftsmen to re-gild the memorial arch to virtuous widows in the village who refused to remarry by chastely refusing 'to drink the tea of two families'. The Family Elder reminded her that virtuous widows in any righteous household were not supposed to marry again, and if they did they departed to the new household empty-handed save that their daughters might accompany them. Sons and whatever property the woman had brought to the household continued to belong to her husband's family and the widow lost all rights and all voice in that family once she married again. Despite all these injunctions, however, the widow Chou-li continued in her desire to marry, and the Lin family elders had to receive the jolly proprietor of the restaurant with all the courtesy that custom demanded should be accorded to an honourable suitor for a bride. The House had to accept his proffered wedding gifts, and give Chou-li to him but she went without a bride's chair and without a procession of any kind. One afternoon she walked out of the House of Exile with her second husband followed two hours later by her childhood nurse, who was accompanied by what seemed to Nora to be an enormous amount of luggage for a servant to possess. No one in the Lin household took any notice of or any interest in this wedding and even those who went to wait at the gate for the servant and her luggage to pass through to the outside declared they had not noticed her!

The third wedding within the year, and one which was also unusual, occurred when Ching-mei, one of the Lin twins who had been betrothed at birth, was married to a young student studying in America. Both she and her twin sister, La-mei, accepted marriage as an inevitable event yet they were heartbroken at the thought of separation as they had never been apart for an hour in their lives. Ching-mei was very nervous and fearful of Western habits her betrothed might have acquired in America, yet she knew the contract had to be completed. To give her confidence and to keep her company, and because she was more interested than her twin sister in foreign thought, La-mei went with her although she could not ride in the bride's chair nor bow to the ancestors of her sister's husband. Even so any children born to her would have equal rights with those of her sister and the two trousseaux were similar in every detail.

After three weddings within the year, including a double dowry for one, the resources of the House of Exile were somewhat strained. It was decided that a proposed fourth wedding in the Lin household be postponed. The daughter concerned had advanced the suggestion herself and the family council had rewarded her with a trip south to the Lin household in Canton.

The family elders should have been suspicious. Su-Ling, the daughter, had been studying in Paris and unbeknown to her family she had acquired modern ways and thought of which the House of Exile had heard but thoroughly disapproved. When the young returned student sons of the household had expressed their disapproval of family-arranged marriages, Mai-da's mother had quickly retorted:

> When this Republic gets itself established, girls will have to go out and hunt for their mates! If their families cannot help them get married, then they will have to become bold and deceitful, preying on any man they can get, yet pretending that they are not wanting one. Only the most artful will mate! Shy, plain, good maids will wither away into a fruitless old age.

Little did the family realise that two weeks after Su-Ling went to Canton, she would slip over the wall of the House of Lin one night and marry a young Chinese lawyer. They had met while they were both students in Paris and after the example set by many of their peers, they repudiated the marriages contracted for them by their elders, and simply set up home and announced their marriage in the newspapers. By breaking a contract signed by her elders, Su-ling was considered to have dishonoured her family and for this she was officially censored and received no dowry. However the independent, wayward and winsome Su-ling had never been long in disgrace and some months after her marriage she knocked at the To and From the World Gate of the House of Lin in Canton and was later received by its First Lady of Authority. Thereafter Su-ling wore her famous pearls as a token of her favour. Su-ling's husband was also received by the Elder of the Canton homestead and after communication between the two Lin households no word of criticism was ever heard of Su-ling again, nor was it long before the marriage was also publicly recognised and accepted by her husband's family.

There was one more wedding yet. Nora herself had met an Englishman, George Edward Oswald Hill, who had been eighteen years in the British government service. She had met him on one of her brief boat trips back home to Pennsylvania, and after their marriage in Shanghai, they settled in Nanking where Mai-da also now resided. Nora and her husband lived in a house set in three acres of lovely walled gardens in Big House Road which had been built by the Chinese government to command respect. A long-time bachelor's household, it had been very efficiently run by a variety of servants used to full authority and control who were now inherited by Nora. When she arose at seven o'clock each morning she always found that the floors had been polished, fresh flowers arranged in the vases, new fires laid in the grates; there was never a suspicion of dust when she ran her fingers under chairs or along a shelf at the back of her books. She and her husband came to a breakfast table covered each day with a freshly laundered linen cloth, set with shining silver, glittering china and sparkling glass. Although it might sound a life of leisure and ease, Nora thought that such perfect service had its disadvantages. If at any time she moved things or took out her sewing, a book or a cushion from their allotted places and left them for but a few minutes, they were quietly and quickly returned. The household was geared to her husband's needs and timetable. As her husband enterd through the front door, the midday soup was placed on the lunch table. The household was run with clocklike precision as if Nora was herself not even there. As she concluded: 'The house is handsome, the service perfect, but I was soon dissatisfied.'

She sought to establish her personal authority and control over the household, but time and again her own wishes were thwarted and her own needs ignored by the servants. If she wished to use the car, make a purchase or humorously play a practical trick on her husband she was hindered. If she took responsibility for the comfort and diet of the household as she had been trained in Pennsylvania she was thwarted. If she ordered fruit jelly then she got peach pie, if she suggested lamb with mint sauce she was given beef and Yorkshire pudding, and if she asked for biscuits she was given rolls. If she should order a house-cleaning of the west rooms, then it was almost certain that they would start in the east. In anticipation of forms of female control, authority and interference, senior servants in charge of bachelor households frequently departed once their master married, but in Nora's case their staying power was equal to her own and there was no peace in the household until she resolved not to disturb their pattern of doing things. Instead Nora turned to entertaining and on Home Days received women from Nanking families related in any way to the House of Exile and from Chinese official households. She divided her days receiving Chinese women as guests from eleven to one o'clock each morning and foreign guests from four-thirty until seven o'clock in the late afternoon. She found both Chinese and European callers exceptional in their wit and charm and she had nothing to do but sit, listen and answer while the tea-table was provided with welcome delicacies. In these circumstances, Nora enjoyed learning from her visitors, or rather she enjoyed herself up to a point, for she soon tired of constant talking and yearned for a different kind of self-satisfaction which was more solitary in nature. Within her own courtyard walls she turned to gardening and to writing.

Like many of the other women writers in this book she sought a refuge for herself within a room of her own. From among the many rooms Nora chose the smallest in the house with its own balcony commanding a view of the Purple Mountains and from where she could survey happenings in the street below. Although the room had been set up as a guest room for persons of lesser importance, there were already more than enough guest rooms and Nora set about to organise 'her room'. She pressed the electric bell, her orders were listened to with the utmost servility and she waited with happy excitement instantly to move her own wedding furniture into the room in order to surprise her husband when he returned home. She waited and waited until it became quite evident that the servants were not going to budge until they were clear that their master knew about this change in household arrangements. She had to acknowledge that 'our master' did not know, and as a result no furniture was to be shifted until he returned and gave the order. When she went upstairs again to do what she could herself, she found the doors locked. When 'our master' came home, it was too late to do anything that day and only when he gave his orders was the room arranged to her complete satisfaction – except for the curtains.

The story of the curtains illustrates the difficulty Nora had in arranging for her own needs within her own home. In her husband's locked cedar box which had travelled with him from house to house, Nora found curtains of many textures and colours. To cook's wife who oversaw this operation, no curtain could be used in Nora's room. The creamy net which had been purchased in Szechwan (Sichuan) in 1911 and not used, since it had fitted no window, was 'too new to cut'; the filmy silk with jasmine blossoms had been secured in Mukdan and used by one moon before the master was transferred; it was the same with some green brocade, an apple blossom print, all of which cook's wife took with some determination and sat on them as a 'queen on a rising throne'. The roll of sunshine gauze, Nora sat on herself. She was informed that its thirty yards had never been cut, it had been put in the cedar box four years after the Boxer troubles, and that it was being saved for the right house. Nora carried it to the balcony room where her own servant Bold-the-Third, who had travelled with her from the House of Exile, tactfully suggested that she make the curtains. She took the gauze, went down for some matching thread and sewed the curtains which were then hung although the material 'did seem a little thicker'. It was not until nine years later, when Nora happened to find the roll of thirty yards of sunshine gauze in the cedar chest that Bold-the-Third confessed. She had bought the near-matching material with her own money and returned the gauze to the cook's wife uncut. Otherwise, she gravely told her, 'I should not have been to make a road of peace here for you and me'.

Peace in her own room Nora did achieve, and she spent some time each day writing. She wrote several short stories for the *Pictorial Review* and later, after the birth of her own daughter, began to write of her unique experiences as a 'daughter' within a Chinese household. Her interest in writing was the subject of some discussion back in the House of Exile. On one occasion her adopted mother, with whom she engaged in long correspondence, admonished her for her rebellion within her own household with the words:

> Whether or not a wife finds personal pleasure in the activities which occupy the society surrounding her husband, it must be her pleasure to do them. Writing stories or verse is a vocation to woman well enough if she has time to spare from her vocation which is marriage.

She recommended that Nora be first and foremost a good wife and engage in the accomplishments of bridge, tennis, golf and ballroom dancing and other such activities of daily life on which the reputation of a wife rests. Only after establishing such foundations should Nora take up the occupations that she herself preferred. Like most of the women writers, Nora enjoyed gardening, but it could be a frustrating occupation. She had just planted several hundred tulip bulbs when her husband received transfer orders to take up residence in Canton.

The giant house which was rented and furnished for Nora's husband was located on the island of Shameen linked to Canton by two bridges. Shameen was so small that even a leisurely walk could not occupy more than twenty minutes in encircling it. In addition to the paved bund which curved around under the shade of the wide-branched banyan trees, there was just one central avenue with Western banks and shipping offices running the length of the island. The two- or three-storeyed houses with the wide verandas were all built facing the water and had a long frontage which was kept planted, pruned and mown as communal lawns with a children's playground, a cricket pitch, tennis courts, a football field and a bowling green. Today the lawns, flowering shrubs, tall trees and handsome shuttered and verandaed houses can still be seen as durable reminders of European presence. A motorway now skirts the island, but earlier this century the sedan chair carried by barefoot or sandaled men was the only vehicle permitted on Shameen. Vendors, not permitted on the island, were limited to selling from their boats at the water steps of each house. On this island most of the European nations were represented:

the French flag flew over the east end, the Japanese over the west, the British over the middle and the American flag over the American consulate. In contrast no Chinese person could put a foot on Shameen except in despatch of business or as a servant to a Westerner. The existence of a European Shameen excited much indignation and bitterness and its return to China provided a popular platform among the revolutionary groups in Canton in the early 1920s.

Within the small formal society that was segregated Shameen, Nora and her husband like the rest of the foreign community walked on the bund to take the air every evening before dinner. Her husband was almost entirely occupied by the delicate political situation and Nora seldom saw him outside the brief hour of exercise and conversation on the bund. Soon after they had been formally introduced into the foreign community they were frequently invited to dinners at which they were carefully seated according to 'rank', the highest places reserved for government officials with the longest service, with the next ranking places allocated to merchants according to the date of establishment of their firm's China trade. Nora found that in contrast to Nanking there were no Chinese persons included in the dinner invitations and that the wives of Chinese officials did not call. With no Western friends and a busy husband, Nora spent most of her considerable leisure hours within the Canton House of Lin and with her two adopted sisters, Mai-da and Su-ling, who were both coincidentally also residing in Canton. Here in contrast to her life on Shameen Island, she lived as a domiciled daughter within an entirely Chinese world. It is a sign of the times that now she was received into the House of Lin not as a European but solely because she was a daughter of the House of Exile. In the words of the First Lady of Authority:

> It is unfortunate that you are to live in Shameen. One foot can't stand on two boats. But all through life one must make compromise. You have to live in Shameen because it is your duty to dwell where your husband dwells. There is no social intercourse between Shameen and Canton. Yet it has been decided in Lin Family

Council that you are to be treated here as any other
married daughter of the House of Exile. The Elder of
Exile made formal request for this and we agreed to it.

Since no Lin family members except the incorrigible Su-ling
and Mai-da ever entered her Shameen house, Nora spent most
of her time at the House of Lin.

Within the Canton Lin homestead, which was similar in
plan to the House of Exile, Nora found industry and pru-
dence, kindliness and affection. Daily she joined the wives in
attending to all the household duties in rotation while her own
infant daughter played with the younger sons and daughters
of the household in the Garden of Children. On most days
after their work was done, they all sat round the Elder in
the cool deep shade of the library courtyard and listened
to music, poetry and a recital of the dramatic incidents in
the clan's history. Often the children repeated legends they
had heard from their nurses and occasionally maidens of
the Springtime Bower enacted historical pageants, dressed
in costumes from the old family chests. Life in the House
of Lin was more self-contained than in the House of Exile; it
was also more urban than rural in that it leased out land but
cultivated no home farm for itself, had no intimate relations
with the tenants and was less concerned with the weather.
The house was very much occupied with clan activities, clan
incidents and clan celebrations and no one other than kin
entered the high walls; if the family had to entertain others
they hired a city restaurant for the purpose. National events
were important only if they personally affected any member
of the family. The House of Lin made a liberal donation to
each government as it came into power, and the Family Elder
counselled against any other involvement and participation in
politics in this generation 'because the affairs of the family may
be ruined'. The young did not always heed this advice.

Su-ling was independent. She had had her hair cut in a new
fashion which was called the 'windblown bob' and wore an
orange voile dress which had been sent her by a friend in
Paris. She called the straight sleeveless and low-necked sheath

which came just to her knees 'the new dress of freedom' and enjoyed its effect on her family and servants. She had secured a handsome allowance from her husband's family and lived with him alone in a modern flat where she was 'at home' four afternoons a week. Nora and Mai-da assisted her by pouring tea and passing cake for the young Chinese women and men of means who had been educated in Western universities. Depending on their inclinations, they wore Western clothes, followed Western fashions or wore soldier uniforms and Chinese dress. They danced to victrola records, played tennis, raced speed boats, flirted and theorised continuously about what they would do with their learning as soon as they got the opportunity. They were restless and dissatisfied and fumed at China's fragmentation and passivity in the presence of the Western powers. Nora found them to be bright, attractive, energetic and young who, at loose ends, had been drawn to Canton from all the provinces both because they could not fit comfortably within their households and because Canton was the headquarters of the new and exciting Republican movement led by the idealistic Sun Yat-sen.

One afternoon Sun Yat-sen, who had devoted himself to the Republican cause in the attempt to unify and free China, arrived at Su-ling's house for tea. After asking for silence he made the finest call to leadership of the masses that Nora had ever heard. He was held in the deepest veneration by the young people present and she could understand why:

> One felt his spirit was steady, true and undaunted. His eyes were bright, his cheeks flushed, his countenance illuminated, his body straight and vigorous. . .his speech was conversational, yet it rang a louder call to unselfish service than any dramatic oratory could have done.

Deeply impressed, the young women and men eagerly offered their services in the various organisations of the Nationalist Party. The news spread among the Western educated students, who flocked to Canton, that they had but to appear in

Su-ling's drawing room to find their life's work. At Sun Yat-sen's invitation, Russian advisers, experts in different types of organisations, came from Moscow to train this new leadership for specific, usually propaganda enterprises aimed at winning over labourers to their cause. As a result of these labours, it was soon evident to observers that serious trouble was brewing between the Nationalists and the merchant citizens who feared the Communist leanings of the Nationalist Party. Even the defiant Su-ling gave Nora a close hug before saying 'You are a darling, but you were a fool to marry an Englishman. So as a good Republican Chinese I must hate you violently, aggressively and noisily'. To avoid such an unhappy ending, Nora was advised by her Chinese family to take her child and leave China. She had no choice, for as the fighting in Canton erupted, she was evacuated along with other European wives and children to Hong Kong to await the ending of the troubles.

Like the writers Alice Tisdale Hobart and Pearl Buck, Nora found herself increasingly caught up in the tumultuous events of the Nationalist Revolution of 1925–7 and the Japanese invasion 1931–2. As a European woman she went to and fro between Canton and Hong Kong and later she went to England for an interval before returning in 1927 to Tientsin (Tianjin) where her husband had since been transferred. The civil war and violence of those years touched all families and the Houses of Lin were no exception. Mai-da's brother was Chiang Kai-shek's agent responsible for securing American military and civilian advisers to help the Nationalist Party shed its Communist members, and Mai-da's own husband on an errand to secure peace within the Nationalist Party was sent home dead from a dinner party. One of the sons of the House of Exile, Shao-yi, was arrested along with several of his classmates when his school was searched for evidence of Communist leanings. Quotations from a book which Su-ling had given him at New Year were found in his notebook. Shocked and sorrowed even as powerful a family as the House of Lin dared not intercede on his behalf. There was no trial and Shao-yi and seventeen others were put to death; Nora had spoken to him on the previous afternoon and found him to be in a philosophical mood. He calmly accepted the fact that Communism must go and he must be used as an example to help it go. Shao-yi's last words were to beg Su-ling not to cry.

On the eve of the anti-Japanese war in 1932–3, Nora left Tientsin for America, but before doing so she paid a return visit to the House of Exile, setting out on a journey very like her first. In the House of Exile she found the familiar daily and annual rhythms intact but not indifferent to the uneasy political situation and the threat of war. Nora stayed in the courts of the House of Exile sharing a courtyard with Mai-da as she had always done, but perhaps unbeknown to her for the last time. As 'sisters' the friendship between the two young women had been unique, and as a 'daughter' Nora had been privileged with access to the daily and social life of a Chinese household. On this last visit she took with her the completed manuscript of *The House of Exile* which she had written from the notes made at the time of her first long residence. Apparently the entire family read the manuscript and their criticisms were none too amicable. In the end however they permitted her to submit it for publication and it was published a year later in 1933. It immediately became a best seller and was translated into many languages. Described many times as a 'classic', it was republished in 1986 by Penguin Books.

After leaving China, Nora's husband resigned from British government service and in 1934 the family took up residence in Germany so that he could study music there. Never idle, Nora made it her self-appointed task to observe and write of Germany during the first years of Hitler's leadership, to document the rise of Nazism and to study the response of the German people of her acquaintance. Once *The House of Exile* was translated into German, she enjoyed a certain notoriety and met and was introduced to many Germans of all political persuasions and occupations. Even the Führer numbered himself one of her readers and ordered thirty-five copies of her book on China to give to his personal friends. However when it became known that Nora Wain was writing a book about her impressions of Nazism the number of invitations declined. Before she left Germany, she mailed separately to her publisher three copies of her manuscript 'Reaching for the Stars', but not one copy ever arrived in England. She had to rewrite the entire book from memory and from the few notes she had managed to smuggle out on her person. The rewritten book was one of the first on Germany to be published under Hitler, but her attempt to understand and report on the German as opposed to Nazi experience led to accusations that she was unduly sympathetic to the German people whom she admitted to liking and admiring. Although at the time her indictment of their government was too gentle for many readers, in its quiet manner the book was a quite damning account of the Nazi cause.

Her habits of observation and detailed note-taking continued in England where she wrote and took part in a series of radio plays for the BBC entitled 'If you were an American in 1941'. During the war she was the European administrator of an American war fund for mothers and children and a member of the Friends' Ambulance Unit. In 1947 she became a *Saturday Evening Post* correspondent where she remained until 1951 when she spent the last six months on the Korean battlefields. After a short period as a correspondent for the *Atlantic Monthly* in Germany and Scandinavia, Nora Wain became a freelance journalist touring Asia and America. Fittingly, in 1956, eight years before she died at her Buckinghamshire home in England, she was awarded the Gold Medal, as a 'Distinguished Daughter of Pennsylvania'. Despite this and other honours, it is for her 'inside' story of the domestic and social life of a Chinese gentry household observed and detailed from the vantage point of 'adopted daughter' that Nora Wain has been best remembered and appreciated.

7

A Chinese Peasant Household:
Missionary Daughter and Popular Interpreter of China, Pearl Buck

M rs Pearl Buck, you have in your literary works, which are of the highest artistic quality, advanced the understanding and appreciation in the Western world of a great and important part of mankind, the people of China. You have taught us by your works to see the individuals in this great mass of people, you have shown us the rise and fall of families, and the land as the foundation upon which families are built. In this you have taught us to see these qualities of thought and feelings which bind us all together as human beings on this Earth, as you have given us Westerners somethings of China's soul.

This speech, made at the banquet following the award of the much coveted Nobel Prize for Literature in 1938, could not have better pleased Pearl Buck whose literary and public activities both before and after the presentation of the Nobel Prize were primarily devoted to increasing the mutual understanding and appreciation of Eastern and Western cultures and peoples. She was easily the most popular writer of novels about China and Asia and in particular she gave millions of Europeans their first images of and insights into the domestic and social life of China's peasants. Her childhood memories of a world of *amahs*, servants, playmates and school friends, neighbours and

Chinese family friends together with her later observations, insights into and knowledge of the Chinese peasant household were incorporated into her first book, *The Good Earth*, which enjoyed immediate and immense success. Indeed the impact of the book and film combined was such that for a whole generation of Europeans, Pearl Buck created the Chinese peasant as an identifiable person in much the same way as Charles Dickens had created recognisable individuals and families living in the slums of Victorian England. The writing about Chinese persons not in relation to Europeans but in relation to one another was something new in European writing about China. Perhaps Pearl Buck's ability to write so intimately of the details of earthbound peasant domestic and local life can be partially attributed to her unusual experiences as a child living in two worlds – an American world and a Chinese world.

Pearl Buck herself always felt that she grew up in a 'double world', embracing both the large white clean Presbyterian manse inhabited by the American world of her parents and the large living merry and 'not too clean' Chinese world of her servants, neighbours and playmates. Quite accidentally she was born in America while her parents were on a longer than usual leave in order that her young mother Carie might convalesce. Her mother had been only twenty-three years of age when she first went to China as a young bride. She had four children closely spaced and as rapidly lost three of them from tropical diseases which at that time no one understood how to prevent or cure. During the last few months of rest in her grandfather's house in a West Virginian homestead of Dutch stock and design, Pearl Buck was born in 1892. She was later to write that if she had been given the choice of place for her birth, she would have chosen exactly where she was born; in her grandfather's large white house with its pillared double portico set in the beautiful landscape of rich green plains and with the Allegheny Mountains as a background. However at the age of three months, her mother's health being restored, she was transported across the seas to live and grow up in China. Thereafter she lived in an American home with dreams of America as a country 'entirely good' and 'from whom all blessings flowed' but encapsulated in a Chinese town with Chinese playmates and friends.

Pearl Buck's American home was the creation of her mother Carie who, wife of the dedicated missionary Andrew, forever yearned and longed for her own family and country. She was very anxious that her own children, though living in China, should have an American childhood and be conscious of their cultural heritage. Pearl Buck's memories of her father were of a slender, slightly stooping but noble American travelling and belonging in the streets of Chinese villages and market towns, whose thoughts were almost entirely concerned with his Chinese translation of the New Testament and with the souls of his beloved Chinese converts. Her memories of her mother were different and almost entirely home-centred. She was either at her Chinese kitchen table where she made her own bread turning out big brown sweet loaves and little crisp southern rolls as she talked to the children; alternatively she was dressed in a rough white dress that swept the grass as she walked in her beloved garden, a big old straw hat with a red ribbon tied round it on her curly brown hair and carrying a pair of garden shears for snipping roses by the armful. She grew flowers that reminded her of home for enjoyment and a variety of American vegetables for the table. At other times she spent long hours at the organ sent by her best beloved brother from America where, singing in her clear and full soprano voice which seemed to rise to the very rafters, she sang all her favourite old hymns and oratorios which were nearly all of a triumphant type. Indeed the tones of her voice were more fitted for mirth and triumph than for sorrow, although of sorrow she had more than her share. She never forgot, and her children knew that she never forgot, the four small children who had one after the other been snatched from her as the result of a swift and sudden illness, and it says much for her spirit and indomitable will that the children who had survived had memories of a gay and smiling mother who was both fun and very American.

The first family home in Chiukiang on the Yangtze River was located some distance from the treaty port's foreign settlement and was pressed amid and against surrounding dark-tiled Chinese houses, but within a short time they moved to a small brick cottage with a veranda, an old garden and trees high on a hill above the city. Within the mission home, Carie made the little square living rooms familiarly American with white curtains at the windows, fresh flowers and wicker chairs. At meals the family all sat at a large oval teakwood table purchased from an old small and dusty secondhand shop in Shanghai. Carie had found it among heaps of rattan, broken rope and old split bamboo furniture, and after buying it for a few dollars polished it and thereafter all her years sat at the foot of this oval table. She doted on it and her daughter knew why when she first saw the dining table in the Virginian homestead of her mother's family. Pearl Buck later recalled that as a child her fairly decorous American self arose early in the morning from her bed, washed herself, put on her clothes and tied on the apron that all little American girls wore in those days. After brushing her hair she went downstairs to join the rest of the family at the oval table, including her father, who had already risen at five o'clock, bathed, dressed and prayed for an hour in his study. Sitting down and in a solemn voice peculiar to his prayers, her father said his grace always asking divine blessing that the food might strengthen them all to do God's will. Breakfasts were always solid and always American to equip all the members of the family for the hard work of the day.

The first meal of the day usually started with fruits – great varieties of oranges for most of the year except in summer when they were supplemented by loquats, apricots, fresh lychees, strawberries, peaches and varieties of melons. After the fruit came a special sort of porridge of roasted, stone-ground whole wheat which was cooked long and slow and was eaten with sugar and white buffalo cream which was richer than cows' cream. It was followed by eggs and coffee from Java with hot rolls or hot biscuits as her parents came from the American south and seldom had their bread cold. After breakfast and family prayers to which the children had to contribute a verse, the business of 'being American' went on. Her mother planned the lessons for her daughter's day. She taught her music and painting and saw to it that every week a long composition was written in order that the young Pearl might learn to write well. The children had to do exercises to strengthen their bodies and they were encouraged to perform feats of physical bravery. Years later Pearl Buck remembered climbing higher and higher up a wind-tossed slender tree trunk to reach the crow's nest for which her mother had offered her silver coins. There were few aids to help her mother teach, but teach she did very conscientiously the lessons of her own country – American history and literature, the history and literature of England and Europe and of Ancient Greece and Rome – which at the time seemed to Pearl to have little to do with the world in which she lived. As for Pearl, she had few thoughts beyond getting through the lessons as quickly as possible so that she might have plenty of time for play and for dreaming. Lessons were only postponed when a Chinese visitor was with her mother or on festival days.

All such American days as 4 July and Thanksgiving were carefully observed and provided an occasion to teach the children about their country. Hallowe'en was faithfully observed with a jack-o-lantern made from a yellow Chinese gourd and kindly Chinese neighbours pretended to be terrified when a fiery grinning face shone through their window on the October night. Except for one year when there was famine and so much want outside their wall, Carie made Christmas a happy and merry time for her children. The decoration of the house with holly and green and the stirring of the plum pudding had always been rites in the mission home, but here she had to ingeniously provide all the trimmings for there were no toy shops and no Christmas displays to help her. She could make Christmas a very orgy of gingerbread men and cookies and toys she had manufactured, of things both useful and nonsensical, of stockings hung at the hearth on Christmas eve, and on Christmas morning there was a tree trimmed with little bits of twisted and twirled bright paper and ribbon she had saved throughout the year. Seldom was anything allowed to spoil the pleasure of the season, and to recreate the sweet mystery of the first Christmas Carie told the gathered family the manger story about an open hearth fire with carols sung at the organ at bedtime. At dawn her brilliant voice rang through the house, welcoming the special day for her children.

Even more memorable for the children of the household was the annual arrival of the Montgomery Ward boxes from America. As for other American children in the interior of China, the Montgomery Ward store took its place alongside Santa Claus and even God, and certainly it was one of the most tangible links with their own country. Pearl and her sister anticipated for weeks that morning when their father, looking up from the letters before him on the bare breakfast table, would say solemnly, 'The boxes have come.' There was a regular but always exciting routine to be followed. While their father went to the customs office on the bund to present the bill of loading and get the boxes through customs, the children at home were waiting at the gate to welcome the four to five coolies carrying the boxes slung on ropes upon their shoulder poles to the sound of their rhythmic step-keeping call. As their mother prepared a place in the back hall for the boxes, one of the children had always found the hammer and big nail puller that had been bought for such days, and breathless they all watched as the nails came up screeching with reluctance. Every board was saved as it came off, for they were of good American pine and dry as no wood in China was ever dry, so that bookcases, bureaux and chests of Montgomery Ward boxwood featured in every foreign home.

Perhaps ordinary, to the children the contents were the extraordinary and all the more luxurious because they could not be bought anywhere around them. There were precious foods to be savoured, utensils and tools that seemed magic in their complexity and ready-made marvels of garment fashion. Really there were tins of coffee and bags of sugar, cakes of yeast and soap, molasses for Carie's famous gingerbreads and spices which had perhaps grown in the Orient and now were back ready again for use. There were needles and pins, hair-pins, ribbons, threads and other small things not to be found in Chinese stores. For clothing there was the necessary long warm underwear to keep at bay the damp Chinese winters in badly heated houses. Lastly but most importantly there was always the one special item costing no more than one dollar that each child had chosen out of the fabulous catalogue. As an adult Pearl Buck could still remember the lovely childhood hours spent poring over the catalogue that was America.

For Carie and her children, Sunday was most nearly 'an American day'. For six days the mother taught in mission schools, cared for the sick women and received Chinese sisters, but the seventh was a day when she, who never lost the longing for her own home and country, 'rose with a look different from that of the other days on her face'. There was less of purpose and planning and more of peace; over breakfast for many years she expressed a wish that once more she might hear the church bell ringing clear and simply over the giant houses of her home village. In later years she persuaded folks back home to give her a little cheerful church bell which for years tinkled out its brisk tones along the Chinese street – as American a greeting as can be imagined and which often surprised a stately old Chinese gentleman below. For Carie there was nothing so quick and so clear in the whole city as that bell on Sunday and she never failed to smile and cry out 'Now isn't that nice, it sounds like home.' Twice she went to church in the morning in the Chinese chapel and again in the afternoon she joined the small gathering of European women and men who came together to worship the God who had brought them to China. It was at the end of this day that their mother talked most to them about America. When she had sung her heart contented and eased it of its homesickness and quiet, she sat down by the fire, if it was winter, or on the long veranda in the garden in summer and retold her story of herself as a young girl in the America she had known. In doing so she had a gift for anecdote and for descriptions of the physical, the beautiful, the emotions and the hidden, which years later they could recall in almost all her colourful words.

She painted for her children the big beautiful house of her first memories. 'It was a big white house three storeys high,' she would say and a gesture of her hand made them see it so.

There was a deep cool larder underneath where they kept the shallow pans of milk and where they churned. There too on the shelves were the round Dutch cheeses and casks of berry and grape wine. She remembered the berries they gathered in the summer – blackberries, raspberries and elderberries and particularly the red raspberries with a sort of silvery dew on them and the scratches of briars on her bare legs. As she stopped and smiled in the dark or as she sat silent, they saw the little bare-legged girl deep in the berry patch, a sun-bonnet over her head to protect her complexion. They got to know the local families, the days of the pioneers and of the Civil War, and the dreams of the freedom of quiet village streets where disease was absent from the water and the fruits and there were no lepers or crowded alley-ways. Above all it was the snow that captured the children's imagination. They saw the roofs under great snow blankets, windows peering out, cosy and merry from beneath, with smoke curling against the still sky. They saw that the shadows on the snow were blue under the lee of the hills and felt the clean air which crimsoned the cheeks and brightened the eyes of the robust girls and boys of the town who had gathered at the maple sugar camp for the sugaring, tobogganing and games. They wanted to hear time and time again the tale of maple sugar. They learned the whole procedure from collecting and thickening the syrup which after passing into giant kegs was further boiled to just the right moment for pouring the hot stuff into the great round moulds for big cakes of sugar and into the hundreds of little heart-shaped twin tins or into tins crescent- or star-shaped. Best fun to imagine and most delicious of all was to pour the hot syrup out on the snow and eat it suddenly, after cooling and sweeping up the handfuls of snow and stiffening hot sugar. When her children first visited America, they found few surprises; their mother had shown it all to them years before and given them dreams of their own country from 10,000 miles away. But if America was for dreaming about, the world in which the young girl lived was China.

Writing of these early childhood years, Pearl Buck once described how she slipped simultaneously out of one life into another, depending upon the geography of the moment. Her own childhood home had a Chinese side to it. From her earliest years she was tended by a Chinese nurse, Wong Amah, who besides her mother was the one other clear figure of her first memories. She could to her grown days remember the small blue-garbed woman with a brown wrinkled face bending over her and a fairly constant attachment to her hard brown hand, its forefinger roughened with needle pricks from constant sewing for them all. At night when it was suddenly too dark to breathe, she remembered the comfort of her presence and her own insatiable thirst for Wong Amah's seemingly inexhaustible store of old tales of woman, man and gods. These tales included Wong Amah's own life story – the binding of her feet, her girlhood beauty, her marriage bargain, the cruel fate of her husband and parents-in-law at the hands of the Taiping rebels and her own escape and rescue from the clutches of an evil man by Pearl's mother. Wong Amah's gods became Pearl's own gods and she participated in all the forbidden foods and pastimes of the servants who were prone to protect the children from the rules and punishments of their stricter parents. From the servants too she learned of a different cultural tradition:

> In our home our parents taught us to be as mannerly to the servants as we were to guests and elders, and each side maintained its pride. We kept our servants for years and belonged to them and they to us; how many happy childhood hours I spent with them and how lonely might I have been at evening when the gates were locked for the night had I not been free to sit in the servants' court, to play with their babies and listen to the music of a country flute or two-stringed violin. Sometimes our cook would tell us a story from the past because he could read. And he read *The Three Kingdoms, All Men are Brothers, Dream of the Red Chamber* and other classic books he kept in his room.

Pearl Buck learned to speak the language of the servants and her neighbouring Chinese playmates and their families. Close by were all the daughters of her Chinese 'sister' adopted by their mother at the behest of a dying Chinese friend. She married at about the time Pearl was born and bore six daughters in close succession. They were such an embarrassment to her pastor husband that the Christian church even prayed for a son to rescue its religion from association with such a fate! Underneath the big white-washed brick bungalow, were honeycombed haunts, cool and dry in the beaten earth, where the young girl loved to play with her playmates, the daughters and sons of the servants and neighbours. Wonderful, unsupervised play was to be had by the hour there and on the grassy grave mounds of the nearby hillside where they all imagined themselves at the court of the Empress Dowager Tsu Hsi. She was the central figure as familiar to every child as if they had seen her themselves. Did not everybody know how she looked? In games every little girl was proud to represent her and each took for a throne the tussock of one of the tall-pointed earthen graves that dotted the hillside. Just as her Chinese friends referred to the Empress as their venerable ancestor so also Pearl Buck long supposed that she had the same venerable ancestor just as she supposed she was sufficiently Chinese to eat sweets from the Chinese marketplace with impunity and to celebrate the Chinese festivals.

Pearl Buck was fortunate that she had the kind of parents who were one of the few missionary families she knew to welcome Chinese friends to their house and to their table. Instead of the narrow and conventional life of other European children in China, she lived closely associated with Chinese adults, spoke their tongue before she spoke her own and their children were her first friends. Their Chinese neighbours were in and out of the mission homestead, and their laughing curiosity, their unabashed ignorance of Western ways and their pleasure in observing their house, their food and how they dressed were all part of a day's amusement. The adult Pearl however did doubt whether her parents knew just how much she shared in the domestic life of their neighbours. She received instruction alongside her Chinese friends from their Chinese grandmothers in the ways of girlhood, and at one point even wondered whether she should have her own feet bound if she was to get a good husband! She learned the intimate details of the customs, hopes, disappointments and loves in neighbouring Chinese families in whose homes she was free to come and go. With them she celebrated the feast days of the Chinese moon years, each with its particular delicacy to be made and eaten and each with its special toys and delightful occupations. At the Feast of Lanterns, the servants brought the children paper rabbits, lotus flowers or butterflies pulled upon little wheels and lit within by candles. In the spring there were kites to be made in every imaginable shape out of split reeds, rice paste and thin red paper. They spent their days upon the hills catching the huge intricate kites perhaps in the form of a mighty dragon, a thirty-foot centipede or a pagoda that might need a dozen grown men to get it to fly. They played with birds in cages – black macaws, white-vested magpies or nightingales that would talk or sing if they were taught carefully enough. In the company of her friends she listened to the wandering storytellers who beat their little gongs upon the country roads or stopped at night at villages and gathered their crowds upon a threshing floor. They went near and far to see the troupes of travelling actors who performed the plays in front of the temples from which she learned her Chinese history and became familiar with the heroes of all the ages. For young Pearl as for her friends, the Chinese New Year was still the annual highlight with the exchange of gifts and the receiving and making of calls between the mission household and their Chinese friends, everyone dressed in their best and bowing and wishing Happy New Year and riches everywhere they went. On this day alone, it seemed to Pearl Buck that her two childhood worlds came nearest to meeting, for during most of the rest of the year, her parents, despite their liberal attitudes, seldom entered with her into her Chinese world; indeed they remained completely foreign whereas she was not entirely a foreigner either in her own opinion or in the opinion of her Chinese friends.

At the turn of the century in the spring of 1900, Pearl Buck's two childhood worlds unexpectedly split into two. The rising anti-foreign sentiment and the reports of Boxer activities in Beijing meant that the stream of visitors to the mission house thinned, and sometimes days passed without a single Chinese friend appearing before its gate. Pearl Buck later vividly remembered how her playmates often became silent and how they did not play with their usual joy until at last they too ceased to climb the hill from the valley. Even her schoolmates did not clamour to share her desk seat. After years of free play and friendship, the young girl felt first bewildered and then sorely wounded when it was explained to her that though their Chinese friends did not hate them individually, they dared not show their friendship for in this anti-foreign age they would suffer and be blamed. The danger to the lives of the mission women, children and men during the Boxer Rebellion felt very real and immediate, and following reports of murders of missionary families including little children in other provinces and after much discussion within the mission household, Pearl Buck with her mother, brother and sister took temporary refuge in Shanghai and later in America. This trip was to mark the end of a carefree Chinese childhood.

In 1902 a child of ten returned to the mission bungalow on the hills above the Yangtze River; in this new age Europeans were to be allowed to go freely about their business whether it be the education or the saving of souls or the wrenching of further commercial or other concessions from the Chinese. As Pearl Buck passed into her teenage years, she continued to enjoy the freedom of the city streets and the country roads, but she had few companions of her own age either European or Chinese. She was too old to play childhood games, and she was not allowed to run down the hill any more to visit the women and girls in the valley farms. She was getting to the age when she required chaperoning by either her mother or her nurse on all occasions bar visiting the six or seven families the family knew well. She did spend long hours in the nearby family courtyards, playing with the babies, listening to the young wives' gossip and sharing the thoughts of schoolmates. She also learned Chinese philosophical truths from her Chinese tutor, Mr Kung, who visited her home every weekday afternoon when the weather was fine; he would not come on rainy days because his mother forbade it lest he wet his feet and fall ill and being a filial son he did not wish to cause her anxiety. To the young girl there seemed nothing strange in that, even though he was approaching fifty and his mother sixty-five! Thus Mr Kung arrived punctually on fine afternoons at two o'clock carrying his treasure of books wrapped in a soft old piece of black silk. From this he unfolded with due care and reverence the book which they were to read and study for the next two hours. It was from him that Pearl Buck learned her early historical lessons linking past, present and future and of the approaching storm in which 'the Chinese would see that justice was done to the European'. He fervently hoped that in that dangerous time, which must surely come, his pupil would be far away in America where she belonged. The truth was that at this time Pearl Buck's world was no longer intensively Chinese, and she was beginning to feel more American than Chinese. America was not just for dreaming, for she had seen America with her own eyes! The divisions between things Chinese and American or foreign and her own world were becoming more clearly differentiated. She continued however to see America and all things foreign through Chinese eyes although as a child she kept silent about and pondered alone with Mr Kung much of what she learned about America from her Chinese friends. After the swift death of Mr Kung from cholera, Pearl Buck was sent to school, first a local mission school for a few hours a week and later to a girls' mission boarding school in Shanghai and eventually to college in America.

Pearl had originally hoped to go to Wellesley and had taken the examinations for entrance there, but her southern relatives, still haunted by the war between the states, had objected so that a compromise had to be made between a Yankee college and the southern finishing schools against which she rebelled. Eventually a smaller southern college for women, Randolph Mason, was chosen for her because the education there was designed for the male student, and her mother, long suppressed in her own household, was determined that her daughters should have every possible advantage over their future husbands. Her college days were chiefly memorable for the energy with which she threw herself into being wholly American. She had soon ascertained that the Chinese world into which she had been born had no interest for her fellow students. Indeed she often wondered at the fact that her college mates asked not one question about China, not even what the people there ate and how they lived. She decided that unless she was to spend four lonely and unhappy years, she would separate her worlds again and live a full college life and learn to talk about the things American girls talked about, boys and dances and sororities and so on, in proper American slang! Although she knew that within her lay concealed another life, she lost her heart to America.

> The cleanliness which made it safe to drink water unboiled, the freedom from the possibility of dysentery and cholera which made it pleasant to pluck an apple from a tree and eat it stone and all, the abundance of the water to bathe in, the spaces wherein one lived, the miles of fields and lawns and countryside, the colouring of the autumn forests. . .

All these won her heart, but once she received her diploma and, although she really wanted to stay in America, she quickly returned to China as soon as she learned that her mother had been ill with sprue, a slowly fatal disease which increasingly robbed the blood of its red corpuscles and which then no physician knew how to cure let alone to treat. On her return to Chiukiang, she divided her time between caring for her now shrunken and tiny white-headed mother, teaching English in a new boys' school and supervising seventeen to twenty young Chinese women who were being trained for various types of work in other schools. She observed and studied the changes in China, the struggle of Sun Yat-sen, the early reforms, the changes in the lives of her students and friends and listened to the arguments for and against change by the different generations. Nevertheless Pearl Buck felt lonely and especially for friends of her own age. The years in college had separated her from the Chinese girls with whom she had been so close. They were now all married and busy with household affairs, and in true Chinese fashion they constantly worried about her solitary state by suggesting not only to herself but also to her parents that she was of an age for marriage.

In 1917 she did meet a young American agriculturalist John Buck who was also employed by the Presbyterian mission board, and once married they moved to a little old-fashioned town in northern Anwhei province where Pearl enjoyed setting up her four-roomed Chinese-style house of grey brick and black tile. She became head of a girls' school and made many new friends. Indeed she soon discovered that one of the advantages of marriage was the greater freedom it gave her to accept invitations to Chinese homes and as a result she learned about the domestic and social life of northern peasant families. It was a complete change of scene – instead of the green valleys and blue hills beside the wide Yangtze River, the countryside stretched as flat as any desert, broken only by what appeared to be heaps of mud but were actually villages whose houses were built of the pale-coloured earth of the region. In the spring however the whole landscape suddenly grew bright. The bare willow trees around the villages put forth soft green leaves, the wheat turned green in the fields and the blossoms of the fruit trees were rose-coloured and white. Most beautiful of all were the mirages, especially when the earth was still cold but the air was warm, dry and bright so that wherever she looked she could see lakes, trees and hills between her and the horizon. It was in the little northern town that she first felt the beauty of Chinese streets at night. The usual streets of northern Chinese towns were dusty, wide, unpaved and they were lined with low, one-storey buildings of bricks or earth, little shops and industries including blacksmiths, tinsmiths, bakeries, hot-water shops, dried goods and sweetmeat shops. In this old and remote area, the life of the people seemed confined not only geographically but also mentally and spiritually to centuries past. Pearl Buck like visitors today walked the streets gazing unashamedly into open doors where families were gathered around their supper tables lit only by thick candles or a bean-oil lamp. She felt that she recaptured some of the closeness to the Chinese way of life which she had shared as a child.

She helped the local American doctor, whose Chinese was limited, with his night calls and made many new friends. Her neighbours were as intensely curious about her ways as she about theirs and, since her little house was readily accessible, a steady stream of visitors came and went and she was soon pressed with invitations to participate in local birthday feasts, wedding and family affairs. She enjoyed it all and was soon deeply engrossed in the details of the lives of her neighbours. She played with their babies and talked with the young women of her generation; and they told her their problems with their mothers-in-law and in their families. She delighted in their humour and their talk and although without exception none of her new friends knew how to read or write, they had an infinite store of knowledge revealed in family talk between the young and old. She had for immediate friends two very different women although each was at the head of a large household. Madam Chang was a tall and ample figure dressed in a full skirt and knee-length coat, as old-fashioned as any family portrait, with her hair drawn tightly back from her round kind face. Unusually she was both a Buddhist and a Christian. She told Pearl that she had joined the Christian church as a kindness to the stranger foreigners whom she wished to encourage once she saw how good were their works. She was a jolly, kindhearted woman who spent much of her time fulfilling her duty to her dead husband. According to the Buddhist priest her husband needed all her prayers and constant gifts to the temple to rescue him from purgatory. By the time she became a Christian she had rescued all but his left foot which she decided to leave to its fate once the missionaries convinced her that the whole rescue operation was part of an elaborate hoax the only beneficiary of which was the Buddhist temple itself. Madam Wang, in contrast, was a thin, beautiful woman past middle age who ruled her large household with absolute authority. Gossip had it that out of sheer jealousy she had driven to suicide the bride of her favourite eldest son who had apparently had the temerity to fall in love with his own wife. She had purposely arranged for him to marry a girl who was not beautiful so that her own hold over him would not be threatened. It was said that the young husband had not spoken to his mother since his wife had hung herself from a rafter. From women such as these Pearl Buck learned much of the local, ancient and time-honoured customs and manners of gentry households, but she also learned of the ways of the Chinese peasant.

Since her husband was an agriculturalist, Pearl accompanied him on many of his trips to the country, he on his bicycle and she in her sedan chair which was the only way for a woman to travel. Although the sight of her attracted comment and crowds on the country roads and in the remote walled towns where few Europeans ever travelled, she was able to sit and talk with the womenfolk of proud old families who had lived in the same houses for hundreds of years totally untouched by modern times. However, the longer she lived in the northern town, the more deeply impressed she became not by the rich folk but by farmers and their families who lived in villages outside the city walls and in simple comfort upon farms averaging less than five acres. They were the ones who shouldered the vagaries of the weather, earned the least income and who laboured long. They were closest to the earth, to birth and death, to laughter and to weeping. To visit the farm families and 'to search out the reality of their lives' became her primary interest, and she felt richly entertained by the sense of drama which seemed always to surround the least quarrel, a festival or birthday. They provided not only for days of talk and enjoyment in the small town, but also the materials for her later books which were thickly peopled with friends, neighbours and acquaintances drawn into composite portraits each very often displaying the raw humour and even the jollity which was never far from the surface of their lives and not entirely overcome by the occasional and inevitable tragedies.

For as long as she could remember the child Pearl Buck had wanted to be a writer. Her mother had earlier required her to write a weekly essay or story incorporating her experiences and ideas. Years later Pearl Buck could still recall something of the wonder of seeing her first letter published even though it was neither of interest nor worth and was much influenced by her missionary environment. The letter was entitled 'Our Real Home and Heaven' and was printed by the *Kentucky Christian Observer*. Dated 5 April 1899 it read:

> Dear Mr Combers,
> I am a little girl six years old. I live in China. I have a big brother in college who is coming to China to help our father tell the Chinese about Jesus. I have two little brothers in heaven. Maudy went first, then Artie, then Edith and then on the 10th of last month my brave little brother Clyde left us to go to our real home in heaven. Clyde said he was a Christian soldier and that heaven was as best as home. Clyde was four years old and we both loved the little letters in the *Observer*. I wrote this all by myself and my hand is tired so good-bye.

Here it is interesting for the perhaps Chinese-derived emphasis on brothers rather than sisters and on heaven as her third world where her brothers and sisters, kept alive by her mother's memories, resided. This early success, for such it seemed, made her willing if not always eager to follow her mother's suggestions and write regularly for the *Shanghai Mercury*; the monthly prizes offered for the best stories and contributions by children became a source of regular pocket money for her by the time she was ten years old. Throughout her school and student days, Pearl Buck continued to write short essays and stories about China which won her school, college and university prizes and money enough to supplement her meagre allowance. It was not until her husband moved to Nanking however to take up a lecturing position at the university there, that she began to write more seriously and even then her writing career was at first constantly interrupted by events both within her family and in China.

First her daughter was born and the young mother fully enjoyed the early years of this apparently whole, beautiful and intelligent child little realising the bleak future in store for both of them. Six months later came the death of her beloved mother Carie which filled her with the need to keep the memory of her mother alive for herself and her own children who would otherwise have no memories of her. It was for them that she wrote a biography of her mother which she then boxed, sealed and placed in a high wall closet to await the time when they were old enough to read it for themselves. Little did she know that hidden as it was, it would be one of her only possessions that would survive the ransacking of her house a few years later and that the portrait of her mother so carefully and faithfully made up of exact memories would be later published and would help to earn her the Nobel Prize. At the time of its completion, she found that more than anything else she wanted to keep on writing. In the siesta hour each day she wrote a series of essays portraying the turmoil that was the China in which she was living. She was devastated to learn that her small daughter was to be forever without speech or comprehension. At the same time she was caring for her widowed and somewhat dependent father as well as an increasingly estranged husband who was without a settled interest of his own. She also taught English to university students who were at once disillusioned and perplexed by the turbulent events around them. Her busy life was interrupted in 1927 by the same violence in Nanking from which Alice Tisdale Hobart fled. Pearl Buck and her family were hidden for the better part of a terrifying day by faithful servants and were then evacuated to Shanghai. After some travelling in Japan and the United States, the family returned to Nanking where Pearl Buck resumed the writing which was soon to make her world famous.

Out of two of her previous articles and stories, Pearl Buck fashioned her first manuscript which she entitled *East Wind, West Wind*. Her friendship with the students in her classes and her sympathy for those who had studied abroad caused her to feel deeply for the young Western-educated and -oriented youth who were both idealistic and patriotic in their hopes for China's future. Educated in Western universities or mission and modern schools in China, however, they had little or no acquaintance with Chinese philosophy or history. She felt that consequently they belonged neither to the East nor the West and that they were bound to be disillusioned, for dedicated as they were to the improvement of their own country, they had themselves lost touch with the wisdom of their people and with their families.

In her novel she represented the conflicts within those caught between the present and the past and between two cultures by writing a story about a young Chinese girl trained for marriage according to long-established Chinese conventions only to find that her husband, who had been educated abroad, disagreed with and disparaged these customs. Gradually and gently her husband encourages her to convert custom into the companionship which he perceives to be the hallmark of a European marriage. Pearl Buck depicts the pains of the young wife as she first adjusts to her husband's ways and then as she in turn experiences her mother's pain when her own brother returns from abroad with an American wife. From her own experience, the young Chinese wife can appreciate the value which her brother places on his relationship with his foreign wife and can sympathise with his intolerable position within the family household. At the same time she can understand and value her mother's feelings of betrayal at the rejection of her wishes and traditions which in the end both threaten the marriage of her brother and her mother's own life. The book is unusual in that it was written by Pearl Buck in the first person as if she were the young Chinese wife and she relates intimately the thoughts of a young Chinese woman experiencing a common dilemma of the times. Already the book, slender as it was, contained the recognised hallmarks of her later writings – an engaging human story and an observant eye for absorbing detail.

The book was published by the John Day Company and unbeknown to the author, Richard Walsh, the president of the company (who was to become her second husband), cast the vote in favour of publishing her manuscript. He believed he saw evidence of a writer who 'might continue to grow'. Even he could have had no idea that Pearl Buck's next book would be at the top of best-seller lists for twenty-two months, be translated into almost every language, win both the Pulitzer and Nobel Prizes and for millions of readers provide their first acquaintance with Chinese peasant life. Pearl Buck embarked on this major novel on her return to Nanking after a brief sojourn in the United States during which *East Wind, West Wind* had been accepted for publication and she had settled her daughter Carol into a carefully selected, progressive but expensive training school for retarded children in New Jersey. Despite friends and family, the house in Nanking suddenly had seemed empty without her little elder daughter and she needed to earn some money to meet the expenses which her daughter's care demanded. This she decided was the time to begin to write:

> So one morning I put my attic room in order and faced my big Chinese desk to the mountains, and there each morning when the household was in running order for the day I set myself down to my typewriter and began to write 'The Good Earth'. My story had long been clear in my mind. Indeed, it had shaped itself firmly and swiftly from the events of my life, and its energy was the anger I felt for the sake of the peasants and the common folk of China, whom I loved and admired and still do. For the scene of my book I chose the north country, and for the rich southern city, Nanking. My material was therefore close at hand, and the people I knew as I knew myself.

She wrote *The Good Earth* in three months, and without anyone knowing tied up the finished manuscript, mailed it off to her publisher in New York and prepared herself for a long wait. At times during the writing, she had felt very doubtful about the value of the manuscript but what had kept her going was her keen awareness of the Chinese peasants who constituted some 85 per cent of China's population and undertook most of the country's burdens and toil and yet had no literary voice of their own. She wanted to portray for others the qualities of the Chinese peasant. At the same time as her husband was undertaking some of the most comprehensive surveys of the farm economy in rural China, Pearl Buck set herself to recount in fictional form that which normally remained unsurveyed and undocumented.

The story of *The Good Earth* revolved around the farmer Wang Lung who with his wife O-lan moves in timeless rhythms between home and fields in a constant round of sowing, tilling and harvesting, periodically but only briefly interrupted by climatic vagaries and the births, marriages and deaths of the individual members of the household as they pass through their life cycles. The novel opens with the marriage of the farmer Wang Lung to the former slave-girl O-lan, and anyone familiar with the conventional three-roomed Chinese house will immediately recognise the lay-out, arrangement of furniture and morning routine of the Chinese homes of their acquaintances:

> The house was still except for the faint, gasping cough of his old father whose room was opposite to his own across the middle room. . .He went into the shed which was the kitchen, leaning against the house and out of its dusk an ox twisted its head from behind the corner next to the door and lowed at him deeply. The kitchen was made of earthen bricks as the house was; great squares of earth dug from their own fields and thatched with straw from their own wheat. Out of their own earth had his grandfather fashioned also the oven, baked and black with many years of meal preparing. On top of this earthen structure stood a deep, round, iron cauldron.
>
> The cauldron he filled partly with water, dipping it with a half-gourd from an earthen jar that stood near, but he dipped cautiously, for water was precious. . .He went around the oven to the rear, and selecting a handful of dry grass and stalks standing in the corner of the kitchen, he arranged it delicately in the mouth of the oven, making the most of every leaf. Then from an old flinted iron he caught a flame and thrust it into the stove and there was a blaze. He had lit the fire, boiled water and poured the water into a bowl. . .Now father and son could rest. There was a woman coming to the house.

The book authentically and intimately describes the small details of daily life which Pearl Buck writes into the story in order to incorporate the reader directly into the world of the Chinese peasant. Thus the reader learns how to light the fire daily, heat the water, prepare food, sweep the earthen floor, replenish the fuel pile and gather manure for the fields; how O-lan took a bamboo rake and a length of rope to roam the countryside, reap here a bit of grass and there a twig or a handful of leaves, so that she might return at noon with enough fuel to cook the dinner; how with a hoe and a basket upon her shoulder she went to the main road where she picked up the droppings from the animals, carried them home and piled the manure in the dooryard for fertiliser in the fields; how she mended their ragged clothes with thread which she herself had spun on a bamboo spindle from a wad of cotton; how she shaped and sewed wads of paper into shoes; how she took the bedding into the sun on a threshold and ripped the coverings from the quilts and washed them and hung them upon a bamboo to dry and how she picked over the cotton in the quilts that had grown hard and grey from years, killing the vermin that flourished in the hidden folds and sunned it all as households continue to do today. When not occupied in the house O-lan helped Wang Lung in the fields where he worked as he had always worked, with his hoe upon his shoulder. He walked to his plots of land where husband and wife cultivated the rows of grain or yoked the ox to the plough.

In the first good years there was plenty and their three-roomed house was bursting. From the rafters of the thatched roofs hung strings of dried onions and garlic and on the eastern floors were mats of reeds twisted into the shapes of great jars full of rice or wheat. Much of this would be sold but not until the time was right for a high price, and from the rafters too there hung even a large leg of pork as well as two of their own chickens dried with the feathers on and stuffed inside with salt. In the midst of all this plenty, a son was born and on his month birthday they had a feast of noodles which meant long life and to each guest who had come to congratulate them, two red eggs were given which had been boiled and dyed. From the produce of the first good year, Wang Lung accumulated a handful of silver dollars which, in a small hole in the inner wall of their room behind the bed, gave both Wang Lung and O-lan a sense of sweet richness as the New Year approached. As the Wang household prepared for the annual celebration, Wang Lung went into town to the candlemaker's shop where he bought squares of red paper brushed in gilt ink with the character for 'happiness' or 'riches'. These squares he pasted upon his farm utensils, including his plough, the ox's yoke and upon the two buckets in which he carried his fertilisers and his water. On the doors he pasted long strips of red paper brushed with good luck sayings and out of the bought red paper he had his old father, despite his shaking hands, cleverly fashion new dresses for the two small gods housed in the temple of the earth; before them he burned a little incense and set two red candles to burn on the eve of the New Year. To celebrate a good year, O-lan and Wang Lung kneaded the specially purchased pork fat and smooth white sugar with their own milled rice flour into rich New Year moon cakes.

Unfortunately not all years were good. For Wang Lung's family and for countless others the earth periodically failed them and on one occasion after years of fortune, it seemed as if the gods had indefinitely turned against man. The rains that should have come in early summer withheld themselves so that day after day the sun shone with fierce and careless brilliance. The hopeful but increasingly desperate Wang Lung continued to cultivate the parched and starving earth, but without water it dried and cracked and the young wheat stalks now ceased their growing and stood motionless, dwindled and yellowed into a barren harvest. Wang Lung carried water to the young rice beds day after day in heavy wooden buckets slung upon a bamboo pole across his shoulders until the day came when even the water in the well was too low. From his fields the peasant farmer reaped a scanty harvest of hardy beans, and from his corn field he plucked short and stubby ears with grains scattered here and there not a bit of which was to be lost in the threshing. Corn cobs were stored, not for burning as in ordinary times but for grinding and eating since they tasted better than grass.

There was a sense of foreboding in these strange brilliant days when the land was failing them, when the ox was reluctantly eaten and when, foraging completed, there was nothing left in the house or on the land for food. The streets and yards were deserted for nobody moved unnecessarily. They agonised whether to stay put and starve or move out of home and village to another if not more uncertain fate; who to sell and who to keep; and finally who to let live and who to let die. Wang Lung refused to sell his daughter whose skeleton-like body and damaged mind broke his heart, but when O-lan again gave birth and there was no second cry, Wang Lung knew she had done what she had to do. He himself took the handful of the girl baby – a wisp of bone and skin, laid her upon the earthen floor and searched until he found a broken mat to wrap about her. Going as far from the house as he had strength, he laid the burden against the hollow side of an old grave, knowing that the dogs would come. Wang Lung felt his legs sinking beneath him and covering his face with his hands he went away muttering to himself that it was better for the child that way. There came a time when there was nothing but to pull the door tight upon its wooden hinges and fasten the iron hasp. All their clothes they had upon them and into each child's hands O-lan had thrust a rice bowl and a pair of chopsticks and thus they started across the fields in a small dreary procession which by some miracle reached a strange southern city, where from a hut of mats backing on to the city wall they eked out a daily living.

There in the city there was food everywhere displayed in the various markets that still survive today. The cobbled streets of the fishmarket were lined with great baskets of big silver fish caught the night before out of the teeming river, with tubs of small shining fish dipped out of a net cast over a pool; with heaps of yellow crabs, squirming and nipping in peevish astonishment; the writhing eels for gourmands at the feasts. At the colourful grain market, there were such baskets of grain that a man might step into them and sink and smother and none know it who did not see it; white rice and brown, and dark yellow wheat and pale golden wheat and yellow soy beans and red beans and green broad beans and canary-coloured millet and grey sesame. And at the less aesthetic meat market, whole hogs hung by their necks, and in duck shops hung, row upon row, over the ceilings and in the doors, the brown baked ducks that had been turning slowly on a spit before coals, the white salted ducks and strings of duck giblets. As for the vegetables there was everything which the hand of man could coax from the soil: glittering red radishes and white, hollow lotus roots and taro, green cabbages and celery, curling bean sprouts and brown chestnuts and garnishes of fragrant cress. On the streets were the vendors of sweets and fruits and nuts and of hot delicacies of sweet potatoes wrapped in sweet oils, little delicately spiced balls of pork wrapped in dough and steam and sugar cakes made from glutinous rice. It seemed then as it does today that there was nothing which the appetite might desire that was not to be found upon the streets and markets of that city. Yet with all Wang Lung's pulling or running before his rickshaw and with all O-lan's begging, they could never earn enough to cook rice daily in their own hut. If there were a penny over and above the rice gruel provided by the public kitchens for the poor, they bought a bit of cabbage. But the cabbage was dear at any price, for the two boys must hunt for fuel to cook it between the two bricks that O-lan had set up for a stove, and this fuel they had to thieve from the farmers who carried the loads of reeds and grass into the city fuel markets. So life in the city, precarious at the best of times, might have continued indefinitely but for a piece of good fortune and the land waiting back home for the family to return to.

Riches they were determined to have so that never again would they have to flee from the land. Wang Lung set himself to build his fortune so securely to last them through the bad years which must surely come again. After a fortunate succession of good harvests, he added to his lands, hired a labourer each year until he had six men and built a new house covered with tiles. The walls were still made of hard packed earth from the fields, only now he has them brushed with lime and they were white and clean. In the new house, he would not now allow his wife O-lan to work in the fields, for he was no longer poor, but a man who could hire labour if he would. Then O-lan worked in the house making new clothes and coverings of flowered cloths stuffed with warm new cotton for every bed. She gave birth to more sons. After the fifth year, Wang Lung himself worked little in the fields for so increased were his lands that he had to spend the whole time upon the business and marketing of his produce and supervising his workmen. Greatly hampered and sorely humbled by his lack of book knowledge he took his elder sons from the fields so that they might go to school. Having thus settled his affairs Wang Lung and his family systematically acquired many of the accoutrements of the upwardly mobile – leisure, tea to drink, food to eat and silver stores aplenty. The leisured and wealthy Wang Lung had been filled with restlessness which his large-featured and unkempt wife of many years could no longer satisfy. To his new eyes her hair now seemed rough and brown and unoiled, her face, feet and hands coarse-skinned and flat and spreading and her eyebrows scattered and hairs too few.

It was not long before Wang Lung was seduced by the hidden joys in the upstairs chambers of the local teahouse and in particular by one small and slender Lotus. In the tradition of a prosperous man 'who need not drink from the one cup', he brought her to his house and built for her a new courtyard to make her his own. The two women took their place in his house, Lotus for his joy and his pleasure and to satisfy his delight in beauty and smallness, and O-lan for his woman of work and the mother who had borne his sons and who kept his house and fed him, his father and his children. And it was a pride to Wang Lung in the village that men mentioned with envy the woman in his inner court; it was as if they spoke of a rare jewel or an expensive toy that was a sign or a symbol that the man had passed beyond the necessity of caring only to be fed and clothed and could spend his money on joy if he wished.

The rich Wang Lung was also however encompassed by troubles. His poor but lazy and unlikeable uncle and his

family came to live in his household and the obligations of
kin and his uncle's connections with local bandits obliged
him to share his riches with them although it angered him
to do so. His sons, restless, leisured and ambitious for new
experiences, had to be settled in occupations and suitable
marriages arranged. His wife, tired and worn out, died a slow
and painful death, and his ambitious sons persuaded him, in
the style befitting a landlord, to establish a house in the town
which soon expanded to include sons, sons' wives, grandsons,
concubines and servants. Feast days, birthdays and marriages
were celebrated with the splendour befitting a large and rich
household but his sons and sons' wives quarrelled bitterly and
disruptively over the allocation of family resources. Eventually
old and tired, Wang Lung gradually returned to the land where
he had toiled and on which his ancestors had toiled and from
which the riches had come. It is the land, the good earth,
which lies at the centre of the endless cycles in life as in
death. The family graves were a symbol of the roots and a
sign of the establishment of his family upon their own land.
At the close of the novel it is Wang Lung alone of the family
who does not lose touch with the earth, remembering as he
does the debt of the poor peasant to his land which is the most
permanent fruit of his own toil and that of his ancestors, and it
is to the old earthen house and the fields that Wang Lung chose
to return and, contented, he awaits his own death comforted
by the daily sight of his carved coffin hewn from a great log of
particularly fragrant wood. He would have had little comfort
if he had known the full extent of his sons' plans to sell the
land in favour of expanding their own town and commercial
pursuits. Even the merest whisper, accidentally overheard,
that the family land might be sold reduced the old man to
a trembling anger:

'It is the end of a family – when they begin to sell
the land,' he said brokenly. 'Out of the land we
come and into it we must go – and if you can
hold your land you can live – no one can rob
you of land. . .if you sell the land, it is the end.'

The novel ends with the two sons, the elder and the second son each holding the old man's arm and reassuring him that the land would not be sold. But over the old man's head the sons look at each other and smile.

The Good Earth documents in fictional form the classic cycles of peasant mobility as households move upwards or downwards in wealth, size and status. It is sometimes sentimental, sometimes overtly dramatic, but the book does paint a detailed, intimate and authentic portrait of region and family, presents strongly-drawn individual characters engaged in human relationships of production and reproduction which the reader can appreciate and enjoy. For its combination of ethnography and soul, the book was justly celebrated in its time. *The Good Earth* was published in 1931 and when the first copy reached Pearl Buck in far China, she 'felt very shy about it since nobody knew of its being or knowing had forgotten it'. She showed it to her elderly father who felt unable to undertake such a long read. The first letter she received from a reader in the United States was from a member of a mission board who sent her several pages of blistering rebuke because she had been so 'frank about human life'. The book was chosen for distribution by the Book of the Month Club and reviewed by Will Rogers, an influential critic of the *New York Times* who recommended that readers go out and get 'not only the greatest book about a people ever written, but the best book of our generation'. Not until then did it become known and talked about. It then won the Pulitzer Prize and sales soared as millions did go out and buy it. It did not win universal praise and on its publication criticism came chiefly from two sources. The first was from Chinese intellectuals in both the United States and China who felt that although peasants formed the majority of the Chinese population they were not representative of the Chinese people and that *The Good Earth* gave a 'common view' of China rather than of the great literary and cultural tradition of Chinese intellectuals. The second complaint was from Christian missions who objected to the 'earthiness' of the book with its frank descriptions of natural bodily functions. They had it withdrawn from the reading lists of some high schools and junior colleges – a factor which only too often helped to increase its sales!

In the midst of much acclaim and some criticism, Pearl Buck continued to write novels, translate Chinese novels and write biographies during the next few years, first in Nanking and then in America where she moved permanently in 1935. She had conceived the idea of a series of novels, each of which would reveal some fundamental aspect of Chinese life. Two of these novels, *Sons* and *A House Divided*, were sequels to *The Good Earth* and continued to feature the story of Wang Lung and his descendants. In one of them, *Sons*, she decided to focus on the warlord, a figure central to an understanding of political events in China at that time, and in another, *The Mother*, she portrayed the life of a Chinese peasant woman whose perceptions and fulfilment were limited by her experience and understanding of these events around her. During these very productive years Pearl Buck divided her workdays into two. The mornings when she created her stories, novellas and novels and the afternoons when she set about researching and translating the great classics. She translated the much-read and recited novel of ancient China *Shui Hu Chang* which is known in English as *The Water Margin*. After four years of work she completed and published it under the title *All Men are Brothers*. After her return to America and needing time and money to settle into her new life, she brought out and published the biography of her mother which she had written years ago. She called it appropriately *The Exile* and also wrote a companion biography of her father called *Fighting Angel*. Both biographies attracted much critical acclaim as 'tender and moving', 'gripping in interest' and written in a style which 'beautifully documented one man's and one woman's story and their mastery of circumstances'. Several critics thought that *The Exile* was better than or at least of the same quality as *The Good Earth*. In addition to the Pulitzer prize she received many additional honours: the Howell Gold Medal awarded by the American Academy of Arts and Letters, and the Nobel Prize for Literature. The latter was awarded her in 1938 for all her literary works and not just *The Good Earth* as is often thought. Indeed several of the judges said at the time that the quality of the biographies of her parents was a significant factor in awarding her the much-coveted prize.

In all the awards heaped upon her for *The Good Earth*, it is clear that it is for her role as one of the first popular interpreters of China, its land and its people that she was primarily acclaimed. She was awarded the Howell Gold Medal for literature for writing:

> a veracious picture of agricultural life in China worked out with distinguished skill and fidelity. In terms of human drama it gave the intelligent world a far better understanding of the common man in China than it ever had before.

Again at the award of the Nobel Prize, a prominent theme in the ceremonial speeches was the recognition of her understanding of China and the Chinese people and the world-wide importance of her role in contributing to Western understanding of Chinese customs and problems. It was for her interpretation of the nature and being of China to Europe and America – at a time when it seemed to be of the utmost importance that the two cultures, nations and peoples understood each other – that she was most often celebrated, although the number of buyers and readers of her novels is also a testimony to her story-telling capacities and powerful imagery. Years later a scholarly study of the images of Asia held by Americans concluded that it was Pearl Buck who had single-handedly and for a whole generation created a new image of China, and of the Chinese peasant rooted in the soil and sharing in the universal experience of mating, parenthood, suffering, devotion, weakness and aspirations. The study concluded that Pearl Buck's achievement was to create the first named Chinese daughters, wives, mothers and grandmothers, sons, husbands, fathers and grandfathers in all literature about China with whom Americans were able to identify, understand and relate one to another. As with earlier fantasy images, this new noble image of the tall, stoic land-loving peasant withstanding hardship with humour and heroism also in turn furnished a new stereotype of China.

Pearl Buck went on to write another fifty books and to lead a very active public life which combined two of her major interests. The first, more public and political, was with the relations between cultures and furthering the mutual understanding between East and West; the second, more private and personal, was with the relations between female and male and furthering the mutual understanding between women and men. These two interests were shared by each of the six women authors in this study and are central to an understanding and appreciation of their lives and writings.

8

A Dual Life:
East Woman,
West Woman

In their books, the women writers commonly desired to present China and especially its hitherto hidden domestic and social dimensions to a European audience in order to add to both their knowledge of and interest in another culture. While the China presented by each of the women writers was still mediated through European eyes, eyes which frequently had unusual but still limited opportunities for observation, they all depicted and explained the role of the Chinese woman within and outside of her home and in her relations with men. Moreover their own experience within and outside of their own homes in China caused them to reflect on their own position as European women, wives and writers.

In writing of these major interests it was Pearl Buck who developed the themes to their full and who became the most influential writer with the widest readership. Of all the women writers who have attempted to depict and interpret the Chinese for Europeans, none have done so with more effect than she who almost single-handedly created the new image which was to govern European stereotypes of China for several decades. Unlike the other writers, she felt able to speak and write from a Chinese point of view because though by birth and ancestry American, she felt that by the years of her life and by sympathy and feeling, she was Chinese. Her 'Chinese' point of view had been imbibed as a child from her parents, her Chinese tutor, Chinese neighbours and playmates and developed thereafter as her own. Even when anti-foreign sentiment directly threatened her family, she had heard her parents sympathising with the rightness of the Chinese cause in the face of a blatant foreign scrabble for land, commercial and railway concessions and huge cash indemnities. In her autobiography she has claimed that even as a child she felt the burden of the history of the whole of the 'white' person's behaviour towards the Chinese and China. As a young girl she herself had often been troubled as she had watched the slender, sweating, half-naked Chinese coolies labouring over the heavy loads at the side of the foreign ships at the river's edge. She was uncomfortable at the quarrels, which the coolies inevitably lost, over the deficiencies between the tally sticks they carried in their free hands and the records of the Englishman sitting in his comfortable chair under the shade of an umbrella. When, understanding more Chinese than the Englishman, and witnessing the manipulations of his interpreter, she had tried to intervene, it had been to no avail and the small American girl had often been told in no uncertain terms to mind her own business. To the end of her time in China she was aware of the superiority which most Europeans felt towards the Chinese people 'though they be guests upon the Chinese soil, not rulers and not even citizens!' She was also aware of the rebellion and anger in Chinese hearts at this ever-present European arrogance and dominance. For this daughter of a missionary home, the tension and conflict between Europe and China was nowhere more evident than in the person and message of the foreign missionary.

Although most of the women writers had portrayed missionaries and discussed the missionary cause in their books, Pearl Buck uniquely had a first-hand experience as an observant child within a missionary household which gave her early insights into mission life, its motivations and experience. Even within her own home and much respected and beloved as her parents were, she experienced some resentment and misgivings. Her father's burning mission to save souls took him away from home for long periods and when he was at home he spent much time locked away in his study to pursue his lifetime's project of translating the New Testament into the simple vernacular Chinese language so that it might be read more widely. For long periods he withdrew yet further from their world, spending days and nights in his inviolable study. The children could hear both the strange music of Greek as he read aloud the text and the chanting intonations of the Chinese. Slowly, very slowly, the heaps of pages in Greek interlined with Chinese characters written in his large script grew upon the table under the Buddha paperweight that one of his converts had once worshipped, renounced and given to him. Ironically it now stood holding together the Christian scriptures. The years of translating and polishing each book cost the family dearly for it was all paid for by pinching, scraping and begging. Certainly much of the housekeeping was spirited away to augment the father's New Testament fund and there was some tension between the father who thought that food and clothes ought not to cost anything and the mother who unbeknown to her husband made miracles out of pennies. To the children of the family, this work took on, as the years passed, the aspect of a giant inexorable force which swallowed their toys, their few pleasures and their small desires into its being and left them very little for their own.

Within her immediate neighbourhood, the young Pearl experienced some conflict between her missionary parents and her Chinese playmates. So as not to hurt her parents she revealed only years later how much she would have liked to invite her Chinese friends to her home so that they could see for themselves how kindly were her parents and how tender-hearted her little sister. It was not that her friends would not have been welcome – indeed her parents' home was one of the few mission households where Chinese families could come and go – but she did not want them preached at. She understood the deep burden on her father's soul, the duty that he felt to preach the love of God and his yearning to save, as he said, the precious heathen souls. While she did not blame her father, she could not cast her friends into that 'white fire of his own spirit'. Moreover would not her friends distrust her if she had them preached at? Naturally courteous, they would not have refused to hear him but would they not say that she had used friendship to win them to a foreign god? She could not risk it and so for years she had many Chinese friends whom she took good care to keep away from her parents not only because she thought it right, but also because quite selfishly she could not risk the doubt. Out of these childish discomforts were borne grave doubts as to whether there was a case for foreign missionaries in China.

She had early appraised and found wanting the missionary message and the quality of the persons who had brought the message to China. She distinguished two types of message. The one which had the Christian religion as the only true path to salvation so that all those who refused to believe would and must descend into hell. This not only lent a sense of urgency to mission goals but also ignored the centuries-old systems of latticed beliefs, explanations and rituals which were already punctiliously observed in Chinese households. The affrontery of this firm message made the young Pearl's own soul shrink. Others more gentle, her own father included, avoided all mention of hell-fire and dwelt only on the love of God for all men, which surpassed the love of man. Knowing what Europeans had done in China, the young Pearl was only too aware of a certain incongruity between the Christian message and their countries' record in China. She early surmised that the missionaries had come to China to claim the superiority of their God and the advantages of their religion not so much because they understood the needs of China and the Chinese but to fulfil some spiritual need of their own.

While her own memories of the half-dozen or so soberly-dressed local missionaries who gathered to meet and worship with her parents were grim and invited ridicule, she came to understand the 'impossibilities to which their human souls were stretched'. In writing the biography of her father Pearl Buck noted that:

> The real story of life in a mission station has never yet been told. When it is told, it must be told, if it is to be told truthfully, with such vast understanding and tenderness and ruthlessness that perhaps it can never be done justly.

She thought that the task missionaries had set for themselves as individuals and small groups so daunting that it generated passions both outside and from within the mission station. To survive these passions the missionaries had to be strong, daring and assailed by no doubts as to the rightness of their case. They could only then carry through their vocation to go forth, to save souls from dying and in ignorance of the Christian God and the way of salvation. It was with a terrible urgency that those who felt the responsibility of saving souls laid their vast plans and drew up campaigns over hundreds of thousands of miles so that China was divided, and even within regions certain areas were allotted to different denominations for 'saving'. There was supposed to be no overlapping, but even her own father was a 'born overstepper' largely because he did what God pleased rather than any man which, according to his daughter, usually meant pleasing himself. Her childhood memories were of missionaries of different denominations quarrelling among themselves in the search for converts to satisfy their mission boards back home and their single-minded sense of purpose. Later she thought that the difficulties of the task they had set for themselves and the cultural isolation and exile of 'their calling' made 'little men' of them. In a particularly perceptive description of the person of the missionary she wrote:

In his own country he had a thousand aids to his spirit. He had fellowship with his own kind of a better, bigger sort, he had contact with a life he understood and appreciated, he had access to libraries and books. But the foreign setting drove him in upon himself and dwarfed him. There were no such sources of intellectual and spiritual food, of the kind to which he was accustomed, and his own springs were too meager. Their resources were soon gone and he was not able enough in the foreign language and not perceptive enough in spirit to find those other springs in another civilisation. He grew empty, therefore, more narrow; less sympathetic, more impatient as his inner resources died. He lived more on formulae. His determination remained but his little power was gone. The vast people, the age-old history, the fathomless difference of race, even the enormous opportunity combined with apparent lack of his own success, dwarfed him. He presented and presents in many cases the spectacle of a tiny human figure standing among tremendous cliffs and bottomless valleys strange to him. He is lost. It is not to be wondered at that he clings jealously to his little idea of God, fearing lest he lose it, fearing to see if it be true knowledge or not. He shouts the name of God aloud over and over, lest it lose reality for him.

The difficulties which the individual missionary faced were matched by the human passions generated within the mission station where she thought the drama potentially quite horrifying. Imagine, she wrote,

that two, four, five, six – rarely more – white men and women, some married to each other, the others starved without the compensation of being consecrated to celibacy. Imagine them being brought together, hit or miss, without regard to natural congeniality of any sort, in a town or city of interior China, living together for hours on end without relief, in the enforced intimacy of a mission compound, compelled to work together, and unable, for the narrowness of their mental and spiritual outlook, to find escape and relief in the civilization around them. Within these compound walls was their whole real world. Their real companionships are with each other, or else they lived entirely alone. They seldom become proficient enough in the language to enjoy Chinese society or literature, even if their prejudice did forbid it. There they are, struggling to maintain standards of Christian brotherhood, struggling against their own natural antipathies and desires, wasting their spirits in an attempt to be reconciled to that which is irreconcilable among them.

She knew there were all sorts of human foibles, tragedies and comedies which were hushed and kept secret from fellow missionaries and the mission board back home. That was not all that was kept back. Pearl Buck thought that American churches and Christians were quite unaware how little influence missions had in China and how few converts had been won to the Christian cause. While missionaries had a voice and sent their reports back home, nobody had given the Chinese point of view and reactions to the person and message of the foreign missionary. This she took it upon herself to provide.

In 1932 on one of her trips to America, the Woman's Committee of the Presbyterian Board of Foreign Missions invited the newly-famous author Pearl Buck to report on the work of missions in China and arranged several hundred speeches for her all over the United States. She consented instead to talk to a group of mission leaders to make some suggestions as to how to improve their mission in China. Her speech, subsequently published in *Harpers Magazine* with the title 'Is there a case for foreign missions?' received much publicity and caused something of a furore in mission circles not least among her own, from which, although she was but a teacher, she was subsequently dismissed.

In the speech she gave voice to the Chinese point of view of foreign missions – a mixture of criticism and compassion. She outlined for her audience the main reasons why there had grown up among younger women and men in China a grave feeling against missions, 'a feeling that was not always prejudice although it was sometimes so'. Rather it was based on the narrow and superstitious form of religion which these young Chinese were loath to see fastened upon the Chinese people even though it was accompanied by a few hospitals and schools, some flood relief and some good works. Whilst a few would object to any form of religion, most did not and did not necessarily wish to see the abandonment of missionary enterprises from which China could benefit. The young Chinese thought that the present missionary was of the wrong type. Did not the case for the proselytising missionary very much rest on the universal right of all souls to hear the gospel and thus have the chance of salvation from hell?

Pearl Buck argued that this was a somewhat strange cause to the Chinese, and even to present-day Europeans, and that it took little or no account of Chinese needs and interests.

Pearl Buck thought that unlike the American missions in China which had had every opportunity to put their point of view to their own people back home, Americans should also know the limitations of the missions. They should accept that, despite the investment in lives, buildings and written materials, Christians were few in China largely because the messenger and the message had been more suited to the artificial needs of a mission station or missionary board than to the real needs of the Chinese people:

> Is it honest to run a hospital in order to inveigle people in to hear a gospel on the pretence of heal- ing, or that agricultural work could be of use to the missions only as a sort of bait to entice people into being preached to and joining the church? Or take the case, easily multiplied, of a small interior mission station in a famine-ridden and poverty-stricken district where the people were in need of the neces- sities of life, where the wealthy American church sponsor, rather than meeting the scores of needs of the famine-ridden little town had an enormous and expensive church built which was not only a monument to absurdity, but was so expensive that the handful of church members could not even pay for repairs to it.

Instead Pearl Buck, reflecting the views expressed to her many times in China, would like to see every missionary sent to satisfy the practical and special needs of a community and not the artificial need of a mission station, mission board or clerical woman or man evangelist. Furthermore she wanted to feel that in satisfying this need, the missionaries were fulfilling the primary need of their religions and that by the example of their lives they would attract others to their creed and cause. This she thought would change the whole basis of foreign missions in that it would shift the emphasis from preaching to a people to sharing a life with them. What might be achieved thereby would be the removal of the insufferable stigma of moral arrogance and the discrepancy between the preached message and the practical behaviour of the messenger. Pearl Buck concluded her speech giving a voice to the views of the recipients with a plea to consider their needs rather than the desires of the missionaries:

> Let us simply realise that the basic lack of success in spreading the spirit of Christianity has been because neither the messenger nor the message was suited to the needs of the people. The truth is we have never considered the people. . .

After the public furore immediately following the publication of her speech died down, she continued to be accused of prejudice against Protestant missionaries. She maintained for the rest of her life that far from being prejudiced she had both 'a profound pity and tenderness for these self-chosen exiles from their own country', and 'an understanding of the fury that lived in Chinese hearts'. Even in moments of extreme danger when only the mud walls of a Chinese peasant hut separated her from a vengeful, anti-foreign mob, she thought that the motivations and behaviour of most foreigners in China were such that this response was justified. By the time she left China for permanent residence in the United States in 1935, she thought that there could be no mediating role in China for foreigners who could or would not recognise the 'fury that lived in Chinese hearts'. Indeed one advantage of her final departure from the country in which she had lived most of her life was the release from the terrible burden and guilt which the superiority and arrogant behaviour of the foreigners in China had laid upon her from childhood. Freed from this burden, she continued in America to work harder than ever before to further the mutual understanding and appreciation between European and Chinese persons and their countries.

In America, in her numerous fiction and non-fiction works, in her correspondence, in her speeches and in the organisations which she founded, she provided channels for information and understanding between persons of different cultures. She continued to write into her many novels themes which made for greater understanding of China by Americans and of East by West, a cause made all the more urgent by the Second World War. In her novel *The Dragon Seed*, she wanted to draw attention to the forgotten war front in China and the demands of war on the courage of the ordinary Chinese peasants. She wrote of the strength and sacrifice of one peasant family – the farmer, his wife, his sons and daughters – so that the war might be understood in human terms. Like *The Good Earth*, *The Dragon Seed* was packed with ethnographic detail drawn from Pearl Buck's considerable experience and empathy for the Chinese peasant family and the universal effect of conflict and war on the human soul, on families and on any community.

In 1941 she and her husband bought the ailing magazine *Asia* which had been founded in 1917 to inform and interest the American public in Asian peoples. They attracted new authors to write for it and subsidised its publication for many years. Although it was never to make a profit, they thought it an important channel of communication about Asia especially throughout the war years. Although Pearl Buck privileged the written word in establishing communication and understanding, she thought also that there was nothing to match the effect that direct human contact might have between persons of different cultures and race. To widen these contacts she founded the East-West Association to bring Asians into America so that everyday Americans could learn about them and they return to their own countries able to foster greater understanding of Americans. Under the auspices of the 300 US branches of the East-West Association, women and men of Asia travelled throughout the US visiting local communities to talk of their culture, the details of daily life in their own country nd their own thoughts, hopes and aspirations. They frequently illustrated their talks with costumes, pictures, musical instruments and daily utensils. In this way the average American might see and appreciate the young teachers, students and technicians who were in America to learn new methods. Instead of confining their guests' American living experience to hotels, dormitories and classrooms, the East-West Association had them stay in American homes, play with American children, share in domestic chores and learn of American domestic and social lives at first hand. Although the programme of the East-West Association was deemed most successful and was indeed the forerunner of President Eisenhower's *People to People* programme, it and the magazine *Asia* suffered when the fears, anxieties and prejudices generated during the post-war McCarthy era caused their closure. By this time however Pearl Buck had a new project and one which, after her writing, was to become the most important of her public activities.

After the tragic circumstances surrounding the birth of her daughter, Pearl Buck and her second husband adopted several children to complete their family. They were all but grown up when in Christmas 1947 she found herself adopting two Eurasian children really because she had been asked to help look for a home for them and found to her surprise that it was very difficult and that this was the reason why few adoption agencies would take on children of mixed parentage. At the same time, and with the help of her neighbours including Oscar Hammerstein, Pearl Buck opened Welcome House to care for and find American homes for such children. The only condition she set for such homes was that they must be able to teach the children to value both Asian and American heritages. Her concern for Asian-American children born in America expanded to a concern for those born in Asia as a result of the increasing presence of American troops in Asian societies, including Korea and later Vietnam, in whose wake lay a trail of mixed heritage children. She saw a certain irony in the fact that while servicemen were sent overseas to make war against the Asian men they themselves made love to Asian women and out of this strange contradiction thousands of Amero-Asian girls and boys were born.

Pearl Buck felt that because America was large enough and already made up of many races, it could incorporate these children more easily than could crowded Asian countries where the children were handicapped not only by the blood of their American fathers but also because in such patriarchal societies a child without a father was severely disadvantaged. To care for the interests of these children in Asia and to aid them in coming to America to study, the Pearl Buck Foundation was launched in 1964 and branches established in many Asian countries so that Americans might assume some responsibility for improving the lot of children of American servicemen and Asian women. She added the pen to the cause and wrote a novel called *The New Year* which took as its theme the fate of Eurasian children in Asia. In that novel, Christopher Winters, a candidate for governor in Philadelphia, unexpectedly receives an airmail letter postmarked Korea which begins 'Dear American Father'. The letter awakens memories of desolation in post-war Korea, of having to leave his young wife of three days after their wedding and the comfort he found with a lovely Korean girl who bore him a son. The novel, acutely understanding the problems of Korean mother and son and American husband and wife, traces the dilemma of each of the characters and their gradual coming to terms with their consciences, their wishes and images of themselves. The boy is eventually settled in and is accepted by his American father and his wife, but not without some pain.

What Pearl Buck hoped for and worked for the rest of her life in word and deed was that these children, combining both East and West in their person, would be placed in a unique position to understand both European and Asian cultures and mediate or reduce the distance between the two. Pearl Buck herself once said that she felt a certain kinship with these children, for though she had no Asian blood in her veins she had Asian memories and years of Asian living which had affected the very way she viewed herself, her family, her country and nature, and East-West relations. Altogether her writings generated a special benevolence and respect for Chinese and Asians which characterised Sino-European images and relations in the 1930s and 1940s. Although her personal influence dwindled in the last years of her life, her books are still in print and widely read; and her deeds – the Pearl Buck Foundation has recently settled Vietnamese children – are her lasting legacies to mediating Sino-European cultures and races.

Along with the other women writers featured in this book, Pearl Buck was also concerned, sometimes with quiet authority and sometimes with passion, about the role of women in all cultures and the relations between women and men whether it be in China or America. Her quiet understanding, empathy and less quiet passion were born of her own observations in both Chinese and European cultures and out of her own experience as daughter, wife, mother and professional writer. As in interpreting and mediating the cultures, Pearl Buck wrote into her books her views on women as individuals and on women in relation to men to a much greater extent and in a much more explicit way than the other five women writers depicted here. In both China and in her own home Pearl Buck had grown up with the feeling that girls and women were somewhat secondary to boys and men. Her father, who based all his acts and words on biblical precedent, followed strictly St Paul's remarks that just as Christ was head of the Church, so man was the head of the woman. As Pearl Buck grew older she observed how her father in his ancestral German fashion rigidly ruled the household so that he did not give her mother credit for own own equally fine mind although she frequently held her ground. She saw her mother hurt innumerable times by her father's arrogance and superiority and how with God on his side he had an unbeatable combination of resources. It seemed to both mother and daughter that God and creed took precedence over their needs and interests. It was a standing family joke that shortly after his marriage, Pearl Buck's father had forgotten to buy a ticket to China for his new wife! Pearl Buck herself never forgot how her father wrote a number of begging letters to patrons in the hope that they might pay for her college education and so benefit the missionary cause in two ways – by training a new recruit for the China field and by allowing him to keep his funds for his New Testament translation. The result of thirty-five years of discrimination and defeat turned Pearl Buck's mother into an ardent feminist determined to teach and equip her daughters differently. As for the daughter, it gave her a heightened awareness of some of the problems of combining a sense of independent self with the roles of wife and mother, and as a professional and popular author she had to struggle to overcome difficulties and discrimination both publicly in society and privately within the home.

Like Nora Waln, Pearl Buck had difficulty in integrating her writing with the busy life of her demanding household. She also chose the attic at the top of the house to be hers alone to live in the company of her 'book people'. Like Nora Waln and Alice Tisdale Hobart, Pearl Buck was also engrossed with the domestic. She only found it possible to escape to her own room once the rest of the household was smooth running and all other needs catered for. She wrote in her autobiography that she was an inveterate home-maker which was at once her pleasure, her recreation and her handicap. She often thought that if she had not been born a woman, her books would have been written in leisure and protected by a wife and other aids. Instead her own writing, a secret occupation, had to be fitted in by the wife of a very busy husband and the mother of a big busy household and only once the house and its routines had been established and between bouts of teaching and servicing. However she did not think this a grave disadvantage, as a stable home and happy family relations were most important and a focal point of her life; they were a source of content which, like the earth, nourished her own creative talents and forced her to confront the still-unused energy within her. For Pearl Buck it was not so much the allocation of a room and time to work which vexed her so much as her own and others' accommodation of her multiple domestic and public roles. In one of her most autobiographical of novels, *This Proud Heart* – written in 1937 during the anxieties following the publication of her first best seller *The Good Earth*, her departure from China and her permanent settlement in America with a new husband and family – she gave expression to some of these female dilemmas. After her heroine married a local boy in a small town she discovers she has a major sculpting talent. She wanted not to be limited by love or guilt and she thus resolved 'to be all she could and to be all she would'. Surely she need not choose between one thing and another, between 'the old ridiculous finalities of woman'. She wanted and did make a home and she would begin, now that her daughter was alive and thriving, to work as she had never worked before. Pearl Buck has her heroine, Susan Gaylord, set aside the attic for her work just as she herself had in Nanking.

> When the house has thus begun its day she went resolutely upstairs to the attic. For this house must be large enough to comprehend all her life, and this, too was her life, though Mark [her husband] and the children did not come here. She shut the door behind her and looked around. There was no reason why she should not make this place into a room where she could really work. It had been until now an occasional place, where for a few hours, months apart, she came to work at fever speed upon a hasty secret thing. She would work so no more. If she gave herself fully to others, she would give herself fully here also, that she might be fulfilled. It would not be so much of a room of her own as simply one of her many rooms, without which her life would not be complete.

It was the combining of the rooms which exercised Susan Gaylord most just as it had exercised her creator. Each day when they opened the attic door they opened it to imagination, creativity, satisfaction and even ecstasy and when they shut the attic door behind them they shut it upon their very creativity. Pearl Buck too has Susan Gaylord tell no one, for there is no one who might understand to tell. It was the consistent hallmark of Pearl Buck's women characters that they experienced tension between the search for and expression of their selves and their frequently conflicting needs as daughters, wives and mothers. Whether they were European or Chinese this was their primary quandary and in the exploration of this theme Pearl Buck captured even the smallest incident or shaped the smallest gesture: that of the young mother who wondered aloud to Susan Gaylord if it was better not to know all that one wanted from life than not be able to have it, not to be able to read and have no books or as in her own case to want to sing and not be able to afford the lessons. On the annual community occasion the young mother, wearing the same dress and singing the same song as in previous years, wore a special look on her face which Susan noticed and for a long time afterwards remembered.

In another culture, at another stage of life, and in another novel, the forty-year old Madam Wu, after a life time of nurturing others, decided to acquire a small room – a small part of a large household – and adopt a routine which allowed her to withdraw a little and to devote some time to herself. She rationalised the step in a manner curiously reminiscent of the literature for feminist women today:

> I think Heaven is kind to women after all. One could not keep bearing children for ever. So Heaven in its mercy says when a woman is forty, 'Now, poor soul and body, the rest of your life you shall have for yourself. You have divided yourself again and again and now take what is left and make yourself whole again, so that life may be good to you for yourself, not only for what you give but for what you get'. I will spend the rest of my life assembling my own mind and my own soul. I will take care of my body carefully, not that it may any more please a man, but because it houses me and therefore I am dependent on it.

She wrote of strong women who expressed both unusual and yet timeless emotions. For them it was their individual and creative strength which often seemed to detract from their other relationships, also essential to their well-being. Their husbands though they did desire could never quite possess all of them, their very energy could suffocate or sap their children and for their friends they did what they did and so much besides. In her books, Pearl wrote as a woman and, over her long writing career as a woman in and at every stage of her life, writing out as if were her own emotions, experience and distilled wisdoms.

Within home and family life she placed the highest priority on the relationship between wife and husband and it was the accommodation of a woman's own individuality or profession within this relationship which exercised her most. She thought that marriage as conventionally defined could never mean everything for the intelligent and creative professional woman, just as it was not expected to do for the same type of man. She wanted these women to have both, just as she had wanted both for herself. Like her characters, Pearl Buck never felt that she had balanced both her individual pursuits and family needs and interests with benefit to both husband and self. She had two husbands. Her first husband was the agricultural economist John Lossing Buck whose series of unique surveys of Chinese land utilisation and farm economies are still used today to quantify and document the size, activities and incomes of the Chinese peasant household in the 1920s and 1930s. Even though his work was the non-fictional equivalent of her novels portraying the life of the Chinese peasant, Pearl Buck felt he shared very little the measures of her soul, and that the fate of the retarded child came between them and her own writing and success pushed them further apart. Later she told her biographer, T. F. Harris, that she had to write for the funds for her daughter's expensive care and that threatened by her profession and assured success her husband multiplied his demands on her time to the point where he expected her to read all his data to him to save his eyesight which he was sure was failing. With the royalties from *The Good Earth* she had him visit a number of specialists who, finding nothing wrong, advised her that it seemed that this was the one means by which he might avoid the trouble of reading, monopolise her attention and hinder her own career as a writer.

Shortly afterwards the marriage came to an end and Pearl Buck married her publisher Richard Walsh who had been her mentor and friend from the time he had read her first manuscript. Richard Walsh played a major supportive role in encouraging her in writing and in helping her make the rapid transition from unknown to best-selling novelist. She had grown to appreciate him as a publisher and person and in him she thought she would find the companionship and the sharing of selves, thoughts and words which she had missed in her first marriage. She did, though she also found that the marriage relationship in which wife and husband were very anxious to share their lives and professional interests had its own hazards. She spent the first few years after her first marriage acting as unpaid reader and editor in her second husband's publishing company, and she frequently found it necessary rapidly to write a novel in order to keep firm and family afloat. He did not always find it easy to accept that she also had her writing, the creative processes and her own independent imaginative and professional worlds which he could not enter. Neither did he find it easy to be known as 'the husband of Pearl Buck' despite all her care and worry not to make it seem so and his own reasonably mature understanding of the situation.

Her difficulties as a woman writer were not confined to the home however, for in her professional and public life she also found it hard to accept some of the discrimination and criticisms directed towards her and her work. She had long grown up in a society where women were deemed to be inferior to men and were expected to have few public roles, but she had not anticipated finding it so similarly apparent in American society and given such explicit expression in her own profession. Pearl Buck's first direct experience of such criticisms came in 1937 when she was awarded the Pulitzer Prize and again in 1938 when she was awarded the Nobel Prize for Literature. The gist of such criticisms, and there were more than a few, was that in comparison with the giant male writers of the literary world, there was no woman writer who deserved to win such prizes and that, of the women writers, Pearl Buck deserved it least because of her youth, because she had written too few books of note and, having lived in and written of China, she could hardly be considered to be an American. Quite some controversy surrounded and still does surround the literary qualities of *The Good Earth* and whether it deserved the Nobel Prize. It is frequently forgotten however that one of the criteria for the award is that it is of the highest possible idealistic tendency and increases the acquaintance and understanding of different peoples and as such was awarded for her China novels and biographies.

In the face of such criticism however it was a rather nervous and melancholy young author who packed to travel to Stockholm to receive one of the highest awards in literature, for the doubts which she had about herself as a writer were magnified by the negative response of the literary world. The one exception was Sinclair Lewis and she always remembered his exhortation never to minimise herself, her profession or her achievements and to enjoy this great moment in any author's life. She herself felt she had reached that difficult period in a writer's career when the reaction which the American public invariably bestowed upon anyone whom it had discovered and praised, had set in. Just as the praise was disproportionate, so the criticism and contempt were indiscriminate and although she understood this process it did temporarily destroy her self-confidence. It was quite some years before she took up her pen again and then she wrote several books in quick succession. In order however not to saturate her market and to prove to herself and to others that she was a writer of some worth, she wrote four novels set not in China but in America, and using a male pseudonym all achieved a certain success and popularity, though not as much as her previous books written on China and in her own name. Despite her new confidence and although it was very important to her that her largest audiences were women, she always felt at a disadvantage in that she and even the more esteemed writer Willa Catha belonged not to a single literary profession but to a separate category of 'women writers'.

In addition to writing of women and men and men and women in her novels, in 1941 Pearl Buck wrote *Of Men and Women*, a short non-fiction pamphlet in which she explicitly and directly set out her views on the public and domestic roles of American women in relation to the men of their homes, community and society. The book was written as a series of first impressions about gender relationships in her own society. There she observed that the 'power groups' or executive groups of business, schools, churches, industries and government had few women members and certainly not in equal proportion to men. The main point of the pamphlet was that women had so far not taken their proper place in the national life of her country and that while she agreed that women might find this difficult to do, she thought that the fault lay largely in women's self-image and the expectations of themselves shaped by American culture.

She wanted women to be wives and mothers and to be at home with their pre-school age children but she also wanted them to evoke strategies whereby they might contribute to the intellectual life and participate in the local and national government of the country. She suggested that women's universities arrange extension courses at different stages of women's life-cycles, and particularly while they were housebound, in order that they might retain interests and invest in institutes and issues beyond the domestic. She believed that if women took a vital interest in world affairs and the social, political and economic structure of society, then their influence which she thought was more humane and more practical than men's would make itself felt for the better. One of the phenomena which dismayed her as she grew older was to observe not the broadening of women's interest but its narrowing to marriage, home and family life. She feared for women and the domestic institutions themselves if they became the exclusive goals or ends of young women's lives and especially when their incorporation necessitated a denial of their individuality, independence and creativity in order that they might be attractive first to young men and then to the man of their choice. She thought there was even more cause for alarm if young men were attracted by such a denial.

In expressing such sentiments openly in the 1940s in non-fiction form and in writing the growth of her own maturing self into her immensely popular novels written over many decades, she anticipated by some decades Betty Friedan's explosion of *The Feminine Mystique* and the birth of a new women's movement, a central focus of which was the fulfilment of both varied and valued combinations of independence and nurturing, domestic and public roles. Although Pearl Buck wrote most explicitly about the combinations of these interests and roles, explorations of their integration characterised the lives and works of all the six women writers featured in this study as a result of their own experiences as women and as writers in two cultures. Indeed, it might be concluded of these women writers that in their own lives and in their writings on the relations between women and men, Europe and America, East and West, they had revealed themselves to be daughters wise beyond their years both in their own and in foreign lands.

Bibliography

MRS ARCHIBALD LITTLE 1845–1925

Alicia Bewicke

Flirts and Flirts; or a Season at Ryde	1868
One Foot on the Shore	1869
Love Me for My Love	1869
Lonely Carlotta	1874
Onwards! But Whither? A Life Study	1875
Margery Travers	1878
Miss Standish	1883
By the Bay of Naples	1883
Mother Darling	1885

Mrs Archibald Little

Intimate China	1899
Land of the Blue Gown	1902
Li Hung-chang, His Life and Times	1903
Round About My Peking Garden	1905
A Marriage in China	1896
My Diary in a Chinese Farm	1898
Out of China	1902
A Millionaire's Courtship	1906

SARAH PIKE CONGER (dates unknown)

Letters from China with Particular Reference

to the Empress Dowager and the Women of China 1907

Old China and Young America 1913

GRACE SETON THOMPSON 1872–1959

A Woman Tenderfoot in the Rockies 1900

Nimrod's Wife 1907

A Woman Tenderfoot in Egypt 1923

Chinese Lanterns 1924

Yes Lady Saheb 1925

Log of the Look-See 1932

Magic Waters 1933

Poison Arrows 1939

The Singing Traveller 1947

The Singing Heart 1957

ALICE TISDALE HOBART 1882–?

Pioneering where the World Is Old 1917

By the City of the Long Sand 1927

Within the Walls of Nanking 1928

Pidgin Cargo 1929

Oil for the Lamps of China 1933

Yang and Yin 1936

Their Own Country 1940

The Cup and the Sword 1943

The Peacock Sheds His Tail 1946

The Cleft Rock 1950

The Serpent-Wreathed Staff 1953

The Promise	1946
Pavilion of Women	1947
Peony	1948
God's Men	1951
My Several Worlds	1955
Imperial Woman	1956
Letter from Peking	1957
The New Year	1968
The Three Daughters of Madame Liang	1969